PREHISTORIC COPPER MINING

IN THE

LAKE SUPERIOR REGION

A Collection of Reference Articles

PREHISTORIC COPPER MINING

IN THE

LAKE SUPERIOR REGION

A Collection of Reference Articles

Edited by
Professor Roy Ward Drier
and
Octave Joseph DuTemple

Mudminnow Press
Copper Harbor, Michigan

PREHISTORIC COPPER MINING IN THE LAKE SUPERIOR REGION:
A Collection of Reference Articles
Edited by Professor Roy Ward Drier and Octave Joseph DuTemple

Library of Congress No. 61-19236
ISBN: 9780983301820

Mudminnow Press
P.O. Box 36
Copper Harbor, Michigan 49918

Web site: mudminnowpress.com
E-mail: info@mudminnowpress.com

This book is dedicated to the Old Timers
whose prehistoric mining pits were sunk
on all the Lake Superior Region's
native copper bearing lodes
known to and mined by
modern man

PREFACE TO 2005 EDITION OF PREHISTORIC
COPPER MINING IN THE LAKE SUPERIOR REGION

In 1961, my father, Octave J. DuTemple, and Dr. Roy Drier published *Prehistoric Copper Mining in the Lake Superior Region*. From its inception, the book was an outgrowth of a passion (some might say "obsession"), and a true labor of love. In our house, 1961 was an exciting time. Dr. Drier's house was always exciting, with its grand display cases of copper specimens, but our house became a beehive of activity. One of my father's colleagues did the manual typing for them, and the two of them handled the printing and marketing. Central command was usually our kitchen table. Both dad and Dr. Drier wanted the book to be readable, yet also call attention to rare papers and research on the subject.

Over the years, the book went through several printings, eventually selling 5000 copies and becoming something of a cult classic. In 2004, a copy of *Prehistoric Copper Mining in the Lake Superior Region* sold on e-Bay for $150, something neither author ever foresaw.

This 2005 soft-cover edition is a response to all the requests our family has received to re-issue the book. It is an exact duplicate of the original 1961 edition, including typographical errors and original photographs. In the years since *Prehistoric Copper Mining in the Lake Superior Region* was first published, there have been archeological and technical advances within the field. They have not been included.

And last, but not least, this re-issue is a tribute to the two authors. Roy Drier died in 1988, and his loss is still felt by our family. My father is still alive and still fascinated by copper. In December, 2004 he directed my attention to an article in the New York Times regarding the discovery of a prehistoric city in Peru, convinced that researchers would discover this was a culture that used native copper. Some passions never die!

Lesley A. DuTemple Lowrie
Eagle River, Michigan
January, 2005

CONTENTS

ILLUSTRATIONS

FOREWORD

Over 400 years ago European white men started travelling the Great Lakes and began to hear of the legends of copper deposits and copper mining. Some of these legends proved true. However, it was not until 1953, and again in 1955, that we began to realize the real antiquity of the early copper mining operations in the Lake Superior region, particularly on Isle Royale. Radiocarbon dating of charcoal found in the bottom of the mining pits indicated that these pits had been worked 3800 years ago, plus or minus 300 years.

In 1930 Professor Roy Drier started doing library research and began collecting copper artifacts and stone hammers which had been used by the prehistoric miners. As Professor of Metallurgy at the Michigan College of Mining and Technology, Houghton, Michigan, he embarked on a program to try to determine whether or not copper that had been mined in the Lake Superior region could be identified if it appeared essentially in its native state in copper artifacts anywhere in the world. While considerable progress has been made, it is not yet possible by x-ray defraction and/or arc-spectrographic methods to positively identify Lake Superior copper from some other coppers. As our analytical techniques improve we are fast approaching the time when we can identify the source of the copper in copper artifacts.

In 1956 I became interested in the history of this region, particularly the prehistoric period. It soon became evident that Professor Drier had the best knowledge of the prehistory and early history of the region, and that he had the best knowledge of artifacts, some of which were his own, and some of which were available to him at The Michigan College of Mining and Technology. Many of the manuscripts that Professor Drier had collected were not readily available and these form the principal core of this book.

Interest in the prehistory of the region naturally increased after the report of the radiocarbon date and it became immediately apparent that these manuscripts should be made available in a printed form for use by scholars and students. While the manuscripts are primarily intended to be reference material the reader will note that all are very interesting to read and in a few instances we have included translations from earlier European works. There are, of course, many other articles in the literature, most of which repeat in some form or other the material that is included in this book. Some articles also have not been included because, in our opinion, they are more readily available, or make no significant contribution of fact that the articles we have here included. The manuscripts cover a period of over 300 years of the written literature. A Selected Bibliography is also included for reference purposes.

Until such time as a formal depository or museum is established in the Upper Peninsula of Michigan, Professor Roy Drier, now retired from MCM&T, will continue to collect and catalogue additional manuscripts and copper artifacts. Every reader is encouraged to submit information and suggestions to him to help us solve this archaeological mystery.

We have talked with many of our friends and in the last year have asked them to clarify specific dates and locations in order to make the manuscripts as factual and accurate as possible. Some of the manuscripts are not referenced as well as we would like, but we did not find it possible to trace every reference.

We would like to give acknowledgement to Mrs. Ruth Farmakes for her special help in preparing and organizing the manuscripts for publication.

Professor Roy Drier and I published this book privately, and in this form and style of type so we could afford the project.

Octave J. Du Temple
15 June 1961

PART I

PREHISTORY

PREHISTORIC COPPER MINING ON ISLE ROYALE AS CONCEIVED
BY THE MILWAUKEE PUBLIC MUSEUM.

Courtesy of Dr. Robert E. Ritzenthaler, Curator of Anthropology,
Milwaukee Public Library, Milwaukee, Wisconsin.

INTRODUCTION - PART I

Copper was known to the Egyptians approximately 9000 years ago and was used quite extensively by them 7000 years ago. The exact source of the Egyptian copper and the method of refining are not definitely known to us. There is no evidence that links the Lake Superior region with Egyptian copper, but as of this date the Egyptian civilization is definitely one that must be considered. It is estimated that 500 million pounds to perhaps more than one billion pounds of copper were mined prehistorically in the Lake Superior area. Where this copper went is still a mystery.

Samples of charcoal taken from the bottom of two pits on Isle Royale in Lake Superior indicate that these pits were being worked at the bottom approximately 3500-4000 years ago. It is estimated that over 5000 of these pits occur around Lake Superior, most of them on the Keweenaw Peninsula. At this point one can only imagine what extensive investigation and cataloguing of information around these pits would do to clarify our understanding of these prehistoric peoples.

As our ability to date and correlate material improves, archaeologists are generally finding that civilizations are older and that people roamed the earth much more widely than believed 50 years ago. It is certainly possible that a copper trade existed several thousand years ago between America, Europe, Asia and South America. Improved analytical techniques, dating techniques, and knowledge of the geochemistry of copper may help us to trace the routes and determine to what extent copper moved in world trade in prehistoric times.

In the summers of 1953 and 1955 Professor Drier headed The Michigan Mining & Technology expeditions to Isle Royale in order to clean out two of the prehistoric mining pits near McCargo's Cove. The carbon samples taken from pieces of burned logs at the bottom of the pit gave us the first definite indication that the mining was truly of prehistoric times, and at least 1000 B.C.

Opposite this page is a picture of a diorama which depicts the method of copper mining used by this prehistoric race. These miners built large bonfires on top of the copper bearing vein in order to heat the rock. After the rock was thoroughly heated the fire was brushed away and cold water was immediately poured on the hot rock to fracture it. The pieces of copper bearing rock were then taken from the vein and broken by stone hammers in order to extricate the native copper which was imbedded therein. It is quite obvious that the work was slow and tedious. It also became more difficult as the pits became deeper. Pits over 30 feet deep have been found. These pits exist on Isle Royale on the Keweenaw Peninsula and on the Eastern end of Lake Superior above St. Mary's River. There are a number of other pits scattered around Lake Superior, some of which have not been catalogued or reported in the literature. It is estimated that there are approximately 5000 known pits, most of which are completely covered with debris which has accumulated since the pits were abandoned by these men.

There are no known burial grounds of these prehistoric peoples on Isle Royale or the Keweenaw Peninsula. There are no pottery, clay tablets, or writings known to be associated with this culture. Professor Drier has uncovered

potsherds from the two Isle Royale pits which he investigated. These potsherds (broken pieces of pottery), because of their location in the debris, are
believed to come from a much later culture. To date it has not been possible
to correlate these potsherds with any other known culture.

The long hard winters and short cool summers meant that these prehistoric
peoples probably did not work these pits more than three or four months every
year.

Native copper exists commercially only on the Keweenaw Peninsula. In the
early 1920's another deposit of native copper was reported in Bolivia but it
has not proved extensive enough to warrant economical mining operations.
Native copper is also known to occur in small isolated pieces in Southwestern
United States, (samples in museum at the University of Arizona, Tucson).

Undoubtedly the easiest copper to obtain by prehistoric man was native copper.
It seems reasonable that native copper would be used for perhaps thousands of
years before the knowledge to refine the copper sulphide and copper oxide ore
was known. The copper ores on the Sinai Peninsula in the Middle East and on
Cyprus are copper sulphide ores.

The prehistoric miners around Lake Superior had some formidable problems
of logistics in order to supply their workers. Travel, at best, was probably
by canoe along inland and Great Lakes waterways. Where these miners came
from, where they went, and the routes they travelled, can only be surmised
with the fragmentary information we have today. Because they left no carvings,
writings, paintings, or art work, except copper tools, it is impossible to piece
together their living habits, eating habits, religious beliefs and other interesting information about their culture. In spite of the large effort (perhaps as
many as 10,000 men working for 1000 years) it is believed that free men, and
not slaves, worked these pits. Apparently these prehistoric peoples carried
their dead back with them which would probably not be the case if slaves were
employed.

These people were undoubtedly good prospectors. Every mine that has been
opened in the Lake Superior area has been known to have been worked in prehistoric times. One can only imagine how long it took these peoples to locate
these ore beds and to work them by the crude methods they used. The magnitude of the operation would indicate a strong metallurgically-oriented culture.
There was undoubtedly a great economic demand to support this operation with
men, materiel, food and transportation. Such effort was probably not put
forth to secure copper for trinkets and ornaments, but rather for working tools,
probably for armaments, and to exchange in trade.

Current estimates about the last glaciers in this area place them at about
11,000 to 14,000 years ago. If one assumes that these pits were opened after
the glacier retreated this would leave a period of something less than 10,000
years between the retreat of the glacier and the elaborate ventures which these
people operated. While there have been some shifts in the lake level of the
Great Lakes over this period of time, it is believed that Isle Royale existed as
an island at least 8000 or 9000 years.

Approximately 3500 years ago the post glacial Great Lakes were in the Lake
Nipissing Stage (Jack L. Hough, Geology of Great Lakes, University of Illinois
Press, Urbana (1958) p. 253 and 296). Lakes Superior, Michigan and Huron

were all at 605 feet elevation above sea level. At this time it was possible to travel east directly to the oceans via North Bay and the Ottawa River, and thence out the St. Lawrence to the sea, or south via Chicago, Des Plaines and the Mississippi River. The route over Niagara Falls was also open.

Edwin J. Hulbert, the discoverer of the Calumet Conglomerate, reports four percent copper in the ore (p. 32, Red Metal. See reference No. 3, Selected Bibliography.). Later stamping and sampling at the Albany and Boston Mine showed 14.5 percent copper (p. 38, Red Metal).

If one assumes that an average pit is 20 feet in diameter and 30 feet deep, then it appears that something like 1000 to 1200 tons of ore were removed per pit. If the ore averaged five percent, or 100 pounds per ton then approximately 100,000 pounds of copper were removed per pit. If 5000 pits existed, as earlier estimates indicated (and all pits are copper bearing), then 100,000 pounds per pit in 5000 pits means that 500,000,000 pounds of copper were mined in prehistoric times - all of it without anything more than fire, stone hammers, and manpower. If the ore sampled 15 percent, and if more than 5000 pits existed, then over 1.5 billion pounds of copper were mined.

Between 1929 and 1949 The Calumet & Hecla Conglomerate mined 509 million pounds of copper under modern technologies with practically all energy from electric power.

More intensive investigation of the area will undoubtedly yield more information. The size and magnitude of this mining operation must have required written records, maps, accounting records, and other written information.

The papers, maps, pictures and stories contained in this book will help the reader to understand how little is known and how fascinating is this archaeological mystery.

The two papers in Part I, written by Professor Roy W. Drier, summarize what is known of prehistoric copper mining. The first paper was written in 1953 and the second paper in 1935.

Octave J. Du Temple

NORTH AMERICA SHOWING GREAT LAKES AREA

MICHIGAN'S MOST ANCIENT INDUSTRY IS
AMERICA'S PREHISTORIC COPPER MINING
by
Prof. Roy Ward Drier
Inside Michigan, July 1953
Volume 3, #7, p. 15

Romance still awaits the traveller to the "isle that of magic partakes." It
is a part of the West that Horace Greeley advised young men to go to and is
but very little changed from the fall when Greeley "missed the last boat" and
hibernated on the Keweenaw Peninsula for a winter. If he had been interested
in that mysterious prehistoric race which had mined copper on Isle Royale
and on the Keweenaw Peninsula and if he could return to Isle Royale now, he
could go right on with his searchings where he might have left off seventy
years ago. The Island is but little changed. Lake Superior, our great un-
salted sea, has here and there victoriously assaulted the giant cliffs, the
battlemented rocks, so characteristic of the island's shores, but step inland
a very few paces and except for the integration and disintegration of nature,
one steps back centuries--to one of the last remaining traces of the only
evidences of the Copper Age in America.

Historical literature abounds with reference to the Bronze Age in foreign
countries, the so-called transition age between the Stone Age and the Metal
Age, but very little has ever been said about that transition age in America.
Here it was a Copper Age, as undoubtedly it was elsewhere. The main
reason for this lack in our literature is the scarcity of information about
these ancient peoples who "mined" copper, and used it as a structural
material, manufacturing it into tools, weapons and utensils, possibly as long
ago as when Christ was teaching his Apostles on the shores of Galilee.

"Picturesque America" reads, "centuries ago copper was mined from the
hills of Keweenaw, and the first white explorers found the ancient works and
tools, and wondered over them; when they were tired of wondering they
ascribed them to the Mound Builders, whoever they were, a most convenient
race who came in for all the riddles of the western country and never rise
from their graves to say to us, "No." The mining has also been ascribed to
the Vikings who might possibly have come in from the East, the Russians who
might have come from the Northwest, the Winnebago Indians from Wisconsin
to the South region, and to the early cultured peoples of Central America and
southern Mexico.

Needless to say, no mounds have ever been found in this ancient copper
mining region. Copper artifacts have been found in the Copper Country, in
the Mounds of Wisconsin, and also in the possession of the Winnebagoes; in
fact in the possession of practically all the Indians who lived in this country,
and the copper can be identified as Lake Superior copper, but factually very
little is known of these Prehistoric Miners more than was known when the
white man first discovered the Ancient Diggings. Cabot, in 1497, wrote of
the Indians possessing artifacts of copper, and most of the later explorers
mentioned the Indians possessing native copper implements.

The first actual mining operations, within historic time, were commenced
near the Ontonagon River in 1771 by Alexander Henry. No success attended
these efforts and no further mining activity took place until 1841 when
Dr. Douglass Houghton, state geologist of Michigan, reported the presence of
native copper in the Northern Peninsula. The Copper Rush which resulted
acted as an excellent work-out for many who took part in the western rush of
the 49'ers. The early excitement had died down by '46 so that only a few
small companies were still earnestly operating. But in 1848 a prospector by
the name of Samuel Knapp, who, in trying to clean out a small cave for a
night's habitation, discovered that the ruble in the cave bottom was not natural.
He kept digging to determine what was at the bottom and the reason for the

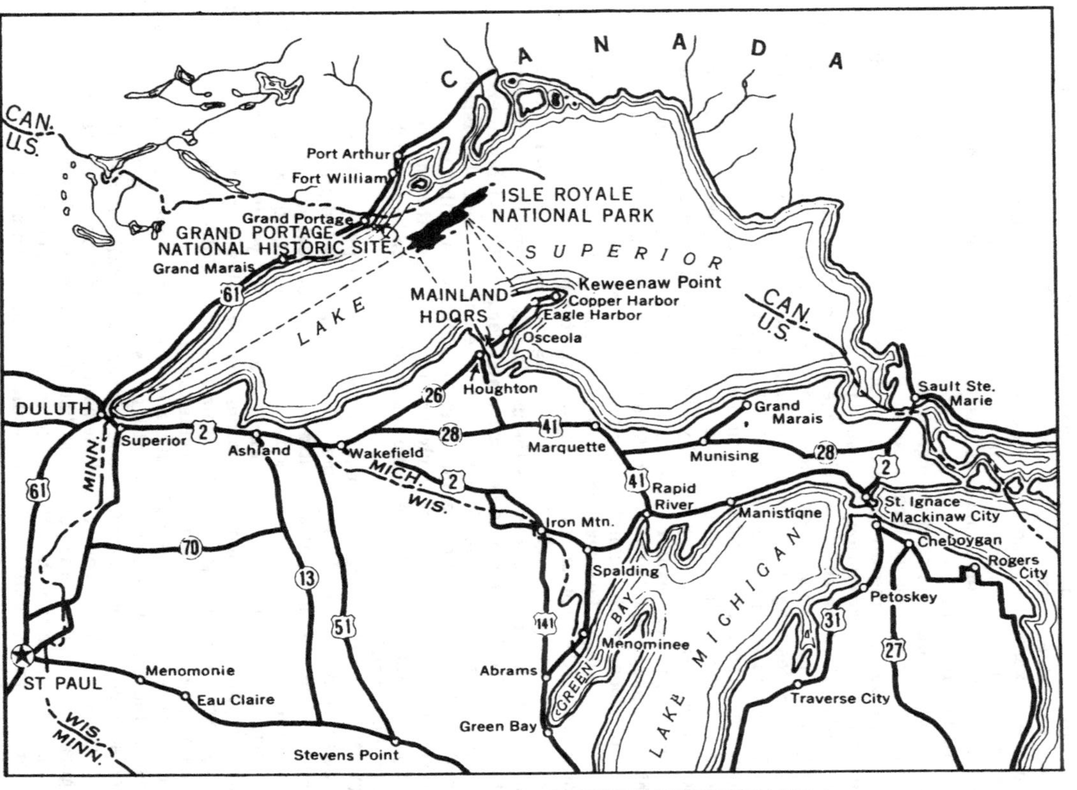

LAKE SUPERIOR REGION SHOWING ISLE ROYALE
AND THE KEWEENAW PENINSULA

hole. At the depth of 16 feet he came upon a "mass" of copper weighing nearly six tons. He instantly realized that the pits and trenches in that particular region were not natural, but in reality were ancient "mines."

This find renewed activity and interest in exploring, not an exploring for copper, but rather a searching for these ancient workings, which, when found, were excavated without any thought being given to the historic value of the pits and the tools and artifacts in them. This resulted in the actual despoilation and destruction of much of what might have been evidence identifying these ancient miners.

As historic mining spread throughout the present Copper Country it was found that these ancient explorers had mined on every productive vein in the region. As some of these veins did not outcrop at the surface but were discovered only upon excavation, it is seen that these prehistoric peoples possessed a gift or an ability which present day man would find very valuable.

Fifty miles northwest across storm-tossed Lake Superior is located Isle Royale, 50 miles long, 5 miles across, and reaching an elevation of 500 feet. Lake Superior lies in a huge syncline or basin and some of the same geological formations outcrop on the island as on the Peninsula but dipping in the south instead of to the north. The lay of the formations caused the early white miners to wonder about the possibility of copper being found on the island, and when the first miners explored the island in the late 1840's they found that these prehistoric people had been there before them and had mined on all of the worthwhile lodes on the island. They found pits (mines) of 0'-30' in diameter and as deep as 60'. For reasons of inaccessability, short season, ruggedness of topography, the problem of food supply, and the poorness of the lodes, Isle Royale was not prospected by historic man as intensively as the mainland and as a result many of the pits are as the prehistoric miners left them, except for the natural filling in due to vegetation and decay. The writer in excavating an old pit in the region of McCargo Cove on the north shore of the island dug down about three feet and came upon a stake which when pulled up was about six feet long. Apparently some early explorer had found the ancient pit and had driven a stake down to determine the depth and when he found out, he quit, just as did the writer.

The McCargo Cove region abounds in these ancient pits, in fact an engineer who was working at the Minong Mine, situated on one of the pits there, estimated from the extent of the ancient workings in that region of a very few square miles, and the mining methods of the ancients, that they represented the efforts of ten thousand men working for a thousand years. In the Rockland region the pits form an almost continuous line 30 miles long; in fact the copper bearing region, extending 100 miles from Keweenaw Point to the Porcupine Mountains was all mined by these prehistoric miners.

The Ancient's mining methods naturally was very primitive. They consisted of heating the face of the formation with fire and then throwing water on the heated surface. This caused the rock to crack and spall and they then worked on the spalled rock and vein with stone hammers and copper wedges, chisels and gouges. By this method they sank "shafts" as deep as 50 feet in solid rock and excavated trenches 100 feet in width. Some trenches of Isle Royale were provided with auxiliary drains, while in some more nearly shaftlike pits were found the remains of wooden and leathern receptacles for removing water and possibly broken ore from the pit. Early investigators concluded that from one million to one and a half million pounds of copper were recovered.

In several of the pits, masses as large as 6000 pounds were found raised up on cribwork. It is difficult to imagine what these miners expected to do with these enormous masses of metal once they did get them on the surface because they had no means of separating or removing any but knobs or pieces of copper

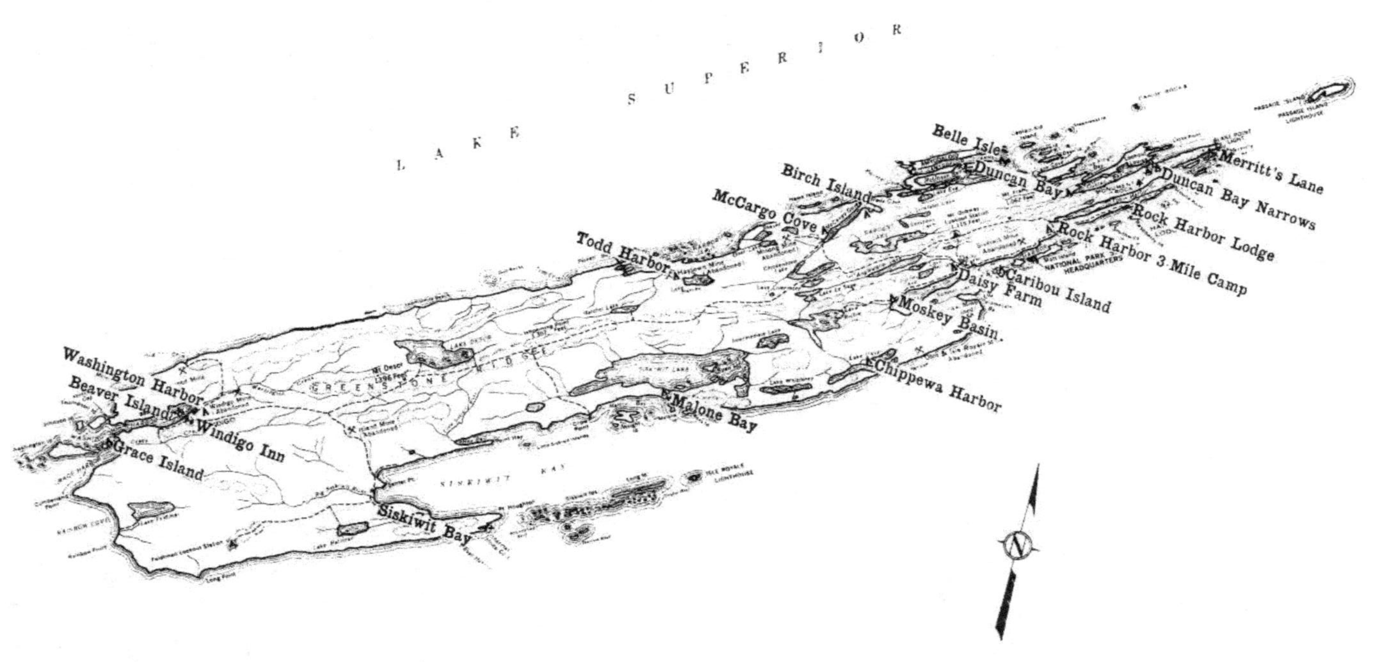

DETAIL MAP OF ISLE ROYALE

projecting out from the main body of the mass. At the location of the Minong Mine on the Island it is said a mass of about 5000 pounds was found elevated on cribwork, though in general the Island miners seemed to be of an earlier or less advanced type.

The most important tool of these miners was the hammer-stone, or maul. These mauls are usually egg-shaped boulders, varying in weight up to over forty pounds, and of the variety found on the shores of Lake Superior or in the glacial drift in the region. With the exception of a few locations in Keweenaw County, all of the mauls found on the peninsula have a circumferential groove, which undoubtedly was used to enable the mauls to be attached to handles by means of thongs, withes or crotches. Some of the larger mauls are found with two grooves. It is thought that these larger hammer-stones were attached to bent over saplings and used as stamps. None, or very few of the stone mauls found on Isle Royale have grooves. Certainly, the grooved hammer-stones are evidence of a later stage of civilization or at least a reversal on the average slope of the civilization curve. Only one copper maul was ever recorded found and that near Ontonagon. In general the character of the Island diggings is older and more interesting.

Samuel Knapp is said to have removed ten wagonloads of mauls from one location near Rockland and walled up a well with them. The mauls in McCargo Cove region were estimated at a thousand tons. Very few undamaged mauls have been found. Most of them show the signs of hard usage, both ends of the grooved mauls being chipped and broken, while the ungrooved variety have only one end chipped indicating their having been held in the hand while being used.

Some of the pits were only half worked and some of the old mining operations were found with the tools left in them, just as though the miners has quit for the day, and planned to return.

Indian legends make no mention of these mining operations which were of a magnificence and a magnitude worthy of being included in the history of any race. The legends do mention that a white race was driven out far back in the Indians history. The fact that Indian legends indicate that pieces of copper were revered as Manitous or gods would seem to prove that they were not the people who mined and used copper "industrially."

Who were these prehistoric users of grooved and ungrooved mauls, whose mine workings extend for 100 miles along the Keweenaw Peninsula and pockmark many square miles of the surface of beautiful Isle Royale? Were they Mound Builders, or does the finding of copper implements in the same formation as the skeleton of a mastodon indicate a more ancient lineage? Were the Peninsula and Island miners the same race or were the operations separated by a long period of time? Why did these miners leave their operations and implements as though planning on taking up their labors the next day, and yet mysteriously never returned? Were the copper implements found at the Canal and the Entry on the Portage Waterway lost by these miners on their journey between the Island the the central part of the country, or were these finds pieces lost by parties traveling between the Ontonagon and Keweenaw regions and the eastern end of Superior? Did the Island miners ever cross to the Peninsula or did they approach their Island workings from the North Shore, possibly after coasting along the shore from the western end of Lake Superior? What native talent or ability enabled them to locate copper-bearing lodes even though the formations were buried? Why did Indian legends surround Isle Royale with an atmosphere of mystery and magic?

The cloud of mystery which veils the answers to most of these questions about our prehistoric, stone-age copper miners of Michigan's Upper Peninsula and Isle Royale still waits to be drawn aside to reveal the secrets of as interesting an era as this country will ever have recorded in its history.

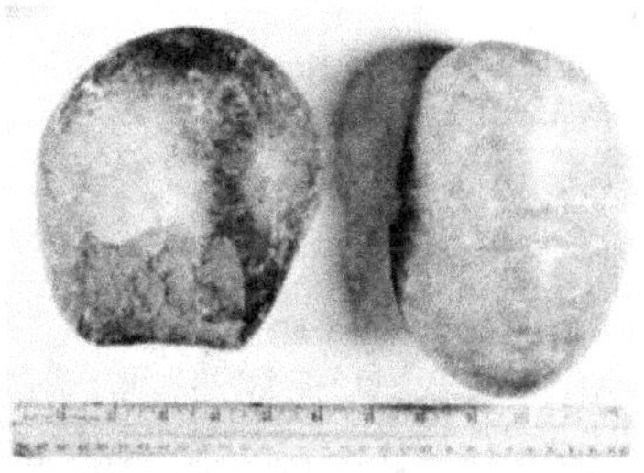

TWO STONE HAMMERS, THE GROOVED ONE WAS FITTED TO A HANDLE; THE OTHER HELD IN THE HAND

The ungrooved hammer was found in 1935 at the MINONG Mine near McCargo's Cove on the northwest side of Isle Royale. It is chipped and damaged from use. In the 1870's a mining engineer estimated that over 1000 ton (200,000 to 300,000 hammers) were in the Minong Mine area. The grooved hammer was found in 1938 on the Keweenaw Peninsula at the Lake Mine near Rockland. This undamaged and apparently unused hammer was found in a crevice high on a cliff, probably hidden there by its original maker. The average weight of the hammers is usually about 7 pounds (as shown), although one has been reported to weigh 40 pounds and to have two grooves. The hammers are usually made of a dense fine-grained ophitic-basalt rock which has been water-worn to smoothness as shown in the photograph.

On Isle Royale all hammers reported as of June 1961, except one, have been ungrooved. On the Keweenaw Peninsula almost invariably all hammers found, with the exception of one location near Copper Falls Mine (about five miles southwest of Eagle Harbor, Michigan) have been reported to be grooved.

It is reported that the stone for the hammers found on Isle Royale came from the north shore of Lake Superior, (Winchell paper #11 in this book). In 1953 and 1955 the Michigan College of Mining & Technology expeditions headed by Professor Drier failed to find on Isle Royale a source of stone used for the hammers. (Roy W. Drier Collection).

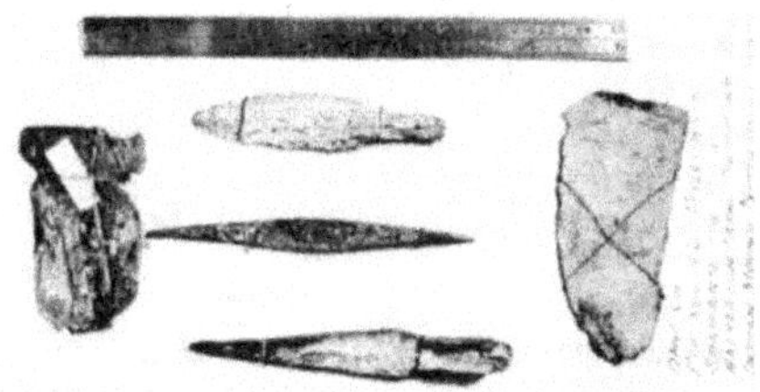

PREHISTORIC COPPER ARTIFACTS

Examination of copper artifacts indicates that these were formed by heating and hammering and not by melting and casting as supposed by some investigators. Some other copper artifacts not shown in this picture have small visible masses of native silver included in the copper. If the copper had been melted the silver would have been dissolved and therefore would not be visible. (Keweenaw Club Collection).

EXCAVATION IN AN ANCIENT PIT SHOWING NUMEROUS STONE SLEDGES
SCATTERED THROUGH THE FILLING. Photograph taken about 1881.
Presumably taken at a pit near McCargo's Cove, Isle Royale.
(Roy W. Drier Collection).

Reprinted with the kind permission of Mr. Arthur O. Heegman, Publisher
of The Great Lakelands, Kalkaska, Michigan, successor to Inside Michigan
Magazine.

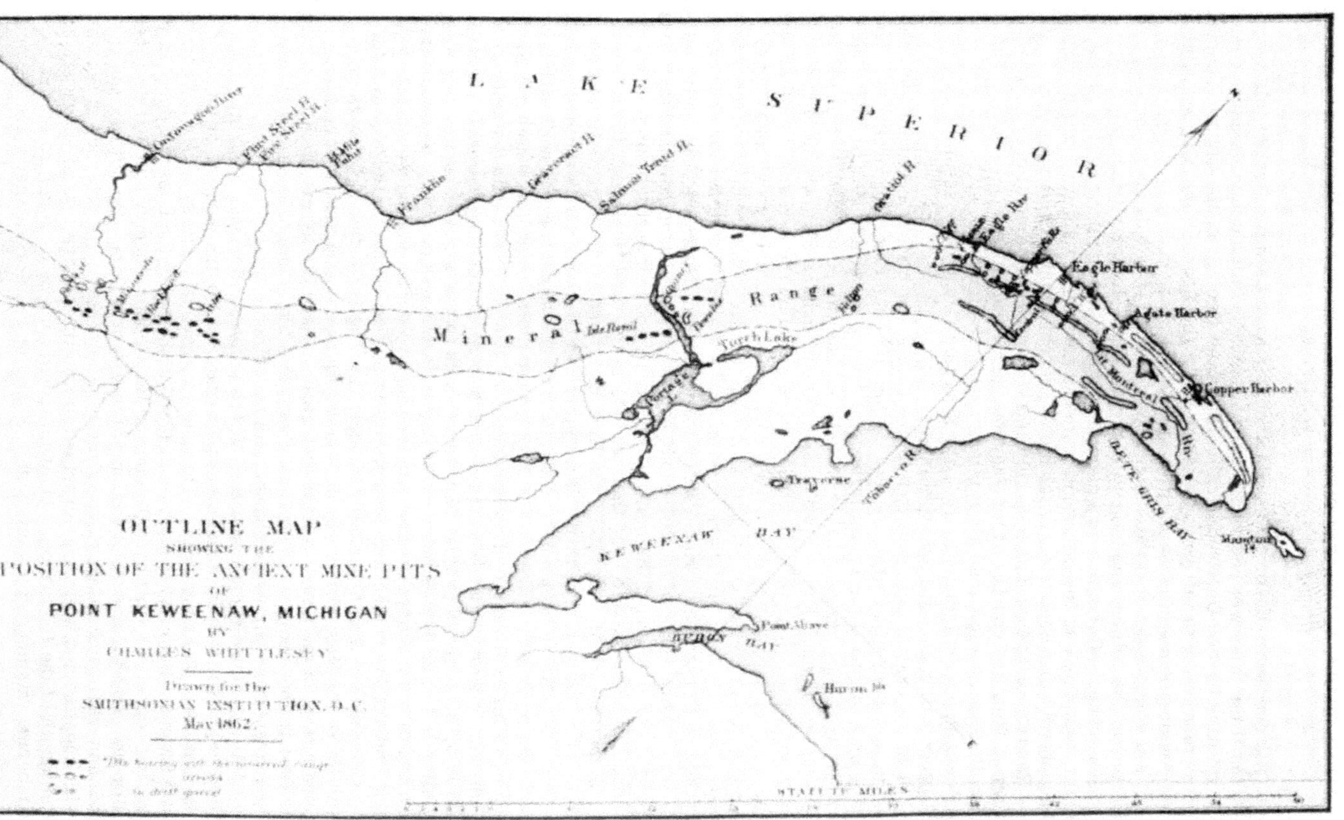

LAKE SUPERIOR
Mineral Range
Keweenaw Bay
Huron Bay
Portage L.
Torch Lake
Isle Royal
Traverse
Tobacco R.
Point Abave
Huron Is.
Confonsqoo River
Flint Steel R.
Fire Steel R.
Misery R.
Franklin
Graverack R.
Salmon Trout R.
Gratiot R.
Eagle Riv
Eagle Harbor
Agate Harbor
St. Montreal
Copper Harbor
B. Ete Gris Bay
Manitou
STATUTE MILES
OUTLINE MAP
SHOWING THE
POSITION OF THE ANCIENT MINE PITS
OF
POINT KEWEENAW, MICHIGAN
BY
CHARLES WHITTLESEY
Drawn for the
SMITHSONIAN INSTITUTION, D.C.
May 1862.

PRE-HISTORIC MINING IN THE COPPER COUNTRY
Roy W. Drier

This evening's discourse should probably have been the first of this year's series if the talks were arranged chronologically, although the subject does not go back beyond Dr. Broderick's talk on the Geology of the Copper Country. I am going to try to tell you womething about the Pre-historic Copper Mining and possibly something about the miners.

I am going to develop the subject by saying a few words about the early history of the subject and then go back to the pre-historic times.

Undoubt edly Columbus or Americo Vespucci brough back copper artifacts - tools, weapons - to the old world from the new. They did not know it but again undoubtedly that copper came from our present Copper Country.

Records of French missionaries and voyagers make mention of copper coming from the country of the Saguenay (Superior) as early as 1636. The Jesuit Relacions for 1660 after missions were established state that Father Allouez found the Indians in the Lake Superior Country, possessing copper nuggets which were looked upon as gods.

It is not exactly pertinent to this discussion but history records again and again instances of superstition and taboos and such hindering progress. We have only to recall the Indian legends of Michipicoten Island to see how such things work out. Legend has it that the island was possessed by evil spirits, and that of a canoe load or two canoe loads of Indians who canoed to the island only one returned alive - the others were killed by the evil spirits either while there or on the journey home. What happened undoubtedly was as follows:

The Indian method of heating water was to heat stones and place them in water which was in birchbark containers. Amongst the stones which they picked up to heat was a round water worn chunk of native copper, on the outside of which were some of the poisonous copper salts. These poisoned the water and it in turn poisoned the Indians. Their legends state that from then on the Indians even refused to head their canoes in the direction of the island.

Sometime in the late 1600's the first mention was made of the Ontonagon Boulder in historical record. It possibly can be classed with the most noted natural objects or phenomena of the world. It was a large mass of native copper resting free from vein or bed rock near the banks of the Ontonagon River about 16 miles from the river's mouth. It too was regarded as a deity by the Indians. History abounds with reference to it. Pilgrimages to see it were made by many noted people. But to get back to our story - one of those who visited it was an Englishman - a voyager - a courier de bois - an explorer. On one of his journeys he saw this Ontonagon Boulder and he went back to England and interested English nobility in mining copper in the New World.

One was Sir Wm. Johnson, Baronet, the English Indian agent for one section of the New World. In 1769 he wrote to the king asking permission to open mines on the Coast of Lake Superior. I have the letter which is the king's answer to that request. The kings then were like some present day rulers and executives. He wrote that he was undecided.

But in 1770 we see a company - which included the King, Sir Wm. Johnson, the Earl of Hillsborough and others - organized for the purpose of mining on the Coasts of Lake Superior. They sent a group of miners, under the command of Alexander Henry to the region of the Ontonagon Boulder for the purpose of mining copper. Henry brought them to the Copper Country and directed them to mine near the present location of the Victoria Dam. He left them in the fall and went back to Mackinac Island for the winter. He returned in the spring with supplies and was very surprised to find the miners on a sit-down strike at the mouth of the Ontonagon. The winter had been cold enough so that no timbering was needed in their adit. When the weather warmed up in the spring the workings caved in and the men quit in discouragement. That was the first organized mining in the Copper Country as far as historical mining is concerned.

The next significant date connected with our native copper industry is 1841 when Douglas Hooughton, our first state geologist, reported to the Governor of Michigan the presence of veins of copper bearing formations. This started a rush which compares favorably with the gold rush of the 49'ers. In fact many of the 49'ers got some of their "rushing" experience in the Upper Peninsula.

In 1848 a man by the name of Samuel Knapp, an explorer and prospector, was searching for copper near Rockland, Michigan. One of the stories states that he cleaned out a hillside cave one evening to shelter him for the night. He noticed that the material he threw out didn't seem like natural filling and his interest was aroused to the extent that the next day he continued his excavation. In the debris he threw out were a number of boulders with grooves around them. At a depth of 18 feet he discovered the top of a mass of copper which upon further excavation was found to be roughly 10' x 3' x 6' and weighed over 6 tons. This mass was supported on cribbing and had been raised at least 5 feet from its original resting place.

Knapp realized by this time that the pits and hollows which pockmarked the mineral region were not natural but were in reality the remains of ancient mining operations. Interest in mining and exploring which had died down after the boom of the early 40's was revived again; but now instead of looking for geological indications of copper the search was for these pits which were called Indian Pits, Ancient Diggings and other such names. When found, these pits were emptied of all they contained. No thought was given to saving any of these for posterity.

In 1862 the Smithsonian Institution sent Col. Whittelsey to investigate and report on these indications of a pre-historic race which mined for copper.

He found areas where these pits were abundant. They were: the region from the present Cliff Mine almost to the end of the point; the Pewabic, Quincy, Isle Royale area; and the region around Rockland. He also recorded pits near Fulton. We now know that practically no mine operating or having been worked was not without its pre-historic workings. Hulbert found pits on the Calumet Conglomerate. These pre-historic miners certainly had the Cornishman's "nose for copper."

In the Rockland Region the pits formed an almost continuous line for 30 miles. In Keweenaw they extended for 15 or 20 miles east from the Cliff. In the Portage Lake Region the pits were more concentrated, some of them being long trenches in the hillside gravel, indicating that these pre-historics knew of the presence of float copper in the glacial debris.

Whittelsey reported that he heard reports of such pits on Isle Royale but he did not visit the Island. We know that on Isle Royale are possible remaining traces of these prehistoric mining operations which date back a thousand years at least and possibly to times preceding the birth of Christ.

Before we can try to place these miners historically we should consider their manner of mining, their tools, their records, geographical distribution of the mined copper, and Indian Legends which might throw a possible light on the problem. Their mining methods were crude and limited the depth of the operations. A fire was built on the lode and the rocks heated. Then water was thrown on the heated rocks causing spalling to take place. If the spalled material contained copper stone mauls were used to break up the rock and liberate the copper. The mauls were probably used in the mining as well. Copper wedges were also used.

The mauls varied in size from a pound or less up to 40 pounds in weight.

LOOKING NORTHEAST FROM BELLE ISLE, ISLE ROYALE
Typical Cove Entrance. (Courtesy of National Park
Concessions, Inc., Photo by W. Ray Scott.)

Some are grooved, some singly and some with two grooves, and some entirely
ungrooved. Though there have been reports of grooved mauls found on Isle
Royale it is generally accepted that the race which mined on Isle Royale used
ungrooved hammers, and that those who mined on the peninsula used grooved
mauls. The grooved mauls certainly indicate a higher stage of civilization
than the ungrooved. This would indicate that the Isle Royale miners were of an
earlier race and that the mines on the island antedated those on the Peninsula.
These hammers or mauls are boulders picked up on the shores of Lake Superi-
or or in local glacial debris. It is thought that possibly the larger mauls were
attached to bent over saplings to be used as a sort of a stamp. Ten wagon
loads of mauls were found in a few pits near Rockland and in the McCargo Cove
Region on Isle Royale early visitors estimated that there were probably a
thousand tons of these stone hammers lying around.

Other tools which were found were wooden shovels, wooden pans or bowls
and a leathern bag, possibly for dewatering. Dewatering was quite a problem
and the workings often consist of a series of pits, the separations preventing
drainage from one pit into the next. The wooden tools tho preserved under-
water were so old that when dried they crumbled to dust, likewise the leathern
big which was said to resemble walrus hide.

Some of the pits were small, some large, some deep and some shallow. On
Isle Royale the pits were reported to vary from 10 to 30 feet in diameter and
from 20 to 60 feet deep. (Personally I think that 60 feet is an exaggeration.)
At the Hilton Mine near Rockland a gap 10 rods wide was cut in a hill making
such a sizeable valley that it was not recognized as a digging until a forest
fire bared it to view. One author mentions a timbered adit on Isle Royale.
Near Rockland an adit or hillside working had pillars of the vein left for support.

Near the old Minong Mine at McCargoe's Cove on Isle Royale the pits fairly
pockmark an area roughly 1/4 mile x 5 miles. An early engineer estimated
that everything considered, the workings represented the efforts of 10,000
men working for 1000 years. Others have remarked that centuries and centuries of labor were represented by the area.

These pre-historic miners left no records that we can translate to tell who
they were. Apparently they did not winter in the region and apparently, too,
none but the hardy and strong made the trip. No graves have been found which
can be definitely ascribed to them. They made no drawings, no carvings, and
they left nothing in the way of mounds, ceremonial or otherwise, to indicate
their lineage. The pits and the tools are all and they are not enough.

Father Allouez said that the Indian Legends contained no reference to mining or the miners. In fact the Indians did not know where the mines were. A
report of a Chippewa legend says that an old one states that their forefathers
drove out a white race who might have been the miners.

Native copper from Lake Superior has been found in the possession of
Indians all over the United States and also in Mexico and Central American including the Aztecs, Toltecs and Incas. The mounds of the Mound Builders contain much copper particularly those in the Great Lakes region.

In Illinois the remains of a mastadon were found and a copper knife found
along with the remains, indicating copper mining was carried on when the
mastadon lived in America. It is though that the animal became mired and was
killed by the Mound Builders, whoever they were.

Who these miners were, where they came from and why they left their
operations as though expecting to return the next day - but didn't - are the
questions which are still bothering archeologists. We know from the depths of
grooves which have been exposed to the weather as compared with the other
sides of the mauls that great antiquity is indicated. The same is very evident

when one examines the depth of corrosion on the surface of the copper tools
used and made by these pre-historics. Trees found on some of the old "poor
rock piles" and in the pits themselves indicate an age of 400 years and more.
If the 10,000 men for a thousand years were discounted 90% and made a
thousand men for a thousand years, it would take us back to the beginning of
the Christian Era. The mastadon and the copper knife would indicate still
greater antiquity. Stone tools would mean the Stone Age.

Were these miners the Mound Builders, or were they Scandinavians from
the northeast   or Russians from the northwest, or Aztecs from the southwest
or Indians from the south and east?

We do know that the evidences of mining in the Upper Peninsula take us back
to prehistoric times when a race of intelligent men, of whom we know very
little, mined copper here and on Isle Royale and that all attempts to trace
their origin to a common fountain of life involves the investigator with mazes
of conjecture.

This paper was originally written for delivery by Prof. R. W. Drier before
the Calumet Michigan Congregational Men's Club about February 1935.

PREHISTORIC COPPER TOOLS - SPEARHEAD AND WEDGE
Roy W. Drier Collection

The spearhead shows greater corrosion than the wedge probably because
of the combined conditions of the depth in soil condition where the artifacts
lodged for thousands of years and because of the extensive cold working
required to form this spearhead. Cold working increased the internal
strain in the copper grains which in turn made the spearhead more
susceptible to corrosion.

Hardening of both artifacts is the result of cold working. There is no
evidence of intentional alloying.

PART II

EARLY HISTORY

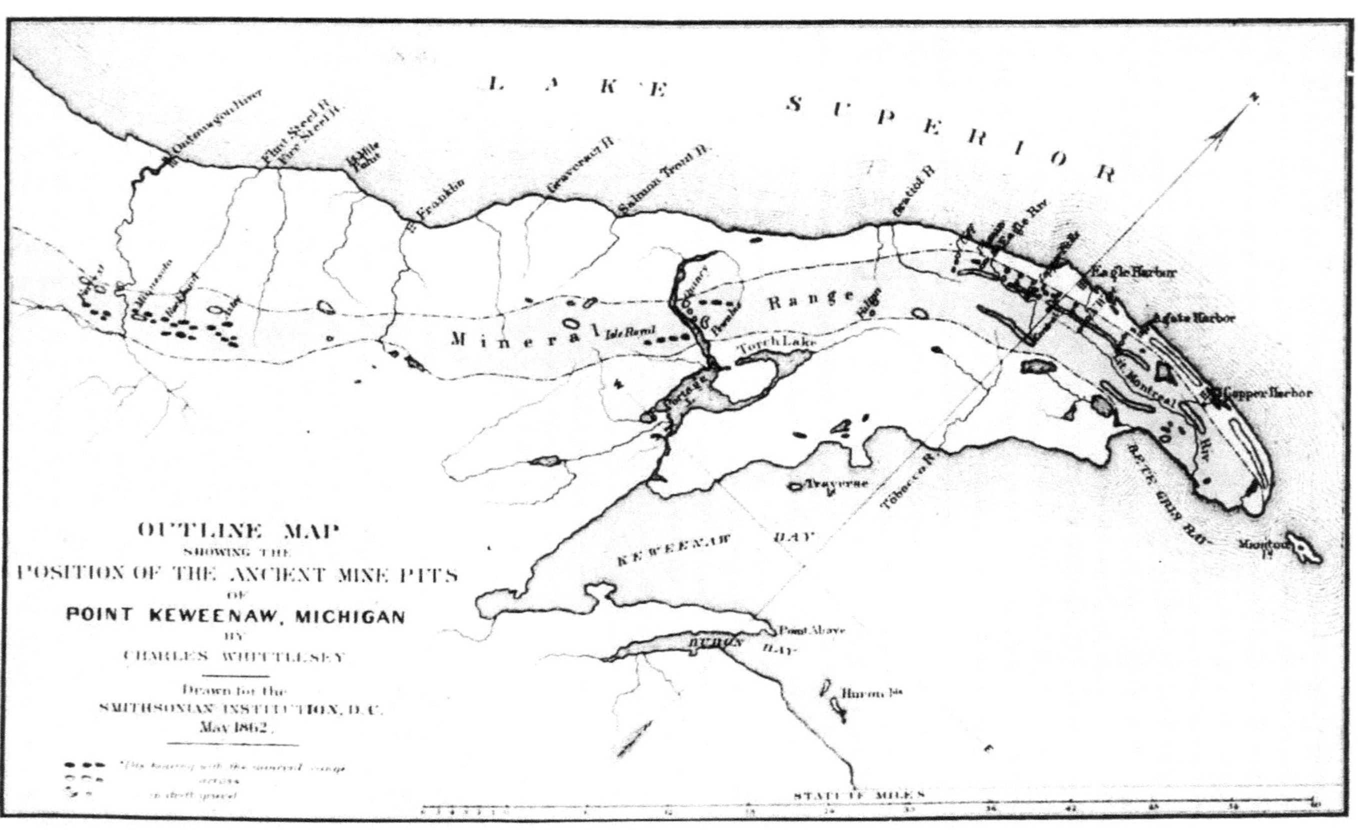

LAKE SUPERIOR
Ontonagon River
Flint Steel R.
Fire Steel R.
14 Mile Point
E. Franklin
Graveraet R.
Salmon Trout R.
Eagle Riv
Eagle Harbor
Agate Harbor
Copper Harbor
Mineral Range
Quincy
Portage
Isle Royal
Torch Lake
Portage
Mt. Montreal
Riv
B. PTE. GRIS BAY
Traverse
Tobacco R.
KEWEENAW BAY
Point Abaye
HURON BAY
Huron Isd
Manitou Is
OUTLINE MAP
SHOWING THE
POSITION OF THE ANCIENT MINE PITS
OF
POINT KEWEENAW, MICHIGAN
BY
CHARLES WHITTLESEY
Drawn for the
SMITHSONIAN INSTITUTION, D.C.
May 1862.
STATUTE MILES

INTRODUCTION - PART II

The early history of the Lake Superior Region is covered by
23 papers dating from 1636 to the early 1950's. These papers
give an accurate account of mining in historic times and
interesting and factual observations of the early historians
and writers of this area. The reports discuss mining on the
Keweenaw Peninsula and Isle Royale. Little attention is paid
to the prehistoric mine operations which are known to have
taken place north of Sault Ste. Marie.

Some of the information and observations are repeated in some
form or other in a few of the papers. It is interesting to note
how closely the reports correspond, especially when one
considers that in most instances the authors and their works
were not known to each other. The text of the original papers
has been carefully reproduced with no known alterations. Some
of the papers refer to figures and diagrams that have been lost
or were not available to the editors. However, the reader will
find that other appropriate drawings, maps and references do
exist either in other papers or as separate inserts in this book.
The papers are generally arranged in chronological order
according to date of publication. In a few instances the papers
have been rearranged to provide better continuity and organization of the material. The pictures have been arranged within
the manuscripts for the convenience of the reader. Some of
the maps and charts have been repeated for this same purpose.

Octave J. Du Temple

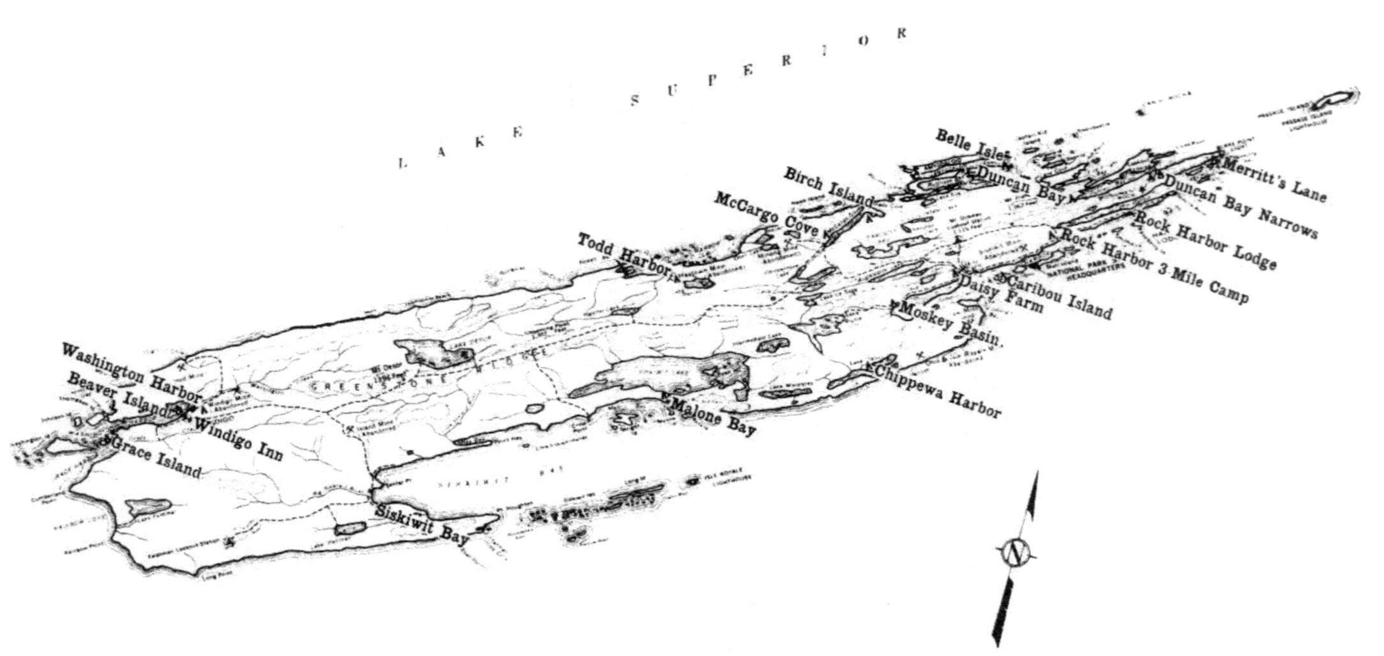

DETAIL MAP OF ISLE ROYALE

FIRST ACCOUNT OF COPPER COUNTRY
PUBLISHED IN FRANCE IN YEAR 1636
Clippings sent to Dr. Dillman*by Mr. James R. Dee**
May 17, 1944
Probably from a tourist edition of the Gazette,
date unknown

The first known account of the Copper Country of Michigan was published
at Paris, France, in 1636 by Lagarde. Writing of what is now the upper
peninsula of Michigan, he said:

"There are mines of copper which might be made profitable, if there were
inhabitants and workmen who would labor faithfully...About 80 or 100 leagues
from the Hurons, there is a mine of copper from which Truchement Brusel
showed me an ingot, on his return from a voyage to the neighboring nation.
It is pretended also, that near Soguenay, gold, rubies and other precious
stones are found. I am assured that, in the country of the Sourigois, there
are not only mines of copper, but also of steel; also certain blue transparent
stones, which are as valuable as turquoises."

In 1640 Pierre Boucher published in Paris a small volume in which he
mentioned this region as follows:

"There are mines of copper, tin, antimony and lead. In Lake Superior
there is a great island which is 50 leagues in circuit, in which there is a very
beautiful mine of copper; it is also found in various places in large pieces, all
refined."

In the "Relations de ce qui s'est passe dens le pays des Hurons," 1655-60,
one of the Jesuit fathers wrote:

"It is enriched on all its borders by mines of lead almost pure, and of
copper all refined in pieces as large as the first, and great rocks which have
whole veins of turquoses."

In a French publication of 1666-67, "Relations de la Mission du St. Esprit,
aux Outaovees dans Lac Tracy (Superior) dite auprarant le Lac Superieur
Journal du voyage du Pere Claude Allouez dans de Paris Outaonacs," the
following is found:

"The savages respect this lake as a divinity and its magnitude, for it is
200 leagues long and 80 wide; on account of its goodness in furnishing them
fishes, which nourish all of those people where there is but little game. There
are often beneath the water pieces of copper, all formed and of the weight of
10 to 20 pounds. I have seen them many times in the hands of the savages,
and they are superstitious, they keep them as so many divinities, or as
presents from the gods beneath the water, who have given them as pledges of
good fortune."

An early English account was written by Alexander Henry, who was a
trader in the early times of the English occupation of the peninsula. In his
"Travels" written between 1760 and 1776 he states:

"On the 19th of August, 1765, we reached the mouth of the Ontonagon
river, one of the largest on the south....(missing)"

*Dr. Grover C. Dillman, President, 1936-1956, Michigan College of Mining
& Technology, Houghton, Michigan.
**James R. Dee, Resident and early business man of Houghton, Michigan

REPORT ON THE GEOLOGY AND TOPOGRAPHY
of a portion of
THE LAKE SUPERIOR LAND DISTRICT
in
THE STATE OF MICHIGAN
(Circa 1850)

Evidence of ancient mining, excavations, implements.- High antiquity to be ascribed to them. - Whether they can be traced to the mound-builders. - Ancient works at the Minnesota mine. - Nature of the materials found in the pits. - Bones. - Evidences of tumuli. - Extent of these workings in the Ontonagon region. - On Keweenaw Point. - On Isle Royale. - May they not be traced to the aborigines?

That this region was resorted to by a barbaric race for the purpose of procuring copper, long before it became known to the white man, is evident from numerous memorials scattered throughout its entire extent. Whether these ancient miners belonged to the race who built the mounds found so abundantly on the Upper Mississippi and its affluents, or were the progenitors of the Indians now inhabiting the country, is a matter of conjecture.

When all of the facts shall have been collected, the question may be satisfactorily determined. The evidence of the early mining consists in the existence of numerous excavations in the solid rock; of heaps of rubble and earth along the courses of the veins; of the remains of copper utensils fashioned into the form of knives and chisels; of stone hammers, some of which are of immense size and weight; of wooden bowls for bailing water from the mines; and numerous levers of wood used in raising the mass copper to the surface.

The high antiquity of this rude mining is inferred from the fact that the existing race of Indians have no tradition, by what people or at what period it was done. The places, even, were unknown to the oldest of the band until pointed out by the white man. It is inferred from the character of the trees growing upon the piles of rubbish - between which and those forming the surroundings forest no perceptible difference can be detected - from the mouldering state of the wooden billets and levers, and from the nature of the materials with which these excavations are filled, consisting of fine clay, enveloping half-decayed leaves, and the bones of the bear, the deer, and the caribou. This filling up resulted, not from the action of temporary streamlets, but from the slow accumulations of years.

Traces of tumuli, constructed in the form of mathematical figures, have been observed, but not sufficiently explored to determine absolutely whether they be the work of art, and, if so, for what purposes they were intended.

It is well known that copper rings, designed for bracelets, are frequently met with in the western mounds. We have several of these relics in our possession. There is no evidence that the race by whom those structures were built possessed sufficient knowledge of the metallurgic art to reduce and purify the ores of copper. Admitting that they did, should we not naturally refer to this region, instead of seeking a more remote one, as the source from which these materials were derived? Are not these copper rings a strong link in the chain of evidence to connect the ancient mining of this region with the earthworks of the Mississippi valley?

We will now proceed to the details of the discoveries thus far made. The most extended excavations are found in the vicinity of the Ontonagon River; and to Mr. Samuel O. Knapp, the intelligent agent of the Minnesota Company, belongs the credit of having first laid before the public an account of their nature and extent.

In the winter of 1847-48, while passing over a portion of the location now occupied by the Minnesota Mining Company, he observed a continuous depression in the soil, which he rightly conjectured was caused by the disintegration of a vein. There was a bed of snow on the ground three feet in depth, but it had been so little disturbed by the wind that it conformed to the inequalities of the surface. Following up these indications along the southern escarpment of the hill, where the company's works are now erected, he came to a longitudinal cavern, into which he crept, after having dispossessed several porcupines which had selected it as a place of hibernation. He saw numerous evidences to convince him that this was an artificial excavation, and at a subsequent day, with the assistance of two or three men, proceeded to explore it. In clearing out the rubbish they found numerous stone hammers, showing plainly that they were the mining implements of a rude race. At the bottom of the excavation they found a vein with ragged projections of copper, which the ancient miners had not detached. This point is east of the present works.

The following spring he explored some of the excavations to the west, where one of the shafts of the mine is now sunk. The depression was twenty-six feet deep, filled with clay and a matted mass of mouldering vegetable matter. When he had penetrated to the depth of eighteen feet, he came to a mass of native copper ten feet long, three feet wide, and nearly two feet thick, and weighing over six tons. On digging around it the mass was found to rest on billets of oak, supported by sleepers of the same material. This wood, specimens of which we have preserved, by its long exposure to moisture, is dark colored, and has lost all of its consistency. A knife-blade may be thrust into it as easily as into a peat-bog. The earth was so packed around the copper as to give it a firm support. The ancient miners had evidently raised it about five feet and then abandoned the work as too laborious. They had taken off every projecting point which was accessible, so that the exposed surface was smooth. Below this the vein was subsequently found filled with a sheet of copper five feet thick, and an undetermined extent vertically and longitudinally. The position of the copper block, and the extent of the exploitations along a portion of the lode, may be seen by reference to the plan of the Minnesota mine, on page 133. The vein was wrought in the form of an open trench; and where the copper was the most abundant, there the excavations extended the deepest. The trench is generally filled to within a foot of the surface, with the wash from the sur- rounding surface intermingled with leaves nearly decayed. The rubbish taken from the mine is piled up in mounds, which can readily be distinguished from the former contour of the ground.

A few rods to the west is another specimen of ancient mining, where they have left a portion of the veinstone standing, in the form of a pillar, in order to support the handing wall. The rubbish in this excavation has not been cleared away, so that its extent is unknown. These evidences are observed on this location for a distance of two and a half miles. Upon a mound of earth we saw a pine stump, broken fifteen feet from the ground, ten feet in circumference, which must have grown, flourished, and died since the earth in which it had taken root was thrown out. Mr. Knapp counted three hundred and ninety-five annular rings on a hemlock, growing under similar circumstances, which he felled near one of his shafts. Thus it would appear that these exploitations were made before Columbus started on his voyage of discovery.

The amount of ancient hammers found in this vicinity exceeded ten cart- loads, and Mr. K., with little reverence for the past, employed a portion of them in walling up a spring. They are made of greenstone or porphyry pebbles, with a groove, single or double, cut around, by which a withe was attached. One of the larger class had the dimensions of 12 x 5 1/2 x 4 inches, and a weight of 39 1/2 pounds. The smaller class, weighing five or six pounds, were probably wielded in one hand.

In addition to these relics, a copper gad, with the head much battered, and a copper chisel, with a socket for the reception of a handle, were brought to light. It contained the fragment of a wooden handle, when discovered, which crumbled very soon after being exposed. The timber in the excavation before described showed the marks of an axe, the bit of which must have been about two inches in width.

Mr. Wm. H. Stevens, the agent of the Forest mine, has discovered other workings on the southwest quarter of section 30, township 50, range 39, almost of equal extent and interest. They occur on the southern slope of a hill, and consist of a series of pits, some of which, on being opened, are found to be fourteen feet deep. They are arranged in four lines, following the courses of four veins or feeders.

In cleaning out one of these pits, at the depth of ten feet, the workmen came across a fragment of a wooden bowl, which, from the splintry pieces of rock and gravel imbedded in its rim, must have been employed in bailing water.

Remnants of charcoal were found, not only there, but at numerous places, lying on the surface of the rock. Some have supposed that fires were kindled for the purpose of melting the copper, but the more reasonable supposition is that heat was employed to destroy the cohesion between the copper and the rock. Before the introduction of gunpowder, fire was the great agent in excavating rock; and even now, in the Harz and at Altenberg, two of the old mining districts of Europe, this agent is employed to break down rocks of extreme hardness. It is quite as economical where fuel abounds as gunpowder in destroying silicious rocks.

We can hardly conceive it possible for them to have made such extensive excavations with such implements simply as they have left behind, without availing themselves of the aid of fire.

In one of these pits - southwest quarter of section 35, township 51, range 38, were found the bones of a deer, in a pretty good state of preservation. Fragments of the cranium, humerus, and of one horn (which, to use the language of sportsmen, was in the "velvet" at the time of the destruction of the animal) were taken out. The smaller bones had mouldered away. They reposed on clay, a foot above the surface of the pit, and were covered with accumulations of clay, leaves, gravel, and sand to the depth of nineteen feet. It would appear that the animal either fell into the pit or ventured in to procure water, and, unable to extricate himself, perished.

These pits, filled as they were with water, would not become the dens of carniverous animals, and to no agency of theirs are we to attribute the position of these bones.

In the northeast quarter of section 16, township 50, range 39, near a small stream, there is a mound which has the appearance of having been the work of art. Mr. Hill, from whose notes much of the above information has been derived, states that from the want of tools he was unable to penetrate it, to determine whether it was stratified or not. It is about ten feet high, in the form of a square, the sides of which are fifteen feet in length, flat on the top, and slope regularly to the base.

There is another tumulus on the right bank of the Ontonogon River, six miles above its mouth, forty feet high, and nearly circular, which has been supposed to be artificial, but has not been explored with a view to determine the point.

From the northeast quarter of section 31, township 51, range 37, to section 5, township 49, range 40, a distance of nearly thirty miles, there is almost a continuous line of ancient pits along the middle range of trap, though they are not exclusively confined to it.

Upon Keweenaw Point they have been found extending from Eagle river eastward to range 28, a distance of twelve miles, along the base of the trap range. A great number of hammers were discovered on the present site of the Northwest Company's works, which first led the explorers to suspect the existence of a valuable lode of copper. They have also been found at the Copper Falls mine, and at the Phoenix, formerly the Lake Superior, mine. At the latter place a copper knife was discovered, in the early explorations of that tract.

Mr. C. G. Shaw pointed out to us similar evidences of mining on Isle Royale. They occur on what is known as the Middle Finger, and can be traced lengthwise for the distance of a mile. Mr. Shaw remarks that, on opening one of these pits, which had become filled wp with the surrounding earth, he found the mine had been worked through the solid rock to the depth of nine feet, the walls being perfectly smooth. At the bottom he found a vein of native copper eighteen inches thick, including a sheet of pure copper lying against the foot-wall.

The workings appear to have been effected simply by stone hammers and wedges, specimens of which were found in great abundance at the bottom of the pits. He found no metallic implements of any description and is convinced, from the appearance of the wall-rocks, the substance removed, and the multitude of hammers found, that the labor of excavating the rock must have been performed only with the instruments above named, with the aid perhaps of fire. From the appearance of the vein and the extent of the workings, he conjectures that an immense amount of labor had been expended. He endeavored to find some evidences of the antiquity of these workings, but could discover nothing very satisfactory to his own mind, except that they were made at a remote epoch. The vegetable matter had accumulated and filled up the entire opening to a level with the surrounding surface; and, in a region where it accumulates as slowly as it does on the barren and rocky parts of Isle Royale, this filling up would have been the work of centuries. Upon this vegetable accumulation he found trees growing equal in size to any in the vicinity.

All will admit that the facts above set forth assign to these excavations a high antiquity; but whether they were made by a race distinct from the Indians now inhabiting the region, it is a matter of extreme doubt, although all traditions with regard to their origin have perished.

A race like the Indians, dependent principally on hunting and fishing for the means of subsistence, would employ copper, where it was accessible, in the construction of their weapons of capture, in preference to stone, it being more easily fashioned and less destructible. This would naturally be expected in the rudest and most simple state of society.

Among the earliest benefits derived from their contact with the whites would be the introduction of iron implements, which would soon supersede those of copper. They then would have no interest in maintaining a communication with the copper region, which abounded in few animals of the chase, or in preserving among their tribe a knowledge of the places from which the metal was obtained. The lapse of a century or two would obliterate all traditions. We have seen that the first missionaries arrived on the borders of Lake Superior as early as 1641, and it is probable that the tribes which they there found had established an intercourse with the whites at Quebec and Montreal years before. If, from the scanty records of the Jesuits, we could gather what amount of skill was displayed by the savages in the art of making metallic implements, and the kind of material used, it would throw much light upon this point.

Skulls form the most distinguishing feature between the several tribes of the human family, and hence their discovery - which may be looked for among these excavations - will afford authentic testimony of the character of the race by which they were made. (pp. 158-163, Chapter 7, Doc. No. 69, 1850)

Note: - According to Kalm, (Reise, th. 3, s. 416) M. de Verandrier, who in 1746 was sent upon an overland expedition intended to reach the Pacific, by Chevalier de Beauharnois, then governor-general of Canada, in the prairies 900 miles west of Montreal, found enormous masses of stone, placed in an upright position by the hand of man, and on one of them was something which was taken to be a Tartar inscription. It was engraved on a small tablet which had been let into a pillar of cut stone, in which position it was found. Some of the Jesuits in the city of Quebec assured Kalm that they had seen and handled the supposed inscription. It was afterwards transmitted to Count Maurepas, in France. Humboldt, from whom we derive this information, (Aspects of Nature, title Steppers and Annotations,) adds: "I have asked several of my friends in France to search out this monument, in case it should really be in existence, and in the collection of Count Maurepas, but without success." May not this carved stone have been the work of the old copper miners? Verandrier further affirmed that, throughout entire days' journeys, traces of the ploughshare were discernible; but Humboldt remarks that "the total ignorance of the primitive nations of America with regard to this agricultural implement, the want of draught cattle, and the great extent of ground over which the supposed furrows are found, all lead to the conjecture that the singular appearance has been produced by some effects of water on the surface."

The surface of the island of Mackinac, which lay in their route, presents the appearance of a ploughed field. It arises from the removal of blocks of stone from their place of bedding in the strata by the agency of water, during the drift epoch. The earth is not evenly distributed, but lies in ridges like graves, and well might be mistaken for the remains of aboriginal tillage. (p. 163).

According to the statement of Mr. Knapp, the agent of this mine, whose energy and zeal in exploring this tract we have noticed under another head, there were taken from this mine, last year, (1848), eleven tons of copper, seven and a half of which were included in the mass raised by the ancient miners, the position of which is indicated in the plan.

<u>Plan of the mine.</u> - An adit-level is now being driven from the base of the hill to intersect the vein, at nearly right angles with its course, at shaft No. 3. Its length, when completed, will be 375 feet. Thence, it will be extended along the course of the vein so as to strike the several shafts. Shaft No. 1 will be intersected 77 feet below the surface; shaft No. 2, at 87 feet; and shaft No. 3, at 86 feet.. The shaded portions represent the present workings, while the light portions show what remains to be accomplished. The ancient workings are indicated by a series of oblique lines. (p. 134, 1850).

(See page 222 of this book.)

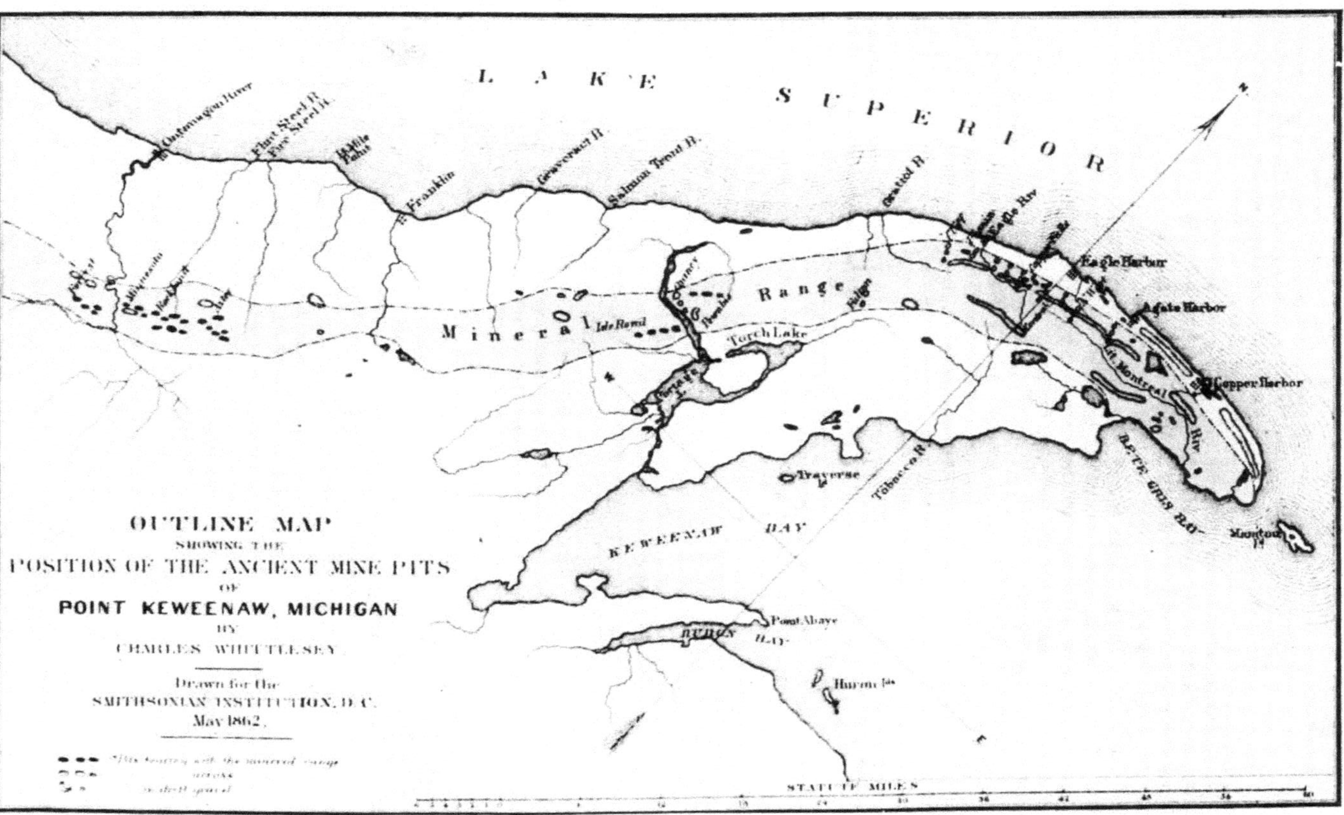

LAKE SUPERIOR
OUTLINE MAP
SHOWING THE
POSITION OF THE ANCIENT MINE PITS
OF
POINT KEWEENAW, MICHIGAN
BY
CHARLES WHITTLESEY
Drawn for the
SMITHSONIAN INSTITUTION, D.C.
May 1862.
Mineral Range
Torch Lake
Isle Royal
Ontonagon River
Flint Steel R.
Fire Steel R.
Mile Point
E. Franklin
Graveraet R.
Salmon Trout R.
Gratiot R.
Eagle Riv
Eagle Harbor
Agate Harbor
Copper Harbor
Ft. Montreal
Portage
Traverse
Tobacco R.
Tobacco R.
KEWEENAW BAY
Point Abaye
HURON BAY
Huron Ide
Manitou Id
Montou
STATUTE MILES

THE ANCIENT MINERS OF LAKE SUPERIOR
By Charles Whittlesy
Cleveland, August 1852
From The Annals of Science, January, Cleveland
Harris & Fairbanks, Herald Building Bank Street, 1854

I shall not enter into a description of the extensive mining operations that have been carried on in very remote periods, on the shores of Lake Superior. They are of great magnitude and are found extending over a wide space. As far as at present known, the most striking remains of the ancient miners, are on the Ontonagon River, extending 15 or 20 miles along the trap range each way from where it crosses the course of that stream.

They are also very apparent in the vicinity of Portage Lake. On Point Kewenaw they may be seen extending from the Forsyth location, (now Fulton), eastward along the range about 20 miles, and across the lake on Isle Royale, are abundant evidence of mining operations of the same era. The details, concerning the mode in which these mines were worked - the depth and extent of their excavations; the tolls, implements, etc., used - may be seen in the Reports of the Government Geologists, and in Mr. Foster's paper on that subject, in the Smithsonian Contributions.

I shall confine myself to the evidences which show the connection, or rather the identity of the people who wrought these mines, with the "race of the mounds," which anciently occupied the State of Ohio, and from them to the Aztecs, the ancestors of the Mexicans.

The part of the discussion which connects the "race of the mounds" or the "mount builders" with the Aztecs, will be brief. The foundation for this relationship, is the learned work of Mr. Delafield, upon the Antiquities of America, where all the points bearing on the question are most ably presented. If Mr. Delafield does not establish the point that the Mexicans are descendents of the "mound builders," he succeeds in giving his opinion as near the character of a demonstration, as the nature of the subject allows. Many of his proofs, must, of necessity, rest upon tradition, which is always vague, upon symbolical paintings, sculptures, and characters, such as all the ancient, ignorant, and half civilized nations made use of and which constitutes their history, and their only history. We cannot expect, in such enquiries the strictest conviction, which is required under oral testimony in a court of law; if we did, there is little of written history that would command our belief. In affairs of such remote antiquity we must of necessity, deal in speculations, and deductions, or we must abandon the subject altogether.

Nothing is better settled in ethnology, than that the North American Indian, or Northern Aborigines, belongs to the Mongolian or Tartar family, which inhabits Northern Asia.

On the basis of craniology, according to which the human race is divided into families, by naturalists, the race of the mounds is unequivocally distinct from the North American Indian. Mr. Delafield's inquiry into the origin of the "race of the mounds," and the excellent work of Squier and Davis, upon the Ancient Monuments of the Mississippi valley, are the same as those of Mexico and Peru.

They have been examined from the western part of New York, southerly and westerly through the States, on the Mississippi, to Texas, and thence through Mexico and Central America, to Peru, and are found to have a common external appearance. The same elevated platforms of earth, are seen in Ohio and in Mexico, on which it is presumed, the same religious rites were once celebrated.

In Peru, the Spaniards, when they conquered that country, found lines and circles of embankment, with exterior ditches, situated on the summit of

46

difficult hills, having the form and structure of the so-called "Indian forts,"
that are so numerous in this State.

At the South, these works are built on a larger scale than they are here,
but after the same general pattern.

The mounds at Grave Creek, Virginia; at Miamisburg, Ohio; at St. Louis,
Mo.; and at Moorehouse Parish, Louisiana, are exceeded in bulk by the
Pyramid of Cholula, in Mexico: but all belong to the same system. The similarity of the earth-works, over so large a space, is one of the links in the
chain of evidence, adduced by Mr. Delafield.

Another point is supported by historical proof. There are among the
Indians, national annals, which say, that about the year 600 of our era, their
ancestors, migrated from the north, under an Emporer named Citin, or Votan.
There have been comparisons made between three skulls, taken from ancient
mounds in the valley of the Mississippi, and that belong to the race of the
mounds, if any of the relics which are found here, do; and three others, which
were procured from ancient tumuli in Peru. - <u>Ancient Monuments,</u> see
pp. 291-292. Their anatomical proportions, correspond so well, that crani-
ologists pronounce them to be of the same family.

The pyramid of Cholula, which our officers visited during the war, is built
of unburnt brick and of clay. The ruins of Azetlan, on the Rock River, Wisconsin, show that brick were used in the construction of the walls, but which were
partly burnt.

The Mexicans believed in, and worshipped, an evil spirit, which they called
Tlacalecalatl or the "rational owl" and had made images of this bad deity in
the form of an owl. The "mound builders" also made and deposited in their
tumuli, images of the owl, which doubtless had some connection with their
superstitions, probably the same as the Mexican owls.

These are the principal proofs that the race of the mounds were the ancestors of the Aztecs, and of the Toltecs, a branch of the same family, who inhabited the country about Copan. There is, moreover, a tradition, and also
hieroglyphical maps, among the Mexicans, and credited by them, showing that
their progenitors, like the Mongolian ancestors of our Indians, were emigrants
from Asia, by way of the Behring straits.

I adopt the conclusions of Mr. Delafield, as to the mound builders, because
it is not merely an hypothesis; but is based on strong analogies, and upon many
facts.

To suppose that the "race of the mounds" has become extinct, would be far
more unreasonable, because it is contrary to the history of nations, and is
sustained by no evidence.

Here I leave the subject of identity, between the ancient Mexicans and the
ancient race of the mounds; and turn to the consideration of the question whether
they are the people who wrought the copper veins of Lake Superior, in ancient
times.

Mr. Delafield observes, that there are traditions among the Indians, that
their ancestors drove out a people who inhabited North America, and who occupied the ancient earth-works of the west. I have never been able to verify the
existence of such a tradition; but in numerous cases, where Indians have been
questioned upon the subject of the mounds, they have replied, that they knew
nothing about them, or the people who built them. The most probably theory on
this point, is, that the country was abandoned voluntarily by the Aztecs. These
military works show no signs of having been attacked, or of having undergone
protracted seiges. If they had been attacked, certainly would have been resistance; for a people so numerous, so well fortified, would not have fled like
cowards, before an enemy, however numerous, in the open field. An enemy
could not have invested these fortifications, without constructing similar works

of attack. A permanent fortification, of any kind, cannot be carried by storm; but only after a tedious approach, sustained by works of a like kind, such as trenches of circumvallation and contravallation. Of works of attack, there are no remains, so far as I am informed, and but one instance where earth-walls appear to have been demolished in their day; this occurs, in a short line of embankment, separating the great fortification, on the Little Miami, into two parts. The double walls across the narrow part of the works, inside, appear to have been thrown down, violently, as though a party in the north portion of the fort, had succeeded in breaking into the southern portion.

There is no proof, that our Indians erected works of defence, until after the French and Spaniards had taught them to do so, by building stockades in their midst. Before this time, they had no need of such defenses, under their mode of warfare, against each other. Of what value would picketed forts be to wandering tribes, who make war with knives and arrows; by long journeys and sudden surprises; who never accumulate provisions or attack in an open field? Much less, would they build permanent works with walls and trenches.

There are cases, where our North American Indians, after the appearance of the whites, and the introduction of fire-arms, as a matter of necessity, fortified themselves against other tribes, as the whites, who had musquetry as weapons of attack; but even this rude picketing which they have been forced to set up, is of very rare occurrence. They make war now, in general, as they did 250 years ago, by surprise; striking a secret and terrible blow, securing the scalps of the enemy, and making a sudden retreat. They have, and always have had, too little industry and forethought, to make permanent defences, preferring, like the wild animals they resemble, to make strongholds of jungles and swamps - provided by the great spirit - in preference to the artificial works of their own hands. A people that does not cultivate the soil, will not be likely to construct works to protect them in the possession of it.

If the Mexican history is true, according to which the Aztecs arrived in Central America, about the year A. D. 600; or 1200 years ago, there has not been time enough since their departure from the banks of the Ohio, and the Mississippi, for another people to rise, to occupy the same ground and to disappear. If there was such a people, the present Indians would be more likely to know something of them, than of their predecessors.

In the year 1001, the Icelanders sailing westward to Greenland, and coasting thence southward, visited the shores of New England. They found upon the Atlantic coast a savage people, who, from the descriptions given, were the same as our Aborigines. Only five hundred years after, when Sebastian Cabot, and Americus Vespucius, navigated the same seas, the same tribes inhabited the New England coasts.

About the same time Pamphileo De Navarre and Hernando De Soto, (1528 to 1540), traversed the interior of Florida, Mississippi, Tennessee, Arkansas, and Texas, and found there tribes that remain to this day.

The bones, and particularly the skulls, that Mr. Brainerd and myself exhumed last year in a sandstone cavern, in Elyria, Lorain Co., Ohio, noticed in the proceedings of the American Association, at the Cincinnati meeting, are in all probability of those of Aborigines, and are from 1000 to 2000 years old.

All these facts go to show that the present Indian family has occupied the country, from which the mound builders emigrated, more than 1000 years, and that they were their immediate successors.

It is not probable that they withdrew suddenly, leaving a beautiful and well cultivated country, which they owned and had strongly fortified, in one night as the Israelites did Egypt. They gradually changed their position for a still more fertile and more genial region, upon the gulf of Mexico and the Pacific Ocean. In time the Northern Indians, who lived upon the wild game and fish,

and not upon the products of the soil, finding the country south of the Great
Lakes unoccupied, and growing up to be again a forest, where game could exist,
extended themselves over it.

But, admitting that the Aborigines were the next occupants after the mound
builders, is there any substantial grounds for attributing to the Indians, the
ancient workings of the copper mines of Lake Superior?

If they did possess the skill to plan, and the industry to execute the immense
rock excavations, which are observed there, it is evident to all who know them
in the present state that they have lost both their skill and industry.

Is it rational to suppose that the same people living upon the same spot, under
the same influences, would have thus changed?

The working of such extensive mines would require not only the persevering
labor of many hundred men, but the labor of as many more employed elsewhere
in the cultivation of the soil, or in some other mode, collecting provisions for
those who wrought in the mines. Is the North American Indian capable of
dividing or carrying out any such prolonged and systematic plan of operations?

By what influences did he rise to that condition, so much above his present
one, that would not have operated to keep him there?

In his history, from the landing of the Spaniards in 1528 to this day, he has
exhibited as a great family of the human race a most dogged indisposition to
improvement, and even to change of pursuits.

He is fond of giving traditions, both fictitious and real, extending back in the
history of his people many hundred years. Would he have lost, or pretended
to lose, the memory of such a fact as the working of these mines?

There is an old Indian of the Chippewa nation who lives at the mouth of the
St. Louis River, at Fondu-Lac, of Lake Superior, by the name of "Loons
Foot," who traces back his ancestors by name, about 400 years, during which
time they have been like him, hereditary chiefs in his tribe.

In September, 1849, I caused him to be questioned by a gentleman from
Canada who is his nephew, in relation to the copper mines that have been worked
of old, on Lake Superior. He made a long story, as Indians generally do, with
many gesticulations and embelishments, which was in substance as follows:

"A long time ago the Indians were much better off then they are now. They
had copper axes, arrow heads, and spears; and also, stone axes. Until the
French came here, (1641) and blasted the rocks with powder; we have no traditions of the copper mines being worked, and don't know who did work them.
Our forefathers used to build big canoes and cross the Lake over to Isle Royale,
where they found more copper than anywhere else. The stone hammers that are
now found, in the old diggings, we know nothing about. The Indians were formerly much more numerous, and happier, than they are now. They then had
no wars and such troubles, as they have now."

The earliest French Missionaries found among the Indians, a very few, but
very rude and illy formed copper knives. But there is no difficulty in distinguishing the implements of copper which they had, from those that are found
in the ancient mounds of Ohio. They are much more rude, and less perfect, in
their construction. One of these knives may be seen figured by Mr. Squier, on
page 201 of the <u>Smithsonian Contributions</u>, vol. 1.

The Indians knew of the existence of boulders or detached masses of copper
and when they found small pieces of it in the gravel, or on the pebble beach,
they made the best skill of which they were possessed to fashion it into some
useful implement.

Mr. S. W. Hill, of Eagle Harbor, Lake Superior, informed me that in digging the foundation for a house, at that place, at about four (4) feet below the
surafce in the water washed sand of the lake, there was found evidences of an
attempt to melt by fire some pieces of copper from a neighboring vein. This

was doubtless the work of our Indians.

Mr. Bailey, of the same place, described to me an instrument of copper which he found in the gravel within Fort Williams that appeared to have been used either for skinning animals, or for dressing and working the skins. It resembled, somewhat, the circular knife of a saddler without its wooden handle.

I have found in the soil or loose materials pieces of native copper that with a little beating in a cold state might be fashioned into a rude knife or cutting instrument, and it is from such masses that I conclude all the implements known to the Indians were made. Those taken from the mounds of Ohio are much more finished and entirely different in form.

According to the relations of the Jesuit Missionaries, the Indians often preserved pieces of pure copper which they picked up on the beach as "manitous" or Gods, which they would not have done had this metal been so common as the working of the mines would make it.

The conjecture that the Indians knew of and worked the mines, but concealed them from the French, is not very plausible.

The length of the excavations now known must be 25 or 30 miles, some of them on the coasts and navigable waters, and not easily concealed. Although the Indians are reluctant to disclose minerals to white men they have done so in many cases of copper masses, but never of veins or ancient mines. They would be as likely to do one as the other, if they knew of them. But all of the ancient works yet explored show that they have been abandoned more than 500 years, and not only before the French first heard the Indians speak of copper, but before Columbus landed on the continent.

If copper utensils had been common among the Indians, they would have been preserved, and handed down to our times, or at least to the times of the Jesuits; for, before then, they had no iron or steel, and no metal but copper. If they had the ingenuity and skill which has been claimed for them in providing themselves with implements, they would have manufactured something like an axe, as the Aztecs did, and would never have lost the use of it. As the Jesuits mentioned only stone axes, and say that the Indians had neither hatchets nor kettles, I conclude that "Loons Foot" is mistaken when he asserts that they had copper axes. I will now give some reasons for ascribing the working of these ancient mines to the Aztecs or "mound builders."

The character of the mining works is that of a people having about the same advancement and intelligence as is exhibited in the construction of the earthworks and fortifications that are visible throughout the west. There is in neither any evidence that they had iron or steel, or the art of hardening copper, as the Egyptians had. In the mounds, and in contact with the skeletons that were interred at their base, are found copper ornaments, axes, and tools of great variety and in great numbers. They are all fully described in the work of Messrs. Squier and Davis, to which I have referred.

The copper is apparently cold wrought and does not show that it has been melted. It must, therefore, have been found by the mound-builders in its native state, and there are no mines in North America known at this time from which native metal can be had, except those of Lake Superior.

There is a peculiarity of this copper not known in any other mines, which serves still farther to identify the locality from whence the Aztecs procured theirs. The silver which it contains is also in its native state, in particles, blotches and masses of pure white studding the surface of the native copper.

Copper has been found in the mounds in which specks of silver are plainly visible. Dr. Locke, of Cincinnati, has a rough sheet of it taken from an ancient work at Colerain, Hamilton Co., Ohio, where there is a spot of native silver of the size of a small pea. This shows conclusively not only that it came from Lake Superior, but that it has not been melted.

50

In the old works on the "Minnesotah" location near the forks of the Ontonagon
River, there was found, at the depth of 18 feet, a mass of copper weighing
11,588 pounds which had been taken out of the vein by the ancients. It had been
raised a few feet along the slope of the vein by means of wedges and of cob-
work made of logs laid up in the form of the body of a small log house. I had a
piece of one of these logs which was cut from a black oak tree about 6 inches in
diameter showing distinctly the marks of a narrow axe, 1 3/4 inches wide, and
very sharp. The character of the cut or stroke of the axe struck me at once as
such as the copper axes would make, similar to that I had seen in Ohio, which
were taken from the mounds.

Although the timber beneath the mass of copper in the old Minnesotah works
was very soft and tender, by reason of its age, it had not rotted from exposure
to the atmosphere, having been always covered by water. The timber was of a
dark color, and shrank very much on drying; but the marks of the instrument by
which it was cut off were as plain and as perfect as they were on the logs and
stumps recently cut in the vicinity. Directly over the mass, and over the timber which supported it, there stood on the rubbish that covered the mass, about
12 feet in depth, a hemlock tree that had recently been cut down, on the stump
of which I counted (290) two hundred and ninety annual rings, or layers of growth.
Other older and larger trees had come to maturity, fallen and rotted away on
the same ground.

I have another piece of timber which I take to be white cedar that I procured
from an extensive ancient rock excavation in the side of a mountain, forming an
artificial cave, about (4) four miles south east of Eagle Harbor on section 17,
T. 58, N.R., 30 west. It was presented to me by Dr. Blake, the Agent of the
Company who was engaged in reopening the mine, and who found among the
rubbish a wooden shovel, a part of a wooden bowl that had been used to bail
water, and troughs of cedar bark for carrying off the water.

This shrunken and withered wooden "bat" or shovel, is more decayed than
most of those found by Dr. Blake because it was a part of the time out of water.
Some others that I saw were less rotten, in fact, were merely water soaked,
and showed the marks of the knife or other shaving tool by which the handle was
fashioned. They generally resemble an Indian paddle in size and form, but
some of them are worn unequally, as though they were used sidewise. The one
I have was taken from the loose materials thrown out brom the cave so long
since that trees, of the usual size and kinds, were growing upon the "burrow"
or spoil bank. A birch about (2) two feet in diameter stood almost immediately
over this shovel, the lower roots of the tree scarcely reaching to it through the
ancient rubbish. The marginal cut represents in outline one of these shovels,
length 3 1/2 feet aa form one after use, from the Aztec cave 4 miles S.E. of
Eagle Harbor; bb form of the one I have, showing it had been used for scraping
sidewise.

They have been found at the Copper Falls mine and all of them are made of
white cedar which is abundant on Lake Superior.

The end of the stick or skid has the marks of a tool like a narrow axe, but
not as broad or as perfect as those on the Minnesotah specimen which I was
obliged to leave at the Ontonagon River, and which has been lost.

The cuts on the piece I now have are made with a duller tool, and apparently
having a curving edge like an adze. An axe or adze of that kind has been found
in one of the mounds in Ross county, Ohio. It is figured and described by Mr.
Squier, and also two other kinds of axes and the mode of fastening a handle or
helve to them, on pages 197-8-9 of the "Contributions." As yet no such axes
have been found on Lake Superior. The only implements found there which are
made of copper, and which are from the rubbish of the old works, were found
at a depth of 5-15 feet below the present surface.

One is a chisel an inch wide, with a bevel edge and socket to receive a wooden handle, and is 5 inches long. Another is a "gad," or wedge, such as quarry men now use, and is four inches long, both of which are figured and described in the report of the Geologists, for 1850, and are from the Minnesotah ancient workings.

The third is a spear-head, in the possession of S. W. Hill, Esq., of the Copper Falls mine, 4 1/2 inches in length, which had the remains of a handle on it when found.

The "gad" is the only implement of metal as yet known which was then used in mining. The rock was excavated principally by the use of fire by means of which the mass was softened and fractured. The main implement made us of to break up the wall rock and vein stone, after it was calcined, was a stone maul or "hammer," shown in this cut which represents a maul with double grooves, weighing 39 1/2 pounds, 12 inches long, 5 1/2 inches wide, and 4 inches thick.

These broken and cast away mauls are seen in great numbers among the rubbish of all the old works, weighing from 2 to 36 pounds. They were handled, in all probability, by putting a withe around the middle at the groove. The wall rock that is left standing on each side of the vein appears to have been bruised and worn away by incessant pounding with these mauls. One from the Copper Falls mine, broken by use and having but a single groove, is in the possession of Mr. S. W. Hill.

No distinct marks of a metal tool have been seen in these works. The "gad" must have been used as it is at this day, by driving it into the cracks and fissures of the rocks, to break out fragments. Other mining tools will probably be found, such as picks, or something answering the purpose of them.

The traces of fire and heat are frequently visible, in the remains of charcoal and ashes far down in the wrought veins, and on pieces of blackened rocks among the rubbish.

There are mines of copper now wrought by fire at Rammelsburg, in Germany, and which have been in operation for a great length of time, many hundred feet beneath the surface.

There are also, in the county of Munster, in Ireland, on the Lakes of Killarny, mines of copper supposed to have been wrought by the Danes, which have shafts 300 feet deep, and which were wrought by the agency of fire. In the same mines are found hammers or mauls of stone, the same as those of Lake Superior, with grooves around the middle.

It is therefore, not impossible to work very extensive mines without the use of powder, or even without the use of any instrument of iron or other metal.

The Danes may have had iron tools, for there are marks of wedges on the sides of their shafts; but they knew nothing of the mode by blasting, which we practice, for powder had not been discovered at that time.

The civilization and general state of advancement of the Danes must have been similar to that of the mound builders, if we may be allowed to judge by the monuments they have left behind them.

There has not been observed on Lake Superior any remains that indicate the existence of cities, or permanent houses of earth or stone. Mr. Hill is of the opinion that he has seen two "mounds," or tumuli, near the Ontonogon, that are artificial and ancient. These are the only known works resembling those of Ohio, except the gravel pits about the Portage Lake. There is nothing to show that the country was permanently inhabited by the ancient miners, and as their works were open cuts and not galleries, it must have been almost, if not quite, impracticable to work them in the winters of that latitude.

No graves or human remains have been found here that can be referred to the era of the copper workings. Neither are there any evidences that there were any furnaces, or places where copper was refined or melted, or where it was crushed in the rock, and afterwards separated by washing, as we do now.

It seems most probably that the people did not reside in the country; but came in the summer, from a milder climate, bringing their provisions with them, and taking away on their return in the fall, the metal they had raised.

In that case the numbers who would die in this healthy region would be small, and no large towns would be built, or permanent habitations such as would be likely to survive to our times.

It is thus by analogies and by proofs that we may connect the ancient copper miners of Isle Royale and Lake Superior with the mound builders and the Aztecs.

It is a question of some interest how much time has elapsed since these mines were worked, and also how much time has elapsed since the Aztecs abandoned the valley of the Mississippi. I think there is some evidence showing that the two regions were deserted by them about the same time, and this strengthens the presumption that all was the work of one people.

The timber which remains in the ancient diggings of Lake Superior is in a better state of preservation than that found in the mounds, but not any more so than would naturally result from the coldness of the climate, the greater durability of the timber itself, and the fact that much of the timber of the mines is, and has been, continually covered by water.

In the Grave creek mound, and in others, the crib work, or enclosures of the Aztec skeletons, are of wood, and it is found to be very rotten, but these are, in all cases, above the level of the soil, with the earth surrounding them dry, artificially raised, and into which the atmosphere penetrates.

Although some of the cedar and pine timber from the old copper mines is still comparatively sound, like this piece taken from a pit on the copper falls location 18 feet below the surface, all the well-preserved pieces were from wet places, or under water. The trees from which the mound builders constructed their burial vaults are less lasting than the northern timber if both kinds were placed in the same circumstances.

Timber may be preserved under water and constantly wet earth for many thousand years. I have in my possession many pieces of cedar from the "stratified drift," or "diluvial deposits," on which this city is built that must have been buried many thousand years before men were placed upon the earth, and these specimens are as solid as the old oaken crib work taken from the Minnesotah mines. They are even more solid than this ancient cedar shovel taken from the Eagle Harbor location, and presented to me by Dr. Blake, and which was sometimes not covered with water. The ancient cedar trees beneath our town were from 12 to 20 feet from the surface, and were always either moist or wet. All circumstances considered, the time indicated by the timber remains of Lake Superior, is as great as by that taken from the mounds, and both may have been left there 2000 years ago.

There is a very sure guide that may be followed in determining the shortest space of time since the mines and the mounds were abandoned, and that is the age of growing timber that stands upon them. There are living trees now flourishing on these ruins which are more than (300) three hundred years old.

On the same spot there are the decayed trunks of a preceding generation that have arrived at maturity and fallen down from old age. It is also a matter of common observation that where land has been cleared, and remained a long time under cultimation, if abandoned, a different kind of timber from that which was cut away, first springs up and has its day. It is only by a slow progress of encroachment that the ancient and surrounding forest trees regain their dominion over the soil, and thus it is only after generations have passed away that the new growth is crowded out and disappears. On the ancient earth works, and on the ancient mining sites of the north, the same kind of timber is seen as that which occupies the adjacent forest.

This carries us back through a period of at least 600, and possibly 1000, years, as the limit within which this territory has not been occupied, either by the old copper diggers or the race of the mounds. We have historical evidence, from the Spaniards, that North America was occupied by the Aborigines (360) three hundred and sixty years ago, and from the Icelanders 850 years ago. If they came as emigrants from Mongolian tribes of Asia a long period must have elapsed after their arrival in order to allow such an increase of their numbers.

The natural increase of civilized nations is much greater than of barbarous ones, and in the former case it does not exceed 100 per cent in 40 years. The Mongolians may have passed freely from Asia to America, as the "Esquimauz," or Eskimos do now, in the "kiaks" made of skins; but there is no apparent reason for an emigration more rapid than the surplus population would demand. Upon the whole it seems that it must be since the Aztecs left, and the Indians assumed the possession of the middle States of the west, from 1500 to 2000 years.

A long period must have elapsed between the first appearance of the Aztecs upon our soil and their exodus to the south during which the copper mines were wrought, the mounds, earth works and fortifications built, and the rich lands of the western states cultivated. If we add 1000 years for their occupation of the northern states it does not carry us back beyond the foundation of Rome (753 years B. C.), and when Rome was built the ruins of Paestum were so ancient that no one knew, from history or tradition, the people who erected those fallen structures.

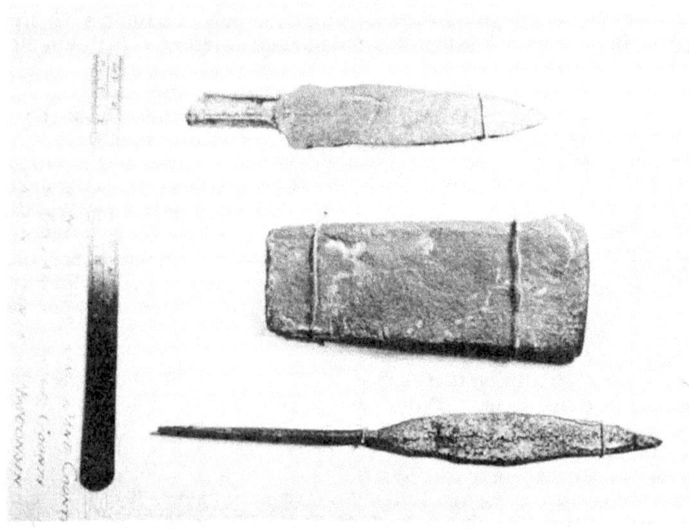

PREHISTORIC COPPER GAD AND SPEAR HEADS

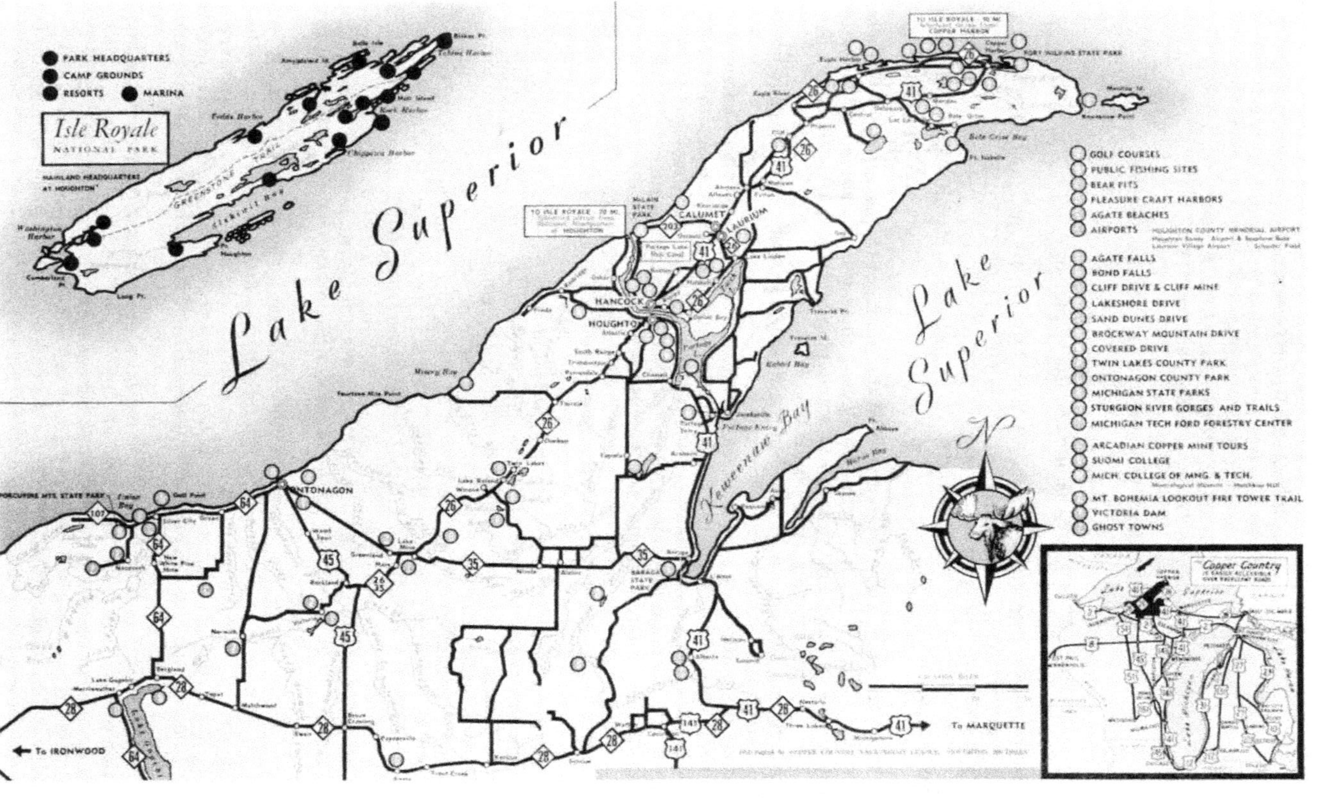

KEWEENAW PENINSULA SHOWING ONTONAGON

EARLY DAYS IN ONTONAGON
Being a translation by Samuel Brady of
CHAPTER XX
REISEN IN NORDAMERIKA
IN DEN JAHREN 1852 und 1853
Von
Dr. Morits Wagner Und Dr. Carl Scherzer
Leipsig
1857
Arnoldische Buchhandlung

THE MINERAL REGION OF ONTONAGON. BIRCH BARK CANOE JOURNEY ON
THE ONTONAGON. THE MINNESOTA MINE. FOREST FIRE. A CITIZEN-
LIKE SERVICE, VISIT TO THE MINE. RETURN TO ONTONAGON. STORMY
SEA. WILD LIFE IN THE FOREST. A MINER AS A METHODIST PREACHER.
INDIAN DANCE.

Ontonagon is a newly located town at the mouth of the Ontonagon River, on
Lake Superior. It is alive with a varegated collection of people, gathered from
all quarters of the Union, as well as wandering Indians, all of whom are dependent upon the trade with the mines.

The Copper Mines lie 15 miles in the interior and can be reached by means
of a comparatively short river journey.

Four of us after engaging a birch bark canoe and two powerful Indians,
started soon after sunrise to ascend the Ontonagon River, the mouth of which
is 331 miles from the Falls of St. Mary, to the Minnesota Mine.

It was a peculiar journey. The dark green mirror like surface of the
Ontonagon contrasting so pleasantly with the cloud decked lake of the previous
day. The banks, the trees, the forest, all had such a virgin like aspect, that
it appeared as if ours was really the first canoe to ruffle the surface of the
river.

Among our travelling companions, we numbered a sad faced figure, a young
but consumptive New Yorker, who in discharge of his duty, as a physician, had
lost his health in the fever exhaling climate of Georgia and now hoped to regain
the same, by inhaling the breath of the pines. He was a sad companion, whose
lips were already kissed by the breath of death, but from whose eyes still
glanced so much of the desire for life. We who sat opposite to him in the
canoe, could but recall to mind that verse from Goethe, "Though I am still so
young so young, I soon must die."

Ontonagon given upon the Jesuit Map as Nantounagon, means in the Indian
language, Cup or Bowl: but to the student of Etymology, the exact meaning of
the word is not known.

One of our canoe men was a full blooded Indian, whose bronze, darkly
painted face, had been touched but slightly by the mark of civilization. His
rough strongly marked countenance, appeared to be seared by the pressure of
want, his strong prominent cheek bones, his irregular nose, the great prominent lips, his careless manner of speech, all proclaimed the aboriginee and
the animal life.

His long black hair fell in plaited pig tails over his shoulders and the open
portion of his thick shirt, that hung shabbily about his hips, exposed a power-
fully developed chest, in all its broad nakedness. He made use of a dark coat
of European cut, that was fastened about his middle by means of the arms,
with its collar resting upon his hips. As pantaloons there served him two blue
colored legs of breeches, reaching from his heel to his hips, which were
otherwise uncovered; finally as shoes he was served by his natural soles.

The favorable position of the sun, the' clearness of the sky, and the radiance

of the perfectly smooth surface of the water, all created a magnificent picture.
The illusion was often so perfect, the reflection of the branches of the trees
appeared as life like that one was frequently involuntarily tempted to try to
pluck them from the water, in order to convince himself of the magic played
by the rays of sunlight.

The river, which in places is 200 feet in width, narrows at other points to
60 feet. At high stages of water a small steamer serves as a method of
communication with the mines, forcing its way against the swiftly running
stream, in a two hour long passage; but this rapid method of travel was for
the time suspended, as we could bear witness to a depth of but two feet of
water in many places. All wares and provision supplies are transported to
the mines by means of barges, which are propelled up the river by means of
long poles, in the hands of a large number of boatmen. The banks of the
river are flat, but most charmingly covered with the most beautiful families
of trees of the American Flora, Birch, Maple, Oak, and especially magnificent Elms - (Ulmus Americana and Fulva) shine in their full natural beauty,
reflecting high in air, with verdant love, the life giving suns rays. Towards
midday we landed in a beautiful spot in the forest, and consumed the cold meal
we had brought with us from the hotel in Ontonagon, beneath a green decked
primitive oak. It was a kind of Diner dans l'herb, with the exception of the
bubbling champagne and the sparkling wit of a merry grisette, that far famed,
indispensable ingredient, of every faithful Parisian, for picnics. But the
water of the Ontonagon tasted good, and the air was so pure, so fresh and so
free.

As we come to the rapids, where the river was often hardly one foot deep
and one must skillfully seek a passage through rugged masses of rock, the
guide, throwing aside his paddle, grasped a long pole to force the canoe
through the confusing masses of rock. Our bronze colored Indian with dark
plaited hair, stands now a wild steersman, half naked, at the head of our little
boat, and as he boldly swung the long heavy pole, now at this end and then at
that side, parrying against the obtrusive and way blocking boulders, he
assumed an imposing and almost heroic appearance. And so we held on.
Often pausing for a moment to regain his strength, the old redskin would squat
himself like a monkey into the bottom of the canoe and with hands between his
feet, would fill a little clay pipe with Kinni-Kinick, which is a substitute for
tobacco, prepared from the inner rind of the Cornux Stolinifera.*

Note* - This much loved smoking material of the Indians is sometimes
composed of the dried leaves of the bear berry or red wort (Arctos sphylus uva
ursi) which is intimately mixed with common tobacco, by rubbing together
between the fingers. The yellow fungus that is found growing in the woods
upon the birch and sugar maple, serves as a means of preserving fire for pipe
lighting and other purposes. Then slowly lighting a small piece of touch wood
by means of steel and flint he laid a piece of the burning match upon the most
primitive of all smoking tobaccos. The aroma of the Kinni Kinick, as it was
brought to our nostrils from the smoking Indian, was not unpleasant and very
far less injurious than the vile compounds made use of, on all sides, by the
half civilized Americans throughout the west.

Some miles before reaching the end of our journey, the river was so shallow and the rock so numerous, that with the exception of the sick doctor, who
was left lying upon the bottom of the canoe, we were compelled to relieve the
situation, by the walk of a half a mile along the river bank. This could not
be helped; as on account of the density of the forest and the extension of the
overhanging growth, well out into the deep water, we were compelled to climb
over fallen timber and through a luxurious growth of thicket, until we were
relieved by a friendly "Halloh," calling us to return to the boat again.

At 3 P.M. we finally reached the Minesota Landing, where we released the Indians and their canoe and were left with a 2 1/2 mile walk to reach the Mine. Our invalid companion remained behind to await the arrival of a horse to transport him upon his back over the crest of the hill to the mine.

The Ontonagon which is formed by the union of two small rivers at a point from six to eight miles above, runs through an everwinding valley, to reach the point of our landing. At high water stage it is navigable for 45 miles; which covers the distance from its headwaters to its entrance into Lake Superior.

We received from the superintendent of the Minesota Mine a hearty welcome, which counts for double the worth in a locality having no place of public reception, that stands between the bed of hospitality and the stony way through the forest. It would have been for visitor as well as host, more comfortable, had we been able to have found an open hotel, where the traveller would not have been put to the unpleasant necessity of feeling, that he an entire stranger, was laying claim to the day long attention of his host.

True it is that at times, one, on account of the great hospitality with which he is received, almost completely loses this depressing feeling, still there are also moments, when one, in spite of the warmest letters of recommendation, meets with a frosty reception, and who like ourselves, have seen the insolent cold face of the Inspector of the Cliff Mine, as we handed him a letter from one of the Pittsburg Directors. At such moments, one is seized with an uneasy feeling, as often as the desire for investigation, takes him into a locality, where in pursuit of lodging he becomes dependent upon the kindness and caprice of such uncouth, baked out block heads.

The vegetation is generally leaved timber,(Laub Holz) and without exception, where such timber is found, the fertility of the soil is greater than where trees of the fir family predominate.

There is also in this locality, a great scarcity of food for cattle. This is not surprising, when one notices the absence of all cows and oxen, as well as of all kinds of domestic animals. Hay which is brought from Detroit (500 miles westerly) costs $30.00 per ton.*

Note* - An enterprising Wisconsin farmer, recently drove 300 head of cattle to Ontonagon to sell. Another speculator brought from Detroit 2 head of Draft oxen and 40 head of sheep. The latter which averaged about 50# each, he expected to sell at 10 cents per lb. The draft oxen he anticipated driving to the mine where he hoped to readily receive $125.00 for both.

Notwithstanding that people were forced to destroy great stretches of forest, on account of the daily pressing want for the products of the soil, the habit of forest burning has become a veritable mania. Dark clouds of smoke that rise on all sides, obscure the sun, and the entire atmosphere exhales the smoky odor of singed vegetation. Even the doctor that shortly after our arrival conducted us to the top of the hill to enable us to obtain a more extended view, could not pass a single burning mass, without setting fire to some remaining group of trees in the neighborhood, and had the appearance of being more like a fire fiend than the consuming flames themselves.

During earlier travels in Western Canada, where we had already witnessed this same drama of burning forests, there as here, the easy preparation of the soil appeared to be the object. Yet many times has it there occurred, that wantoness and negligence in extinguishing the fire of some abandoned encampment, has led to the destruction of noble stretches of forest. Neither on account of the demands of commerce or the scarcity of cultivatable land can such barbarous timber exterminations be justified.*

Note* - Such purposeless and objectless conflagrations, are as a rule only caused by carelessness, as it is the universal custom of the Indians, that all fires shall be extinguished, as often as an encampment is abandoned.

Excepting in such cases where necessity demands, it impresses one with the feeling of the most profound sorrow, to witness the flames sweeping through

the forest, destroying with relentless fury one of natures most magnificent
creations. It always seemed to us as if the young green trees possessed a
sense of life, and that we could witness their terror, as the glowing heat and
ruthless flame advanced upon them, when they could not flee and through a
living love must helplessly await their destruction.

THE PROPERTY OF THE COMPANY

The property of the Company upon which the mines are located, is three
miles long by one mile in width. Already, through the mania of the people for
the destruction of the forests, by fire, 160 acres have been brought under cultivation, and in a few years these aspiring settlements will be completely
emancipated from their present dependence upon the agriculture of the east.
As a rule they have more rainy than dry days in this locality, but this fall
(1852) has been marked by an exceptionally long dry period, no rain having
fallen for three months. The prevailing wind is from the west, the south east
wind generally bringing, according to the season of the year, either rain or
snow.

The lowest temperature of the year occurred upon the 19th day of January,
when the Fahr. thermometer recorder -25 and the highest recorded the same
year was 103. The average degree of cold for that winter having been -12.

The fourfooted dwellers of these forests which are at the same time a source
of food as well as of commerce are the bear, deer, beaver, marten, otter, and
wild swine.

THE MINE

The Copper Mine of the Minesota Company, whose Directorship is located
in New York, was first worked in the spring of 1848. At present the population consists of 400 souls, under which we find 100 miners and 60 children.

Before descending into the mine Captain Harris fitted each of us with a suit
of miners clothing and the necessary lights.

The mine has four entrances, (Ein gange). The deepest point reached by us
was 207 feet below the surface of the earth. The combined lengths of all
levels, (stollen) amounts to 1200 feet. We visited every level, which stretch
themselves out 600 feet to the east and 600 feet to the west. Between each
level is an overhead space of solid rock of 60 feet. The metal veins course
generally horizontally, in a north easterly and south westerly direction, at a
height of about 700 feet above sea level. ("Die metall adern laufen gross-
tentheils horozental"). Their thickness varies from 1-7 feet, with an average
width of about 4 feet. The position of the different beds, from the bottom to
the top is as follows: - Clay, Conglomerate, Sandstone and Trap; in the latter
of which the greater part of the metal in combination with quartz, calcite and
epidote, is found. Frequently copper in combination with silver is found, and
we can estimate the total value of the silver saved in the course of the year at
about $500.00.*

Note* - The largest mass of silver that has yet been brought to the surface
in any of the mines of Lake Superior, weighed 8 pounds, and was found at the
Phoenix Mine, on Keweenaw Point. Beautiful pieces of massive silver in
company with prehnite, have been found along the shores of Washington Harbor,
on Isle Royale.

Note* - In connection with this subject the translator of this article desires
to state that the late Joseph C. Thomas, of the Michigan Mine, informed him
that, in early days he had seen pieces taken from the Cliff Mine that weighed
from 25 to 30 pounds; as much as $500.00 worth being taken out in one night
by the men. Within recent years a piece weighing 12 lbs. was found in the
Mass Mine and Mr. Benj. Cheynoweth informed me that a small boy in cobbing
a piece of Conglomerate, opened up a piece at the National Mine weighing 16
lbs.

In the year 1851 - 275 tons of copper, valued at $20.00 per center, were collected and such advance work completed as guarantees considerably better results for the coming year.

The freight to the smelting points, Detroit and Pittsburg, amounts to $10.00 per ton.

The principal working tools of the miners are the chisel and hammer and drill. At times powder is employed in order to enable them to more easily and quickly reach the copper veins.

The consumption of powder at the present time amounts to 125 kegs of 25 lbs. each, or a total of 3125 lbs. per month.

A miner earns upon the average $36.00 and the surface man $25.00 per month, their expenses for costs and board during the same period of time amounting to $10.00. At present the mine is operated both day and night. The working hours are from 7 in the morning to 6 o'clock in the evening and from 6:30 P. M. to 5 A. M. including a rest for meals. The same rest and repose given to those who labor upon the surface, follows the miner into the dark recesses of the earth.

But one never hears a hearty "Gluck Auf," as the young men pass down the shaft nor sounds a homelike miners song, to the dull beating of the hammer. No happy "Welcolm", no beloved "Fahrwohl."

The character of the product is identically the same as that of the mines of Keweenaw Point. Two thirds of the yearly production of copper being masses, yielding from 75 to 80% of metallic copper. One-third stamp work, barrel or stamp stuff, yields 40 to 50% of copper.

The most common complaint among the mine people are dysentary and eye diseases. Dr. Pratt, an able and learned doctor, who is in possession of a splendid library and a magnificent copy of Rumbolts Cosmos, informed us that during the previous year, an eye epidemic had prevailed among the miners, which he attributed to the fact that after washing the daily accumulation of filth from their hands and faces they were carelessly wiping upon a community towel.

In the past two years there have been 5 deaths and 30 births, 3 miners died from accidents sustained in the mine.

The building of a church for a free common service and of a school house is in project.

Great service to the spiritual welfare of this solitary quarter of the heavens, has been rendered by a Capuchine monk, Father Baraga, an Austrian by birth who lives at L'Anse, on one of the most retired Bays of the Lake and visits from there the dependent missions and settlements. He is often met in the midst of the most rigorous winter weather plodding his way through the forest, with but a single Indian to serve him as a guide and companion, on his way to the different mines to preach the gospel of Christ. As a holy man he is honored. The Catholic believers of Lake Superior, throng with a childlike affection to his services and his benedictions and live in anxious care of the moment when this devoted priest, shall be removed · through a call to fill a higher place and they be deprived of his quiet ministrations.*

Note* - Father Baraga will soon be raised to a Bishop, though he will remain in his present field of labor on Lake Superior.

This indefatigable missionary has just published a valuable Chippewa Dictionary and is now engaged in the preparation of an Indian-English Dictionary. As we were about to start on our return, we were presented by our most hospitable Superintendent, with an interesting collection of minerals and quartz crystals, which we are to have the pleasure of taking with us as a friendly recollection from Lake Superior to the Royal Geological Museum of Vienna. Among the collection we found a very interesting chiseled stone hammer, similar to many that have been found in shaft sinking here. It was the primitive boring apparatus of the Indian, whom numberless cases substantiate as having busied themselves with mining operations.*

Note* - The Jesuit Dablon, relates in the records of the Mission of the Years 1669-70, how wandering Indians upon an island in Lake Superior, probably Isle Royal, as they in their customary manner were cooking their meal by heating stones and dropping them into a water filled wooden vessel, noticed that they were nearly all of solid copper. In their lack of knowledge of the fact that copper ores with which they were cooking their food, exerted a poisonous influence, they ate heartily of the food and with one exception died before reaching home.

To facilitate the manipulation of the greenstone or quartz porphyry hammer the young tough throngs of the willow or the hickory used, Juglane alba, were employed. These they understood how to bind to the back of the hammers in a skillful manner.

Our journey over the road through the forest to the landing was made in a rapid walk of 30 minutes, as it had already grown late for starting and rain and wind were already appearing in the sky. We were met at the landing by our Indians and the canoe. The old fullblood's face was well bedecked with black paint, and he sat smoking a pipe of Kinni-Kinick and looking much like a monkey when he sits resting upon the swinging limb of a tree.

The custom of the Indians of painting or rather smearing the face, the hair of the head and in fact the clothing, appears to be as strange as it does meaningless. During our many months journeying among the different Indian tribes, we have taken extraordinary pains to ascertain why this frivolous race, figure and paint themselves, disfiguring the noble face of man in this horrible manner. We have not omitted to secure all possible information from the most distinguished authorities who have studied the matter; but found to our own personal satisfaction; as well as to the regret of the spirit of investigation that even the learned gentlemen who have made the most earnest efforts to gain enlightenment upon this subject, are prepared to throw but little light upon the matter of the dark painting of the face. The black color is said to denote at the same time, sorrow, want and farewell. The red, when they have in contemplation, during a time of war, the making themselves appear terrible to their enemies. This is about all that we could gain, as a result of our interpretation of conversations with Indian Chiefs. But we shall again allude to this "gendre" decoration, when writing of our intercourse with the Sioux at St. Paul, the Capital City of Minnesota.

Soon after our departure we were overtaken by a frightful thunderstorm, that found us utterly unprotected. Navigating in a canoe, seated upon uncomfortable boards and with water soaked clothing, we mistook the flying minutes for hours and believed the 15 miles ride to be a journey through eternity. We passed the rapids without danger to our canoe and arrived in fairly good shape at Ontonagon. The stormy lake dashed its rolling waves so fiercely against the current of the river that it was only by the strongest effort that our canoe was brought to shore.

We had arrived at the conclusion some days previously to further continue our journey upon the lake as soon as we had completed our visit to the copper mines. But as the equinoctial period was drawing nigh, a time when the anger of the elements, renders the lake often impassible for weeks, we found upon our return to Ontonagon, the weather conditions to be so unfavorable as to prevent the thought of an early continuation of our voyage. No navigator, on account of the delicate construction of the birch bark canoe, would have dared to venture 300 feet from shore.

The entire night the north wind blew in the wildest manner, storming and roaring like an angry lion. We have never heard the Atlantic, the Adriatic or the North Sea give forth such awful tones. What rendered our stay all the more tormenting, was the miserable accommodations that we were called upon to endure. True it is, that we found in our hotel an elegant parlor, provided with a gorgeous carpet, a divan, together with a mahogany table which was decked with a number of gilt edged display books. As Americans more than the English place much importance upon appearances, and seem to deem such ostentations a great necessity, even in the settlements in the midst of the solitary forest. On the other hand the lack of every genuine comfort was all the more pronounced. The doors could not be closed, from the windows panes of glass were missing and the building of the chimney had never been completed. The wind blew so cold and searching through this two storied board house of the back woods, that one could, without flattering the owner, c all it a veritable wind castle. It seemed impossible to believe that a landlord would live for ten long years, fully acquainted with such climatic conditions, without foresight enough to provide for the erection of a stove and the repair of his hou se. At the end of September the chimney was incomplete, "as the bricks had not arrived;" which was the same excuse given his guests of the previous year by this bluffing landlord, for complaints regarding the cold. It may be that this evidence of greed arises from the desire to make money rapidly, by giving as little as possible therefor.

The thermometer which yesterday stood at 66 Fahr. fell to 49; which rapid change of temperature made the cold all the more pronounced. We finally moved out of the big "Weather Cock" of Mr. Paul and into a modest little hut, which to say the least, contained a stove with a good fire and plenty of excellent pine wood close at hand.

And so passed the days, until in the language of the Chippewas, "Four suns had set" ere the turbulent waters of the lake permitted us to end our stay.

Ontonagon is a very young colony. But one year since (1851) the town was possessed of not more than 7 log houses; but up to the present they have erected 103 frame buildings, some of which, if not wind proof, are of an excellent character and serve as a shelter for about 700 souls.

The first settlers, with a few honourable exceptions, are a strange mixture of selfishness and greed, having also a strong tendency for speculation and other swindler like characteristics. They have little in common with the manner and customs of life of the older of cities and form a cast, that must be judged and estimated apart by themselves. Whoever cuts himself loose from the intimate customs and comforts of life, to carve out a new home for himself among strangers, with the aid of the axe and the shovel, must surely have either a very holy or a very temporal object in view, and this temporal object, upon which all their thoughts and aspirations are expended, is gold, ever more gold. To that end the trend of events, in the sparsely settled region of Lake Superior lead; as well as to the annihilation of the Indian race.

Frontier settlements begin with saloons and gambling dens for the whites and with frippery and trash for the red men. The population is a floating, restless, unstable one, who as soon as they have accumulated a little wealth, move to other and more permanent places, making room by immigration for more respectable people.

One must have seen these rough, uncouth, hard figures and observed the misery and privation, with which these stubborn forests are made to yield a fragmentary piece of cultivatable land, in order to enable them to form a true knowledge of the character of backwoods life, as well as to find an explanation and apology for many things. The further however that one journeys northward, the more difficult business and traffic become and the fewer settlers are met with, until in the end one finds only the Indians and the missionary. One of the days that we unwillingly remained in Ontonagon, was the Sabbath. The stores and saloons remained open as upon working days, but this could not well be otherwise, as many have but one lighted room in which they live, eat their meals and conduct their business. Notice was given that during the afternoon

a Methodist preacher would hold services in the school house. The school
house was a floorless and uncompleted wooden building. Pine poles covered
with a few boards, served as seats and in that position where the Catholics
place a holy decorated altar, for meditation, one saw nothing but a table, a
chair and an old much used Bible. The congregation was not numerous, but
was devout, attentive and prayerful. The preacher was a miner from one of
the neighboring copper mines. This pious occupation appeared not to be a new
thing to him; as he improvised an unpretending and highly interesting discourse,
upon the observation of the Sabbath and the idle manner in which the day was
kept in Ontonagon. Only once, when he permitted himself to take a thrust at
Europe, and especially at the godless French, did he make a rude political
blunder. He attributed nearly all of the political sins, which had been visited
upon France for many years past, down to the present date, to their irreligious
condition and to the manner in which they spend the Sabbath. The smooth miner
from Ontonagon appeared not to realize that the French, were never more
contented, church going and sabbath observing than at the present time, and
that the present condition of France, was far from being as wretched and piti-
able as the back woods Methodist preacher in his simplicity pictured.

And on the other hand, that the French people must be considered as happy
and prosperous; since they set up the brilliant following to the Crown.*

Note* - Louis Napolean Coup de Etat, Dec. 2nd, 1851).

A Methodist congregation is always of a solemn character, be its location,
the modest school house in Ontonagon, the dark primitive forests of Western
Canada or the Mammoth Cave of Kentucky. If these brave Christians would
only stop groaning and put aside that forced sigh that is heard on all sides as
the preacher closes, which is an unnatural and studied lamentation and a
disturber of all true devotion.

The following morning about 50 Indians, who in the midst of their poverty,
had in contemplation a journey to the westward with their families, proposed
giving a so-called Beggar-Dance to enable them to secure provisions enough
for their journey. They all appeared in hideous costumes, with their half
clothed bodies bedecked with red blankets, forehead and cheeks to the back of
their ears painted in black, blue and red, and hair loose and plaited, causing
their outward appearance to be diabolical in the extreme. The entire beggar-
dance was more properly speaking but a pretext for an extravagantly good
time, as well as an excuse for being allowed to beg for bottles of liquor from
door to door and then empty the same. For in the licence of the early settlements, the strict letter of the law was not adhered to, especially when it was
known that another day would rid the community of every wandering Indian. To
us it appeared shocking to see the image of God, so profaned and distorted,
while being laughed and sneered at by the white people.

At first the Indian dancers placed themselves in a circle, then one after
another started to hop, and so they hopped closely behind one another around
in a circle; while making unseemingly gestures on all sides with head, hands
and feet. The entire beggar dance has much resemblance to the Parisian
Cancan (dee Chausiere) only here the Gensdarme, with his long moustache,
did not mix with the dancers and call them to order.

During the dance one old Indian sang in a sorry kind of a tone, while the
Chief of the band, pounded with his bare fists upon an old cracked tambourine.
After hopping around the circle for sometime, the dancers gave a wild cry and
pausing suddenly, as if transfixed by an electric shock, while one in their
midst began a short address relating their object in setting forth and their
necessity for provisions for their long journey. Then the dance began again.
In the meantime the idol of the Indians in the form of a whiskey bottle appeared,
and soon were their great necessities as well as their wives and children forgotten and the brandy bottle commanded their undivided attention. The bottles

were passed around the circle in the most conscientious manner, the grey headed Chieftian holding his drinking glass, no more full than the most undeserving young Indian. Up to this time everything had run comparatively smooth, the mischief starting after they had passed the bottle around the circle 15-20 times.

But we cannot but ask ourselves: who is the most blamable and the most deserving of punishment; the ignorant Indian who begs provision for a journey, or the intelligent white man who, in place of the asked for bread hands poison, that depraves and brutalizes, while affording no help towards their journey?

On the 15th of September, we were again enable to resume our journey towards LaPoint, with a south wind, a cloudless sky and a temperature of 37°.

MISSIONARY LIFE
Pitezel
Lake Superior Region-Destiny-Conclusion

An interesting fact is given us as connected with those early explorations; that is, the evidences of the existence of native copper. In several places large boulders of this mineral were found, some of them weighing a hundred pounds. This pure virgin copper was regarded by the Indians with superstitious veneration, and some of the specimens preserved by them were worshipped as gods. After New France had been ceded to the British crown, an Englishman by the name of Alexander Henry, who had escaped the horrible massacre of Mackinaw, headed a mining expedition, which was prosecuted for a time near the forks of the Ontonagon river. But the effort was ill-directed and soon abandoned. Up to the year 1844 no successful effort had been made to develop the mineral resources of the country. Since that period the wonderful discoveries and the untold wealth that have been revealed have been published to the world.

In those mining explorations a very interesting fact has been brought to light - the works of a rude people, who had been engaged in mining, certainly not less than four hundred years ago, probably much earlier. Those evidences may be seen on Isle Royal, at Eagle River, at the North-West Mine, and other places. But the most interesting discoveries of the kind were made at the Minnesota Mine, at the Ontonagon. Mr. Samuel O. Knapp, the then intelligent agent of the Minnesota Mining Company, in the spring of 1848, laid open one of these ancient works. The following is an extract from Messrs. Foster and Whitney's Reports: "The depression was twenty-six feet deep, filled with clay and a matted mass of moldering vegetable matter. When he had penetrated to the depth of eighteen feet, he came to a mass of native copper, ten feet long, three feet wide, and nearly two feet thick, and weighing over six tons. On digging around it the mass was found to rest on billets of oak, supported by sleepers of the same material. This wood, specimens of which have been preserved, by its long exposure to moisture is dark-colored, and has lost all its consistency. A knife-blade may be thrust into it as easily as into a peat-bog. The earth was so packed around the copper as to give it a firm support. The ancient workers had evidently raised it about five feet, and then abandoned the work as too laborious. They had taken off every projecting point which was accessible, so that the exposed surface was smooth." (Part I, page 159).

Proof of the high antiquity of these works is found in the fact that trees growing over these works are as aged as the forest trees around them. Messrs. Foster and Whitney speak of a pine stump, thus situated, "broken fifteen feet from the ground, ten feet in circumference which must have grown, flourished, and died since the earth in which it had taken root was thrown out." Mr. Knapp counted, say they, "three hundred and ninety-five annular rings, on a hemlock, growing under similar circumstances, which he felled near one of his shafts. Thus it would appear, that these explorations were made before Columbus started on his voyage of discovery." (Ibid.)

Ancient stone hammers have been found, in large quantities, in connection with these works. Those taken out of the Minnesota works exceed ten cart-loads, and weighed from five to thirty-nine pounds each. "A copper gad, with the head much battered, and a copper chisel, with a socket for the reception of a wooden handle, were brought to light." These I saw myself, in the possession of Dr. Hickok, of New York, in the summer of 1848. Messrs. Foster and Whitney suppose that this ancient mining was performed chiefly with these stone hammers, with the aid of fire to soften the rock and separate it from the copper.

All is involved in conjecture respecting who were those rude miners. The Indians of the country have no traditionary accounts of this matter. Our authors, quoted above, mention the fact, that copper rings, designed for bracelets, are frequently met with in the western mounds. And they more than intimate that these copper rings are "a strong link in the chain of evidence to connect the ancient mining of this region with the earth works of the Mississippi Valley." (Ibid.)

But with a simple statement of these facts we must leave the reader to his own speculations, respecting the people who, long ago, delved into the mines of Lake Superior, for hidden treasure.

pp. 424-27. Chapter **XXXI**. Edited-1857, a book entitled "Missionary Life" published in 1857 by Walden & Stowe, Cincinnati, Ohio.

ANCIENT MINING ON THE SHORES OF LAKE SUPERIOR
ATLANTIC MONTHLY
pp. 308-315. Vo. XV. 1865

"In the month of March, 1848, Samuel O. Knapp and J. B. Townsend discovered, from tracks in the snow, that a hedge-hog had taken up his winter-quarters in a cavity of a ledge of rocks, about twelve miles from Ontonagon, Lake Superior, in the neighborhood of the Minnesota Copper Mine. In order to capture their game, they procured a pick and shovel, and commenced an excavation by removing the vegetable mould and rubbish that had accumulated about the mouth of what proved to be a small cavern in the rock. At the depth of a few feet they discovered numerous stone hammers or mauls; and they saw that the cavern was not a natural one, but had been worked out by human agency, and that the stone implements, found in great profusion in and about it, were the tools used in making the excavation. Further examination developed a well-defined vein of native copper running through the rock; and it was evidently with a view of getting this metal that this extensive opening had been made.

"This was the first instance where 'ancient diggings'--as they are familiarly called in the Lake Superior region - were ever recognized as such; and this artificial cavern presents the most conclusive proofs that a people in the remote past worked those mines. Upon the discovery of this mine, attention was at once directed to numerous other cavities and depressions in the surface of the earth at this and other points, and the result was that nearly a hundred ancient pits were found, and in all of them mining tools of various kinds. These ancient mines or pits are not restricted to one locality, but extend over the entire length of the copper region, from the eastern extremity of Keweenaw Point to the Porcupine Mountains, a distance of nearly one hundred miles.

"In some of the ancient diggings, the stone hammers have the marks of hard usage, fractured or battered faces, and a large proportion of them are broken and unfit for use; but in other pits the hammers are all sound, and many of them have the appearance of never having been used. These hammers, or mauls, which are of various sizes, and not uniform in shape, are water-worn stones, of great hardness similar in all respects to those that are found in abundance on the shore of the Lake, or in the gravel-banks of that region. They are generally trap-rock, embracing the varieties of gray, porphyritic, hornblendic, sienitic, and amygdaloidal trap, and appear to have had no labor expended upon them except the chiselling of a groove around the middle for the purpose of attaching a withe to serve as a handle. In a few instances, I have noticed small hammers, usually egg-shaped, without a groove; and the battered or worn appearance at one end was all that induced the belief that they were ever used for hammering.

"These hammers are usually from six to eight inches in length, and from eight to twelve inches in circumference, and weigh from four to eight pounds; but I have measured specimens that were twenty-four inches in circumference at the groove, and would weigh thirty pounds. It seems hardly probably that one man could wield so ponderous a tool, and from the fact that some of the large mauls have two grooves around them, it is presumed that two men were employed in using them.

"Stone hammers are found in all the ancient diggings, and some instances the number is almost incredible. From the pits near the Minnesota mines it is estimated that ten cart-loads have been removed; I was informed that a well there was entirely stoned up with them, and from the great number still remaining I am inclined to believe the report. A still greater number are said to have been found at the Mesnard and Pontiac Mines, in the Portage Lake district. Farther east, in the vicinity of the Cliff and Central Mines, they are

also abundant; and it would seem, from the circumstance of their being invariably found in the pits, that the law among the ancient miners was similar
to the one adopted by the adventurers in California a few years since, who
established their claims by leaving their tools upon the land or in the pits where
they were digging for gold.

"In addition to the stone implements, copper chisels, wedges, or 'gads, '
are often found in the abandoned mines; and in the vicinity, as well as in places
more remote, other copper relics are found, consisting of knives, spear-
points, and rings, like the bracelets of the present day. In a collection at the
Douglas House, in Houghton, Portage Lake, are ornaments of this kind, and
also some spear-heads, nicely wrought and similar in shape and size to the
blade of a spontoon. But I have never seen a copper relic that had the appearance of having been melted. They invariably appear to have been cut and
hammered into shape from a mass of native copper.

"Colonel Charles Whittlesey, of Cleveland, Ohio, who has examined these
'ancient diggings, ' has several interesting relics, some of which he has
figured and described in the thirteenth volume of the 'Smithsonian Contributions
to Knowledge. ' In the Vermont State Cabinet is a spear-head of native copper,
about six inches long, which was found in Williston, Vermont, in 1843.

"It may be proper here to remark, that the copper in these relics is tougher
than that which has been fused, and so is the native copper of Lake Superior;
and occasionally in these copper relics blotches and grains of native silver are
found. These circumstances serve to establish the fact, that the material of
which the implements were made was obtained at Lake Superior; for there, and
nowhere else in America, is native silver found in grains, and sometimes in
considerable masses, imbedded in a matrix of native copper. I well remember, when a boy, reading an article relating to the 'Lost Arts, ' in which the
fact was stated, that a piece of metal consisting of pure copper and silver had
been found in Hamilton County, Ohio, and that a copper knife had been found in
one of the ancient mounds at Marietta, which had distinct blotches of pure
silver in it. The writer of the article claimed that the people who manufactured that knife were in the possession of an art, now lost, by which copper
and silver could be melted and indiscriminately mixed, but upon cooling would
separate and remain distinct and pure, instead of forming an alloy. The discovery of native copper and silver similarly associated in the Lake Superior
mines has not only destroyed this theory, but has established beyond a doubt
the locality whence that copper knife, and other relics found in the ancient
mounds and elsewhere, were obtained.

"Billets of wood that bear the marks of a tolerably sharp-cutting tool are
often found in the old mines where water has been suffered to remain since
their abandonment. In the Waterbury Mine wooden shovels were found about
three and one half feet long, some of which were much worn upon the blade,
and appeared as though they had been used for scraping together and throwing
out the refuse rock and dirt from the mine. At the same locality a wooden
bowl was found, the side being so worn as to show conclusively that it had
been used for baling water from the mine. Similar implements have been
found at the mines in the Portage Lake and Ontonagon districts. When first
found, these wooden implements appear sound, and being thoroughly saturated
with water are heavy and can be handled without breaking; but when dried they
often crack and warp so as to retain little of their original form and appearance. It is to be regretted that but few of these wooden relics were saved and
properly preserved by those who found them. In a few instances the wooden
withe or handle has been found attached to the hammers, but upon being dried
they usually fall to pieces.

"At the Hilton Mine in the Ontonagon district, in October, 1863, as the men
were removing the vegetable mould that had accumulated in one of the old pits,

SOCKETED SPEAR HEAD AND WEDGE-SHAPED HAND TOOL
About one-half size.

The wedge-shaped hand tools have a curled-over top which was bent and may have been used as a hook. There is no evidence that these tools were driven with a hammer or rock as a wedge might be.

The spear head is socketed on one end to attach to a stick or shaft and usually designed to have a shoulder which prevented the shaft from sliding through the socket. Many socketed artifacts have rectangular "pinning holes" in the socket to pin the shaft to the artifact.

they found at the depth of about nine feet a leather bag, which was eleven inches long and seven inches wide. It was lying upon a mass of native copper which the ancient miners had unsuccessfully attempted to remove from its parent vein. The bag was in a remarkable state of preservation, the leather being quite pliable and as tough as sheepskin. It was made up with the hair inside, was sewed across the bottom and up one side with a leather string, and near the top holes were cut and a leather string inserted to close the mouth by drawing it together. The bag was empty, but from its appearance I judged that it had been used for transporting copper or other mineral, --the leather in places showing marks of much service, and the hair being almost entirely worn off. I was unable to determine what kind of skin it was, but inclined to the belief that it was from the walrus, as the short, stubby hairs more closely resembled those of that animal than of any other with thich I am acquainted. At the time I saw the bag, --the day after it was discovered, --it was in the possession of C. M. Sanderson, Esq., the agent of the Knowlton Mine; but I hear it has since been taken to Boston and sold.

"In several of the ancient mines considerable masses of pure copper detached from the main lode have been found, which were left there by those who mined it. At the Central Mine, not far from Eagle Harbor, a mass of copper was found in one of these old pits that weighed forty-six tons. Every portion of the surface was smooth, and appeared as though it had been hammered by those who detached it from its original vein. In the Mesnard Mine, in the Portage Lake district, a detached mass of copper was found that weighed eighteen tons, hammered smooth like the mass before named.

"But the most interesting specimen was found in an old pit near the Minnesota Mine. In removing the accumulated leaves and vegetable mouls the workmen, at the depth of eighteen feet, discovered a mass of copper ten feet long, three feet wide, and more than a foot thick, weighing six tons. On removing the earth around the mass, it was found to rest upon skids, or timbers, piled up to the height of about five feet. These timbers, having been constantly covered with water, were in a good state of preservation, and at the ends showed plainly the marks of the tool used in cutting them. It was thought by those who saw the billets when they were plump, that they were a species of oak; but the few remaining pieces which I have seen were so cracked and shrivelled that I have been unable to form an opinion as to the kind of wood. This mass of copper, like all others found in those ancient pits, was divested of all its ragged points, and hammered perfectly smooth. There was nothing in its appearance to show that it had ever been cut from another mass; but upon clearing out the rubbish from the bottom of the mine, which was about twenty-six feet below the surface, a vein of pure metal was found from which this had evidently been taken.

"A few unfinished jobs have been found in these ancient pits, which throw some light upon the manner in which the work was carried on. In two instances there were projecting masses somewhat resembling urns, or inverted short-necked bottles, and completely smoothed by hammering, especially at the thinner portion or neck. It appears that the ancient miners first removed the rock from around the veins of copper. This was done by building fires upon or about it, and, when heated, crumbling it by throwing on water. By means of stone mauls the fragments were broken up and removed. When the vein was sufficiently exposed on all sides a point was selected where the copper was thinner or narrower than the average of the vein. Here they commenced cutting off a mass, and by patient and long-continued hammering severed the two portions of the vein. In all the ancient mines which I have visited there is abundant evidence that fire was extensively used in the removal of rock; for not only did the rocks give proof of having been heated, but charcoal and ashes were invariably found at the bottom of all the rock excavations.

"In general, the mining was done by surface openings along the line of the outcrop of the vein; but occasionally adits are driven into the rock, similar to the one first discovered at the Minnesota Mine before alluded to.

"The surface mines are usually nearly filled with leaves and vegetable mould that have accumulated during the centuries that have elapsed since their abandonment, and till within a few years a heavy growth of timber covered the land; hence the numerous slight depressions that occurred along the line of the vein excited no suspicion that they were artificial excavations. By the closest observers they were regarded as natural depressions, caused either by the disintegration of the underlying rock or the peculiar manner in which the overlying drift was deposited. In many of these depressions, which have proved to be abandoned mines, trees of enormous size are found growing, some of which are ascertained, by counting their concentric rings, to be four hundred years old. At the Hilton Mine, directly over the leather bag before alluded to, there was a hemlock-tree about three feet in diameter. I noticed the stump of a tree nearly four feet in diameter in a gap near the Rockland Mine, where a hill had been actually cut asunder by these ancient miners, and a deep valley formed by the removal of the rock. Until very recently this valley was not recognized as an ancient mine; for, being ten rods in width, and cutting nearly at right angles across the strata of the rock that formed the hill, it was considered too extensive to have been made by human hands, and was supposed to be the result of natural causes. But about two years since, during a very dry time, a destructive fire swept through the woods, and so completely burned up all the vegetable matter accumulated there as to expose the underlying rock, and reveal its true character. After the fire had done its work, it was found that copper veins, which had been worked, ran through the rock in the gap, and that the great bank upon the south side of the hill, which was supposed to be a terraced gravel bank, proved to be a vast accumulation of 'attle,' or refuse stone, that had been taken from the artificial gap and deposited there. The stones forming this immense pile are generally small, and appear to have been broken up by heating to facilitate their removal from the mine, and possibly may have been again broken, with the hope of finding copper in them. In the midst of the pile I noticed several stone hammers, or mauls, some of them measuring twenty inches in girth around their grooves, and one I brought away weighing thirty pounds.

"When examining this locality, I was struck with a significant fact, tending to show the long time that must have elapsed since the abandonment of these mines. I noticed in many instances that the artificial groove around the hammers was nearly obliterated upon the upper side, while upon the lower side, less exposed to the abrading agency of the atmosphere and rains, the groove presented a comparatively fresh appearance, and even the slight markings made by the tool that cut them were quite distinct. When I removed the overlying rock and found a grooved maul in a protected spot, the groove was generally as fresh as though it had been made but a few months before. The compact nature of the stone of which these hammers are made, and their ability to resist the action of weather and moisture, prove conclusively that much time has been required to disintegrate their surface so as to obliterate the artificial work which has been expended upon them.

"I feel unwilling to leave this subject without instituting an inquiry relative to the time when these mines were wrought, and the people who worked them. Many who have been taught to regard the present roving tribes of Indians as instinctively wise in matters of medicine and mining are ready to award to that race the credit of having worked these mines; but, inasmuch as even a traditional knowledge of their existence was unknown to the Indians at the time the Jesuit missionaries visited that region in the sixteenth century, we incline to the opinion that another and distinct race worked them. I am unable to see

why the descendants of a people residing in the same country, and subject to
the same wants, should abandon the half-worked mines which their ancestors
had opened, and even fail to hand down to their posterity a tradition of their
existence. If copper was in such demand that the ancestors of the present
race of Chippeways were induced to work so perseveringly to obtain it, why
did not the children continue to work, at least enough to finish the jobs already
commenced by their progenitors? We cannot consistently attribute the Her-
culean labor expended on these mines to the ancestors of the indolent race of
North American Indians. We incline, rather, to the opinion that the miners
were the mound-builders, who resided south of the mines, and ultimately
found a home in Mexico. The condition in which the mines were left favors
this theory; for in many instances unfinished jobs are found, --as in the case
of the mass copper upon skids at the Minnesota Mine, and the half-severed
veins in other mines. May we not reasonably suppose that the miners came
from the South, and worked during the summer months, returning to their
homes in winter? The circumstance that no traces of their habitations or
burial-places have ever been discovered in the immediate vicinity of the mines
leads to the inference that they came from a distance; and the fact that copper
rings, chisels, and knives, and occasionally stone hammers, are found in the
ancient mounds that extend in an unbroken line from Ohio to Mexico, induces
the belief that the ancient miners and the ancient mound-builders were the
same people.

"It is said that artificial mounds are found in British America; and I was
informed of one upon the banks of the Ontonagon River, about six miles from
its mouth, but was unable to visit the spot. It is well known that they are quite
abundant in Wisconsin, and extend the entire length of the Mississippi Valley.

"It is a noticeable fact that as we proceed south we find the mounds generally larger and more symmetrical than those in more northern latitudes.
It would seem that the people who constructed those in British America, in
moving southward, (for we strongly suspect that this people originally crossed
Behring's Strait from Asia,) improved in their style of building, and, on
arriving at the Ohio River, had so far improved as to be able to construct
those interesting works at Marietta, Moundville, and other points in that
region. It was not till about the time they reached the Ohio Valley that they
manufactured pottery. In that valley, and thence to Mexico, fragments of
earthen ware are very common; and in the mounds entire vessels are not un-
frequently found. Upon reaching Mexico, the mounds are seen to be still
further improved in size and form, and specimens of ancient pottery are more
abundant. The great mound or pyramid at Cholula, which is a fair type of
the mounds in Mexico, is fourteen hundred and seventy-seven feet high, being
larger than the celebrated pyramids of Egypt. This immense structure is
said to have been built by the Toltecs, a people who, according to tradition,
as communicated to the Spaniards, entered Mexico from the North in the year
A. D. 648, and established their capital on the northern confines of the great
valley of Mexico, at Tula, the remains of which city were visible, and a
record made of them, at the time of the Conquest by Cortes.

"This people were said to have possessed a good knowledge of agriculture,
and were well instructed in many useful mechanic arts. They mixed gold and
copper, and were experts in working these metals. For a period of four
hundred years they occupied the territory of Mexico or Anahuac; but secession,
and the attendant evils of war, pestilence, and famine, greatly reduced their
numbers, and the race disappeared from the land to give place to their successors, the Aztecs, who also emigrated from the North. Remnants of the
Toltec race are said to have migrated still farther south, and to have spread
over Central America, and the remarkable correspondence of dates inclines
us to the belief that the famous Manco Capac, whom the Peruvians worshipped

as the founder of their empire, may have been a wanderer from that once happy, but then unfortunate people among whom he settled, instead of originating in the great liminary of the day, and being brought to earth by a 'child of the Sun,' as they were taught, are far more likely to have been cultivated by the Toltecs in the days of their prosperity, and, on the dissolution of their government, transmitted by those who, fearing the result, had fled and taken refuge with the credulous Peruvians. Whether the stupendous ruins of temples found at Mitla, Palenque, and Uxmal were the work of the Toltecs or the Aztecs, is immaterial. It is sufficient for the purposes of this paper to show that a people inhabited Mexico prior to and at the time of the Conquest, who were far in advance of the roving tribes of Indians that subsisted in the more northern and eastern portions of North America.

"At the time of the conquests of Mexico and Peru, numerous cities were found in those countries, and magnificent temples and palaces abounded, some of which were richly decorated with massive images of solid gold, others ornamented with fantastic and sometimes hideous figures carved out of the solid rock. But what is remarkable, no <u>iron</u> implements were used, nor did the inhabitants have the least knowledge of its use, notwithstanding iron ore was plentifully distributed through the country in which they lived. Not a trace of iron has ever been found in those grand ruins of Yucatan visited by Stephens and Catherwood; nor do the ruins of the holy city, Cuzco, give evidence that implements of iron were used in its construction. But the people of these countries were acquainted with many of the metals; and the Spanish invaders found numerous silver, tin, and copper mines that had been worked by them. All the deep, winding galleries of these mines were driven without the aid of iron, steel, or gunpowder. It is said that an alloy of tin and copper was used for their edge-tools; and with the aid of a silicious sand or dust, they were enable to cut and polish amethysts, emeralds, porphyry, and other hard substances. With these implements the elaborate carving in the stone temples of Palenque and the other ruined cities of Central America was executed. The great calendar-stone, which in 1790 was disinterred in the city of Mexico, was nicely wrought out of a block of dark porphyry, that is estimated to have weighed fifty tons, and must have been transported several leagues; for the nearest point where porphyry of that character is found is upon the shores of Lake Chalco, many miles distant from the city of Mexico. In the absence of iron, some tough metal would be in requisition for the tools and machinery necessary in the execution and removal of such a gigantic and elaborate work. In many abandoned quarries in Mexico and Central America unfinished blocks of granite and porphyry are found, which are supposed to have been the work of the Toltecs; and abandoned by them at the time of the invasion of the fierce Aztec. Assuming this to be the fact, we can readily conceive why the half-raised mass of copper in the Minnesota Mine should also be abandoned; for a people suddenly scattered as the Toltecs were--so suddenly as to leave temples half finished, and blocks of stone half hewn--would have no further use for copper tools; and hence the raw material would no longer have a value. In the abandoned quarries near Mitla, amid fragments of pillars and architraves and half-finished blocks of granite, copper axes, chisels, and wedges were found in abundance; but the same inordinate love of money that prompted adventurers to flock to Chiriqui, a few years since, to rob the ancient burying-grounds of their golden idols, induced others to search the old quarries and mines of Mexico and Central America, and take from them any relics that were intrinsically valuable.

"In Mexico, the mounds were built so that their summits were visible from every portion of the surrounding city, in order that the inhabitants might continually have in view the sacred fires that were ever kept burning on each side of the sacrificial altar. The same is strikingly true of the mounds at the West;

for they are invariably placed so that their summits occupy a commanding
position,--a circumstance that has induced many to suppose them to have
been built for military purposes, and to have served as watch-towers. But
when we reflect that the attacks of savage to half-civilized peoples are usually
made in the night-time, we shall hardly suppose these structures were raised
for any such purpose. The Pyramid of Cholula is composed of alternate
layers of brick and clay, or possiblv of burnt and unburnt brick; and others
in Mexico are built of unburnt brick. Many of the mounds in the West are of
clay,--perhaps of unburnt brick,--in situations where clay is not so abundant as other earths.

"I recollect visiting Circleville, Ohio, when it was really a Circleville.
An octagonal court-house stood upon an ancient mound, and the dwellings and
stores were built upon an ancient circular wall of earth that encompassed an
area around the mound. South of this circular wall, and joining it, was a
square inclosure of several acres, surrounded by a wall about ten feet high.
What is remarkable, this square wall--and we presume the same is true also
of the mound and circular wall--was built of clay, perhaps of unburnt brick,
that must have been transported a considerable distance; for no clay exists
upon that alluvial bottom, and the nearest point where it is found is three-
fourths of a mile distant, across a considerable creek. On a subsequent
visit to this place, I found the people using the clay from the wall of the
square inclosure for making brick, and streets had been cut across the circular inclosure, so that the city is no longer entitled to the name of Circleville. In many instances, the ruined cities of Central America have inclos-
ures resembling those at Circleville, surrounding the Teocallis, or sacred
temples, which almost invariably stand upon mounds, or, as they are commonly called, pyramids.

"With these many points of resemblance, the conclusion is irresistable,
that the mounds of the West were but the germs of the more symmetrical
pyramids of Mexico and Central America, and that the people who constructed
them were, in intelligence and civilization, far in advance of the roving tribes
of North American Indians who inhabited the country at the time of its discovery.

"If it be true, as tradition informs us, that the Toltecs were a cultivated
race, even more advanced than the Aztecs who occupied Mexico at the time
of the Conquest, we may reasonably suppose that a metal so valuable to them
as copper would be in great demand, and that mines of it, even at a remote
distance, would be worked by a people, the construction of whose religious
temples and royal palaces, and, it would seem, their nationality even, de-
pended upon its possession.

"Other evidence might be adduced to show that the extensive mining pits
on the shores of Lake Superior were not the work of the indolent and untutored
race of Indians who now inhabit that region, nor of their ancestors, but of a
people comparatively well acquainted with the mechanic arts. Our article,
however, has already extended beyond the limits contemplated. I therefore,
leave the subject with the hope that the few hints here thrown out may awaken
other and abler minds to its investigation."

MINERAL RESOURCES OF LAKE SUPERIOR

A Geological Report Circa 1875

<u>Ancient Mine Works</u>. - All along the Trap Ranges ancient mining works are numerous. The first discovery of one of them was, according to Dr. J. W. Foster, made in the winter of 1847-'8, by Mr. Samuel O. Knapp on the Minnesota Company's grounds. One pit opened by Mr. Knapp, is thus described. "When he had penetrated to a depth of eighteen feet, he came to a mass of native copper, ten feet long, three feet wide, and nearly two feet thick, and weighing over six tons. On digging round the mass, it was found to rest on billets of oak, supported by sleepers of the same material. The wood, from its long exposure to moisture, was dark-colored and had lost its consistency. It opposed no more resistence to a knife blade than so much peat. The earth was so firmly packed as to support the mass of copper. The ancient miners had evidently raised it about five feet and then abandoned the work as too laborious. The number of ancient hammers he took from this and other excavations, exceeded ten cart loads. They were made of greenstone and porphyry boulders. Selecting a stone of the desired size and form, the ancient miner cut a groove, arched it so that it might be secured by a withe, and thus wielded as a sledge hammer."

The instances of similar works elsewhere are too common and well known to be dwelt upon. There is scarcely a productive vein of lode in these districts, that did not show traces of ancient works. Mr. Hulbert found them at the Calumet, leading down to the conglomerate belt. Hon. Samuel W. Hill, some two years ago, discovered pits and trenches on Isle Royale of great magnitude and of surpassing interest. He states that those works exceed in extent all other works of the kind heretofore seen in the copper region put together. The Minong mining company, Mr. A. C. Davis, Supt., is successfully operating in a system of those pits, which covers a space 400 feet wide and 1 1/2 miles long. An army of ancient miners must have wrought there many years.

Float copper is also of common occurrence; it often leads to the discovery of veins in the immediate neighborhood. The largest pure mass found in modern times was cut up by Mr. Jacob Houghton, Agent of the mine on the Mesnard Mining Company's land, near Hancock. It weighed eighteen tons. It was found in the woods, and was covered with moss. It had been worked at by the ancient miner. Much charcoal was found under it; its top and sides were beaten smooth; marks of stone hammers were apparent. All projections, every bit of copper that could be pounded off had been carried away. The ancient man then left the pure, noble mass, doubtless feeling a supreme disgust at his inability to remove the treasure.

This mass had evidently been forcibly torn from its bed, 50 feet distant - the Epidote lode - by an iceberg. Subsequent mining disclosed its original bed, or matrix.   (pp. 52-53)

ISLE ROYALE

This "Lone Isle of the Sea," has been the theatre of active mine operations during the last two years. Under the superivison of Messrs. Hardie and Cole, the Island mine had been partially developed upon a conglomerate belt, near Siskiwit Bay.

<u>The Minong Mining Company of Detroit</u>, was organized December 16th, 1874, with a capital of one million dollars. It owns 1,455 acres of land in sections 22, 23, 26, 27, 34 and 35, township 66 north, range 35 west, lying at the head of McCargo's cove, on Isle Royale. These lands are traversed by heavy

metalliferous belts and transverse veins, carrying copper, elevated one
hundred and fifty feet above the lake, and distant but an average of half a mile
from the cove, which is about two and a half miles long and one thousand feet
wide, forming a perfectly land locked harbor. The exploration on this property, previous to the organization of the company, was induced by the discovery of a very large amount of ancient mine work, which had been done at
some remote period in the past, the date of which was antecedent to the traditions of the Indians, and by a race who worked only with stone hammers and
fire. The cleaning cut of sections of the transverse veins they had worked
to the depth of twenty-five feet, gave fine specimens of barrel copper, and in
the opening of a pit sixteen and a half feet deep on the belt, there were found
boulders of copper, and one mass, weighing 5,720 pounds, bearing ancient
hammer marks, and evidently too heavy for those people to carry away. The
Minong Company did not commence work until about the middle of June last;
they had to construct everything to work with, having but the dense thicket of
brush and timber at their first landing.   (pp. 61-62)

THE ANCIENT COPPER MINERS OF LAKE SUPERIOR
By Jacob Houghton

Geologists now find that the antiquity of man far entedates the era assigned
to his creation by the received chronology, and submit the evidences of their
belief to an enlightened public sentiment. However strange these new views
with regard to the origin and history of our race may appear, they cannot be
disregarded. We must weigh the value of observations, and press them to
their legitimate conclusions. The investigator at this day must not be tram-
meled, in the language of Humboldt, by "an assemblage of dogmas bequeathed
from one age to another"--"by a physical philosophy made up of popular
errors." -- J. W. Foster.

The preparation of this paper is undertaken at the urgent solicitation of the
editor of this work. The limits into which it is necessary to condense the
facts, and the deductions therefrom, are unavoidable contracted. To fully
elucidate the subject, and to present the comparative proofs, would require
a work of many pages, and involve an amount of labor that could be given only
by those who have at their disposal the time to devote to the most fascinating
study of the day -- the prehistoric races of man. This will be the more fully
appreciated when the general statement is made, that the traces which the
ancient copper miners of Lake Superior have left of the work performed by
them, indicate an intelligent and industrious race -- that their mining labors
extended through centuries of time -- that there was a general movement to
the southward, through a vast number of years, of the greater portion of the
people -- that on the route of this transition they have left a wonderful record
of their works, proving an advancing and increasing intelligence, indicated
by the ancient mounds throughout the United States, and the ultimate achievement, in the erection of the massive structures of Mexico and Central America. This advancement is also indicated in the lesser arts, in the gradual improvement in the numbers, forms and embellishments of the utensils of the
household, and of ornaments for the person. Therefore, treating the subject
with the brevity required, the writer will make no excuse for the use of pos-
tulates, while at the same time feeling confident that sufficient connected
proofs exist to warrant the assumptions that may be made.

On the south shore of Lake Superior the works of the ancient miners extend
over a district of country comprising what is known as the Trap range, having
a length of one hundred and fifty miles through Keweenaw, Houghton and
Ontonagon counties, Michigan, with a varying width of from four to seven

miles. They also wrought the copper deposits of the Trap range of Isle Royale,
covering an area of about forty miles in length by an average of five miles in
width. Their mining operations were crude and primitive. The process was to
heat the embedding rocks by building fires on the outcrops of the veins or belts,
to partially disintegrate the rocks by contraction produced by the sudden throwing on of water, and to complete the removal of the pieces of native copper by
mauling off the adhering particles of rock with stone hammers. This is attested
by the presence, in all of the ancient pits, of large quantities of charcoal, and
of numberless hammers, the latter showing marks of long usage. That the
miners had not advanced to any knowledge of the artificial elevation of water,
is shown by the fact that apparently, in all cases, the pits have only been sunk
to a depth where the limit of manpower in bailing out the water is reached.
Between the successive pits are ridges of unremoved rock and soil, rather indicating that they were left as dams to prevent the water from passing from a
pit already filled with water into one in process of being wrought.

The pits, the charcoal, the stone hammers and the implements and tools,
made of copper, are the only relics left of the race that wrought these mines.
Neither a grave, vestige of a habitation, skeleton or bone has been found.
Among the Indians inhabiting the region, from the earliest acquaintance of the
white man, neither tradition or legend remained of these ancient miners. The
Indians themselves had no knowledge of the existence of copper in the veins and
belts, so thoroughly had the debris of ages covered them. Their knowledge
was confined to the float pieces of copper in the soil.

When considering the extent of country previously stated, over which this
mining work extended, the crude and slow process of the labor and the enormous
amount of work performed, it becomes evident that the work extended through
centuries of time, and was carried on by a vast number of people. The largest
aggregation of ancient pits yet discovered is on what is known as the Minong
belt on Isle Royale. Here, for a distance of one and three-fourths miles, and
for an average width of four hundred feet, the successive pits indicate the
mining out of the belt (solid rock) to an average depth of not less than twenty
feet. Scattered over this ground are battered stone hammers, numberless,
but running into the millions.

It is not to be presumed that these ancient people were unacquainted with the
advantages of the division of labor. There were undoubtedly miners, bailors
of water, and men whose part it was to manufacture tools and implements out
of the pieces of rough native copper produced by the miners. Others were engaged in procuring and transporting food and other necessaries of life, and
still others were employed in collecting and transporting from the shores of
the lake the rounded, water-worn boulders of diorite and porphyry, which were
used by the miners as hammers and sledges.

Many of these stone hammers have been grooved by manual attrition or impact for the purpose of fastening them into withes or split handles, but by far
the greater number are unwrought rounded boulders which have been held in
the hand when in use. Mr. A. C. Davis, now of the Minong mine, informed
me that at one place, near the mouth of the Ontonagon river, he had seen quite
an area of ground strewn with stone chips and broken and discarded pieces of
diorite and porphyry, indicating it to have been a workshop for preparing the
hammers before being transported inland.

The ancient miners made few mistakes in the selection of deposits to be
wrought. In almost every instance in the places where they had carried on extensive mine work, have been wrought the successful mines of these latter
days. This fact is often quoted to advance the idea that those ancient people
were gifted with some mysterious knowledge by which they were able to discover and trace out mineral veins or lodes. This day, when the divining rod
is lost to faith, and the mysteries of the alchemist have been opened to full

light by the science of chemistry, should be too late for such a superstition. The explorers of today have, as aids to discovery, the dip and the traverse needles, and still the most experienced and observing of them in the reconnoisance of the surface which overlies beds of magnetic iron ore, where the needles develop the most activity, are simply enabled to approximate conclusions, and are only satisfied when a full development has been made by a system of costeaning. It may be considered improbable that the ancient miners possessed any aid approaching to the value of the magnetic needles of the present day. It is far more reasonable to assume that the ancient miners, following comparatively closely upon the recession of the glaciers, occupied the country at a period before the action of the elements had disintegrated the surface of the rocks, and when the mineral veins and beds or belts were exposed to view. In this connection should be stated the fact that, without exception, the copper deposits of the country are contained between the walls of hard rocks (crystalline trap) that have served the purpose of withstanding, to a great extent, the grinding force of the glaciers. In consequence of this protection, they occupy the high points of the country, and are now covered with a comparatively small depth of soil, the product of the disintegration of the rocks themselves; while the valleys of the rivers and the lowlands bordering the lake have a greater depth to drift, probably the deposits of the receding glacial period. At the time the ancient miners were carrying on their work, under a climate milder and far more inviting than now, these high points were destitute of soil or trees, and for timber and fuel for their mining work they resorted to the valleys of the streams and the lowlands bordering the great lake -- where, also, were carried on their agricultural pursuits.

The implements and tools into which the pieces of native copper thus won from the rocks were fabricated, were axes, knives, chisels, fleshers, spears, daggers, arrow-heads, awls, needles and bracelets. These tools are found scattered in wonderful profusion, from Lake Superior to Central America, and from eastern Pennsylvania on the east, to Arizona on the west. In 1870 I saw, at Pittston, Pennsylvania, several of these tools, that had been recovered from the soil in that vicinity; and in a newspaper correspondence from Arizona, in the winter of 1874-5 (Detroit Free Press), I was not in the least surprised to see mentioned the discovery, in that territory, of what was called by the correspondent a copper fountain. It matters not for what purpose the article may have been used; the fact of the find is sufficient for the present purpose. These tools, however, have been found in the greatest numbers buried in the works of the mound builders throughout Wisconsin, lower Michigan, Ohio, Indiana, Illinois, Iowa, Missouri, Tennessee, West Virginia, Kentucky, Mississippi, and Louisiana.

Bernal Diaz, who accompanied Cortez in his expedition of the Conquest of Mexico, says that upon entering Tuspan they found that "each Indian had, besides his ornaments of gold, a copper axe, which was very highly polished, with handles curiously carved, as if to serve equally for an ornament and for the field of battle. We first thought these axes were made of an inferior kind of gold; we therefore commenced taking them in exchange, and in the space of ten days had collected more than six hundred, with which we were no less rejoiced, as long as we were ignorant of their real value, than the Indians with our glass beads."

When Columbus, in his fourth voyage, was visited at the Gaunaja islands by a trading canoe of Yucatan, the crew, according to Herrara, had "small hatchets made of copper, small bells and plates."

That the copper from which these tools, scattered over such a vast area of country, were manufactured, came from the ancient mines of Lake Superior, does not admit of doubt. Although large and numerous deposits of copper ore are scattered through Arizona, New Mexico, Mexico, and Central and South

America, there is no evidence that the aborigines, of this country, had sufficient metallurgical knowledge of skill to reduce the ores to refined copper. On the other hand, the great Creator, for provision to the wants of that ancient race, had planted on the shores of Lake Superior the only known workable deposits of native copper in the world. The term virgin copper is well used to denote its purity. In this latter day it outranks all others in the markets of the world.

The occurrence of this native metal in segregations of various weights, enabled the ancient miner to easily follow the deposit and to readily separate the pieces of metal from the containing rock. These segregations were peculiarly adapted for the use of the forgers of the tools. The extreme ductility of the metal, due to its purity, was also a provision of great advantage to the ancient artisan. In examining the tools that have been recovered, one is involuntarily amazed at the perfection of workmanship and at their identity in form with the tools made for like purposes and used at the present day, the prototypes of the implements of our present civilization. The sockets of the spears, chisels, arrow-heads, knives and fleshers are, in nearly all instances, formed as symmetrically and perfectly as could be done by the best smith of the present day, with all the improved aids to his art. The sockets of these tools, however, are in all instances left open on one side, showing no attempt at welding or brazing. While acknowledging that the greater portion of these tools were forged from the native metal, several investigators of the subject assert that many of them were cast. Their position is principally based on the observation of certain raised marks upon the tools, which are claimed to be the marks of the joining of molds. The writer believes that the weight of evidence is against the theory of melting and casting. It is probable that the raised marks are due to unequal oxidation, or to incompleteness of fabrication. Had the tools which are made with sockets been cast, it is reasonable to suppose that the sockets would have been cast complete. Without exception the sockets are all open on one side; on the sides of the open part lips are turned sufficient for holding the handles. The presence of spots of native silver in the tools is against the theory of casting. Native silver to a large extent is present with the copper throughout the region, and always as a distinct and separate metal, occurring in macules and strings upon and through the copper. In melting for casting, the two metals would form an alloy, and as the proportion of copper would be the greatest, the silver would not be visible. In all of the relics of the mound builders there is no evidence of any vessels that would serve the purposes of crucibles or melting pots. In excavating the mounds, pieces of galena are frequently reported to have been found lying in the immediate vicinity of the copper tools, but there is no record of any lead implements whatever. When it is considered that the melting point of lead is only 594 degrees, Fahrenheit, while that of copper is 2,548 degrees, it would certainly be remarkable if the ancient race had progressed so far in metallurgy as to melt the latter, and had failed to melt and utilize the former. None of the tools is hardened; they are simple pure native copper. Any process of alloying the copper with tin or zinc for the purpose of hardening, was entirely unknown to the race.

It is an established fact, that in the Old World (a gross misnomer as applied to the age of the Eastern hemisphere, when compared with that of the Western hemisphere) man in the Stone Age existed contemporaneously, with the Siberian elephant, Siberian rhinoceros, mammoth, cave bear, etc., while scientists have been loth to concede the existence of the mound builders as contemporary with the mastodon, mammoth, etc., of the Western hemisphere. The mound builders have been not rightly, assigned to the more recent Age of Bronze.

Mr. J. W. Foster, in speaking of the discovery in Illinois of a copper knife and the bone of a mastodon in the same geological formation, and separated from each other but a few miles, says: "One of two suppositions is true, -- either that here has been an intermingling of the relics of two distinct ages, or that if the synchromism is established, man on this continent, as a contemporary with the mastodon, was far in advance in the mechanical arts of man, as the contemporary of the fossil elephant on the European continent.

The existence of copper tools among the relics of the mound builders has been the stumbling block in this matter. In these metal implements of man in the Stone Age in America there was only the advance over the man of the Stone Age in Europe, that was due to the obtaining of native copper that could be hammered and drawn out into the desired shapes without any resort to the processes of metallurgy. It was with a view to this point that I have throughout this paper endeavored to constantly impress upon the reader the fact of the purity and ductility of the native copper. It was also for this that I so fully discussed above the reasons that lie against the theory of the melting of the copper and the casting of the tools. The relics of the Stone Age left by the mound builders are the stone hammers used for mining copper, and for hammering out copper tools -- axes, hatchets, fleshers, pestles for pulverizing maize, chisels, knives, arrowheads, amulets, pendants, pipes, etc. ,--a list of sufficient extent to warrant the claim for the mound builders of the high antiquity of the Stone Age, and at least of a contemporaneous existence with the prehistoric man of Europe. As proof of the contemporaneous existence in this country of man with the mastodon, the following extracts are given from a paper of the late Dr. Koch, of St. Louis, Missouri, communicated to the St. Louis Academy of Sciences:

"In the year 1839 I discovered and disinterred in Gasconade county, Missouri, at a spot in the bottom of the Bourbeuse river, where there was a spring distant about four hundred yards from the bank of the river, the remains of the above named animals. The bones were sufficiently well preserved to enable me to decide positively that they belonged to the mastadon gigantens. Some remarkable circumstances were connected with the discovery. The greater portion of these bones had been more or less burned by fire. The fire had extended but a few feet beyond the space occupied by the animal before its destruction, and there was more than sufficient evidence on the spot that the fire had not been an accidental one, but on the contrary, that it had been kindled by human agency, and, according to all appearance, with the design of killing the huge creature, which had been found mired in the mud and in an entirely helpless condition. This was sufficiently proven by the situation in which I found, as well those parts of the bones untouched by fire as those which were more or less injured by it, or in part consumed; for I found the fore legs of the animal in a perpendicular position in the clay, with the toes attached to the feet, just in the manner in which they were when life departed from the body. I took particular care in uncovering the bones to ascertain their position beyond any doubt before I removed any part of them, and it appeared during the whole excavation fully evident that at the time when the animal in question found its untimely end the ground in which it had been mired must have been in a plastic condition, being now a grayish colored clay. All the bones which had not been burned by the fire had kept their original position, standing upright, and apparently quite undisturbed in the clay; whereas those portions which had been extended above the surface had been partially consumed by the fire, and the surface of the clay was covered, as far as the fire had extended, by a layer of wood ashes, mingled with larger or smaller pieces of charred wood and burnt bones, together with bones belonging to the spine, ribs and other parts of the body, which had been more or less injured by the fire.

"The fire appeared to have been most destructive around the head of the animal. Some small remains of the head were left unconsumed, but enough to show that they belonged to the mastodon. There were also found, mingled

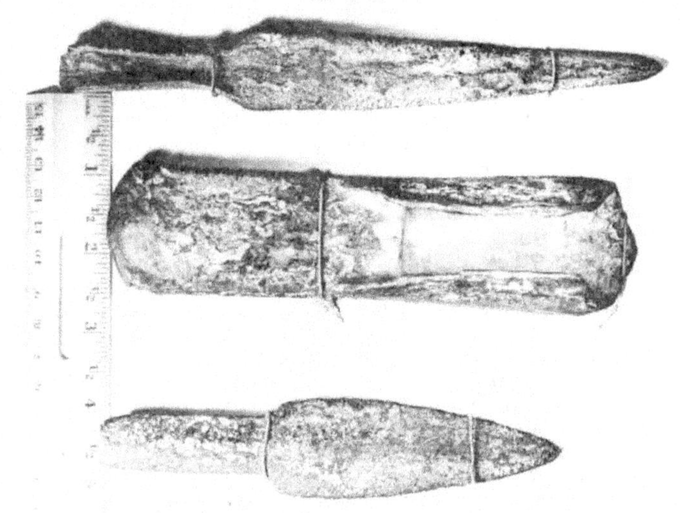

SOCKETED SPEAR POINTS - SOCKETED HOE OR AXE
Approximately three-quarters size.
(Michigan College of Mining & Technology collection).

SOCKETED SPEAR POINTS - UNSOCKETED KNIFE
Three-quarters size. (Keweenaw Club collection)

Note rectangular socket pinning holes in spear points.

with the ashes and bones, and partly protruding out of them, a large number of broken pieces of rock, which had evidently been carried thither from the shore of the Bourbeuse river, to be hurled at the animal by his destroyers, for the above-mentioned layer of clay was entirely void even of the smallest pebbles; whereas, on going to the river I found the stratum of clay cropping out of the bank and resting on a layer of shelving rocks of the same kind as the fragments, from which place it was evident they had been carried to the scene of action. The layers of ashes, etc., varied in thickness from two to six inches, from which it may be inferred that the fire had been kept up for some length of time. It seemed that the burning of the victim and the hurling of rocks at it had not staisfied the destroyers, for I have found also among the ashes, bones and rocks, several arrow heads, a stone spear head and stone axes, which were taken out in the presence of a number of witnesses, consisting of the people of the neighborhood, attracted by the novelty of the excavation. The layer of ashes, etc., was covered by a strata of alluvial deposits, consisting of clay, sand and soil from eight to nine feet thick."

The preceding statements and reasonings are, therefore, sufficient for the position that the ancient miners and mound builders were contemporaneous with the mastodon, and were occupying this country at a period corresponding with the Stone Age of Europe.

The mound builders were not confined to the occupation of the country lying to the South of Lake Superior. Well attested and authenticated statements are made of the existence of the well known artificial mounds in the valley of the Red River of the North, throughout Dakota, Montana and British Columbia. It is possible that future explorers may trace their works still further to the northwest than investigators of this day dare predict.

It is generally conceded that during the glacial period North America was covered with ice between the Rocky Mountains and the Atlantic coast, and from the north pole nearly to the tropics. There is sufficient evidence to suggest the belief that man inhabited the tropics as early, at least, as the latter portion of the glacial period. On the recession and disappearance of the glaciers, probably accompanied with a subsidence, beneath the ocean, of a large portion of the northern continent, and followed by a modified, warm and genial climate, man, together with the mastodon, mammoth, etc., moved north and occupied the land to a comparatively high latitude. This movement, of course, occupied many ages. Subsequently there was a gradual elevation of the land above the ocean - causing a gradual change, through long time, in the temperature of the country until brought finally as it now exists. It was during the changes of this period that the copper miners and mound builders flourished. The effect of the final change in temperature, due to the elevation of the continent, was to drive this race further and further southward, until the seat and center of their power became fixed in the Mississippi and Ohio valleys, and in the region of the great lakes. In this southward movement it is possible that the drones were left behind, and the nomadic people of the far north, and some of the tribes of worthless and shiftless Indians that it is impossible to win to industrious lives, have descended from the outcasts of the people who were the miners of copper and the builders of the mounds.

The Mexican records, as interpreted by the Abbe Brasseur de Bourbourg, are to the effect that the mound builders were finally driven from the Mississippi valley by prolonged and continuous incursions of fierce, predatory and warlike tribes which came from the west. Leaving their long occupied homes, they became dwellers in Mexico and Central America, and leading participators in the work of the early civilization that was the glory of those countries. The beginning of this forced migration, according to Abbe Brasseur, was more than a thousand years before the Christian era. How long prior to this was the first occupation of the Mississippi valley by this ancient people?

is a question the writer will not attempt to answer. The writer, however, does believe, that in the height of their power the population of that portion of the United States occupied by those ancients, was equal in numbers to the present population of the same area. As previously stated, the mound builders were intelligent and industrious people. They followed peaceful pursuits, and their works bear evidence of the efficiency of their government. Their staple food was maize. Their works do not exist on the Atlantic coast except far to the south. Their pursuits being agricultural, they occupied the Mississippi and Ohio valleys and the Lake region as the country most suitable for those purposes, - thus being the precursors of the present race of men who, led by the same instincts, are occupying the same lands, and for the same purposes, but with an advanced civilization which is capable of making the territory once occupied by the mound builders of the Stone Age, the grain producing country for the world, and the center of governmental power. The mound builders being driven out, their territory was occupied by their assailants. Under the sway of a nomadic and warlike people the works of the ancient race were left to decay, and their cultivated fields ran to waste. Thus, through centuries, was test given to the soil, in order to renew fertility and prepare it for the occupation of our present race. After us - is in the future.

pp. 78-89.

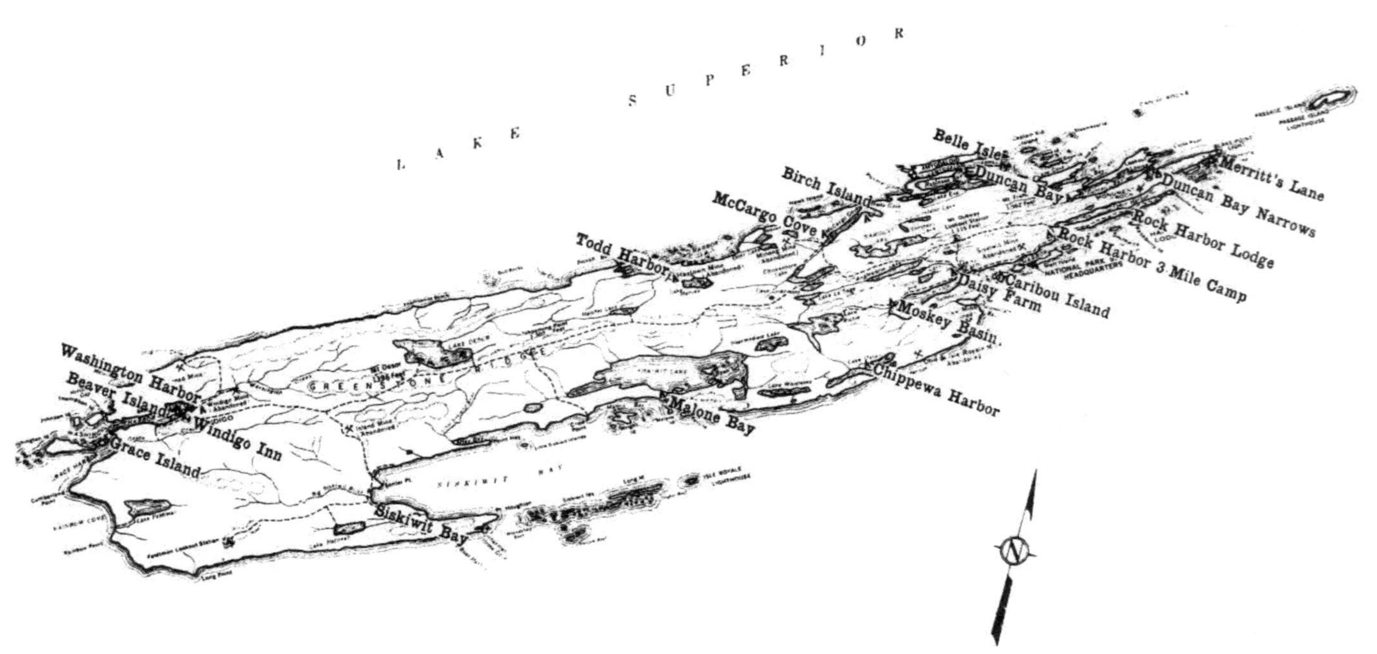

DETAIL MAP OF ISLE ROYALE

ANTIQUITIES OF ISLE ROYALE, LAKE SUPERIOR
By A. C. Davis, Detroit, Michigan
From the SMITHSONIAN REPORT, Washington
Government Printing Office, 1875

I send you three photographic views of a mass of copper found in clearing
some ancient mine-pits on Isle Royale, Lake Superior. The mass was found
in the bottom of a pit sixteen and a half feet deep, and was completely detached from the surrounding rocks. All the wings have been beaten off by the
ancient miner with his stone hammers - evidences of which can be seen all over
its upper surface. The section it was taken from is 27, 66 north, range 35
west. The belt of rock in which it was found is of a sedimentary nature, highly
metamorphosed, from twenty to forty feet wide, and for a distance of two and
a half miles has been completely worked over by the ancient miner. I have
been mining for the last twenty-five years on Lake Superior, but I have never
seen anything to compare with this locality for ancient work.

I am confident that, when this district is thoroughly mined, discoveries will
be made throwing more light than we now have on the character of the people
who did this work.

In the depression in the outlying trap was found clean lake sand, and the rock
thrown out of the pit first was thrown on the sand. There was no sign of vegetable mold between the rock and sand, but over all there was three and a half
feet of made soil or decomposed vegetable matter.

In the pit there are tons of stone and stone hammers, and a large quantity of
ashes and charcoal.

In one I opened on a transverse vein on the same property, I found the scales
of white-fish. At this pit the ancient miner had used large granite boulders to
hold up the hanging ground. These boulders would weigh from 300 to 400
pounds, and were put in where the modern miner would place timber, to secure
the ground. Nearly all the brands and timber we found in the pits were roots
and stumps. This, with the fact of their using these large stones for timber,
leads me to think that the ancient miners had used up all the timber in their
reach, and consequently could not presecute mining further.

There is another peculiarity in the hammers found in these mines - I only
found one that was grooved, while on the south shore of the lake I never saw a
stone-hammer that was not grooved.

MODE OF FABRICATION OF ANCIENT COPPER IMPLEMENTS
By Lyman C. Draper
From REPORT AND COLLECTIONS ON THE STATE HISTORICAL SOCIETY
OF WISCONSIN For the Years 1877, 1878, 1879.
Vol. VIII, Madison, Wisconsin: David Atwood, State Printer, (1879)

The paper in Vol. VII of our Society's Collections, by Prof. Butler of
PREHISTORIC WISCONSIN, describing the collection of ancient copper implements in the cabinet of our Society - the principal portion of which was on
exhibition in the Centennial celebration at Philadelphia in 1876 - has elicited
not a little discussion among our archaeologists as to the mode of their fabrication. Dr. Butler contended that some of them, at least, gave evidence of
having been cast in molds. This view has been stoutly contested by others.
All the light we can get on this interesting subject, pro and con, is desirable.

Prof. Thomas Egleston read, in March 1879, a paper on Prehistoric
Copper Mining at Lake Superior before the Academy of Sciences of New York.
And, in the Proceedings of the American Antiquarian Society, at its semi-
annual meeting, April 30, 1879, was read a valuable paper on Mexican Copper
Tools, by Philipp I: I. Valentini, Ph. D., translated from the German by
Stephen Salisbury, Jr.

These papers throw much light on this discussion. Both of these distant
people, the primitive Mexicans and the Indians of Lake Superior, were unacquainted with iron - the Mexican natives having been ignorant of it until the
arrival of the Spaniards in their country; both were trained in the arts and
practice of war, yet neither had shaped their copper into warlike implements,
the metal being appropriated solely to the uses of peace - in Mexico, apparently, because of its comparative scarcity. "Whilst the Northern Red Man,"
says Valentini, "attained to the highest achievement in the production of the
axe, the native of Central America could boast of important additions to his
stock of tools. He possessed copper implements for tilling the fields, and
knew the uses of the chisel. Besides, when he wished to impart to the copper
a definite form, he showed a superior ingenuity. The Northern Indian simply
took a stone, and by physical force hammered the metal into the required
shape. But the skilled workman of Tecoatega and Tezcuco, subjecting the
native copper to the heat of the furnace cast the wood-cutter's axe in a mould,
as well as the bracelets and the fragile ear-rings that adorned the Princesses
of Montezuma."

The fact of smelting metal is proven by the picture tables, called the
Codices Mexicana, containing representations of their early historical, religious, social and commercial life. Reproductions of these ancient pictures
may be seen in Lord Kingsborough's great work on Mexican Antiquities - one
of which shows a native in a sitting posture blowing apparently a pipe or flute
to increase the heat of the fire on the tripod before him, on which appears a
crucible containing metal.

Metal melting was followed by casting into forms or moulds, as is plainly
indicated by Torquemada, in his Monarquia Indiana, 1613, in which he says:
"The goldsmiths did not possess the tools necessary for hammering metals,
but with one stone placed above another one, they made a flat cup or a plate" -
so the moulds were made of stone. Gomara, another early writer who was
Secretary to Coates, in his Historica General de las Indias, 1552-55, observes
of the native Mexican goldsmiths, "they will cast a platter in a mould."

We learn from Bernal Diaz, in his History of the Conquest of New Spain,
1632, that Cortes had seen for sale in Mexico, "trinkets made of gold and
silver, of lead, bronze, copper and tin," and Diaz, his companion, adds:
"I saw axes of bronze, and copper, and tin." So the great Spanish conqueror
took joy and courage when he now discovered not only a ready means of re-

placing the arms he had lost, but also a source from which to equip his
faithful Indian allies; and Cortes immediately ordered the native goldsmiths
of Tescuco to cast eight thousand arrow-heads of copper, and these weapons
were made ready for delivery within a single week.

It is quite apparent that the Mexican natives were no rude workers in casting metals; and it is not far-fetched to infer that the more northern Indians,
in their intercourse with their southern neighbors, may have learned the art
from them. They had overcome whatever difficulty there may have been in
procuring crucibles, as the skillfulness of their productions sufficiently
attest. The historian, Gomara, writes: "They will cast a platter in a mould
with eight corners, and every corner of several metals - that is to say, the
one of gold, the other one of silver, without any solder. They will also cast
a little caldron with loose handles hanging thereto, as we used to cast a bell.
They will also cast in a mould a fish with one scale of silver on its back, and
another of gold; they will make a parrot of metal so that his tongue shall shake,
and his head move, and his wings flutter; they will cast an ape in a mould so
that both hands and feet will stir, and holding a spindle in his hand, seeming
to spin - yes, and an apple in his hand, as if he would eat it. Our Spaniards
were not a little amazed at the sight of these things, for our goldsmiths are
not to be compared to theirs."

Thus we see that the Mexican natives cast copper implements three hundred
and fifty years ago. Some of the specimens found in Wisconsin show flecks of
silver, proving conclusively that they were laminated; for had they been cast,
the silver would have become amalgamated with the copper, forming an alloy.
But why not others, exhibiting the rude ridges, or raised marks, and quite
uniformly lengthwise of the implement, as if formed by the imperfect joining
of the moulds, have been fabricated, as by the Indians of Mexico, by melting
the metal and pouring it into forms or moulds? Is it any more improbable
that our ancient copper manufacturers of Wisconsin and Lake Superior should
have had the knowledge of moulding, than that the Mexican tribes have prac-
ticed such an art?

This question of the mode of fabrication of the ancient copper implements,
touched incidentally in the preceding papers of Mr. Houghton and Mr. Slafter,
is further discussed by Mr. Perkins, Col. Whittlesey and Dr. Hoy.

By Fred S. Perkins

In January, 1873, I expressed to Dr. John W. Foster, of Chicago, my
belief that many of these ancient copper implements were cast in moulds, and
when I showed some specimens, he became convinced, and re-wrote the portion
of his manuscript that related to the manner in which these objects had been
made. (See following paragraph.)

In "Pre-Historic Races," by J. W. Foster, LL. D., p. 259, the learned
author remarks: "Mr. Perkins, to whose archaeological collections I have had
occasion so often to refer, *** had arrived at the same conclusion as myself;
that, by reason of certain markings, it was evident that the mound-builders
possessed the art of smelting copper, and he has furnished me with the foregoing illustrations, in which the traces of the mould are clearly defined. It is
impossible to infer, after a careful examination of these specimens, that the
ridges could have been left in the process of hammering, or that they have resulted from unequal oxidation." - L. C. D.

In February, 1876, I showed similar specimens to Sir Wm. R. Wilde in
Dublin, Ireland. He examined them attentively, and said they had certainly
been cast, "probably in clay molds." (See two paragraphs following.)

Sir William R. Wilde, a learned antiquary, vice president of the Royal Irish

Academy, and author of a descriptive catalogue of the antiquities of that institution, embracing articles of stone, earthern, copper, and bronze. In describing the copper celts found in Ireland, Mr. Wilde does not, in his work, express any opinion as to their mode of manufacture, but adds: "Upon the steppes of Tartary, and in some of the wildest parts of Russia, the remains of very ancient copper furnaces, of small size, and of the most rude construction, have been discovered."

The fact that bronze implements are found in Ireland, as they were by Cortes and his followers in Mexico, is evidence that the natives knew how to form the amalgam of copper and tin, and this would very naturally lead to the use of molds." - L. C. D.

M. Gabriel de Mortillet, and other French archaeologists, were of the same opinion. I intended to show them to members of the Anthropological Society, in London, but it so happened that I could not stop there on my way home.

Since my return to Wisconsin I have obtained many ancient copper objects, which show to my mind very good evidences of casting, and also some that do not bear any such evidence; but, on the contrary, by their laminar structure, show quite clearly that they were made in a different way, probably by hammering. BURLINGTON, WIS., June 2, 1879.

By Col. Charles Whittlesey

In reply to your inquiry of the 31st ult., I can only say, in brief, that I have never seen a veritable ancient copper implement that was cast in a mold, or where the metal was ever melted. The great bodkin, mentioned by Mr. Foster, from the collection of Mr. Perkins, now I think in your Society collection, I examined at Philadelphia in 1876. The tortuous ridges which were regarded as due to creases in the moulds, are merely the result of irregular oxidation.

A gentleman from Syracuse, whose name I have not in mind, said to me that he had immersed an ancient cold wrought copper implement in weak acids, and the corroded portions were very like those on the bodkin. Cold wrought copper cannot be mistaken for ingot or melted copper. In pounding the native nuggets into shape, they become laminated, and the hardness is irregular. I should expect the oxidation to be irregular also.

It is very strange that the mound builders did not melt copper; but I have seen no evidence that they did. There is a popular belief that they knew how to temper it and make it harder than ingot copper. No people of any age are known to have hardened copper in that way. All the hard copper is an alloy with tin. The Lake Superior copper, in its matrix, is as hard as the ancient implements, and both are harder than the copper of commerce.
COLUMBUS, O., June 4, 1879.

By P. R. Hoy, M. D.
President of the Wisconsin Academy of Sciences, Arts and Letters

I propose, briefly to consider the manner in which the ancient inhabitants of this country fabricated those curious copper implements, which the plow and spade turn up all over Wisconsin and the adjacent states. A few of the specimens, upon a superficial inspection, seem to be cast. Did these rude people possess the skill and intelligence requisite to cast articles of pure copper? Before a cast can be made, it is necessary to have an exact copy moulded in either sand, plaster, clay, metal, or other suitable substances. The formation of sand moulds is by no means so simple a matter as it seems on first thought. It requires long practical experience to overcome the disadvantages attendant on the materials used. The moulds must be sufficiently strong to withstand the pressure of the fluid metal perfectly, and at the same time to permit the escape of the gases formed by the action of the metal on the damp sand. If the material be air-tight, then danger would be from pressure, arising from the rapid generation of the gases, and the casting would thus be spoiled. In moulding, an accurate pattern must first be made, generally in two or more parts. Pattern-making involves much knowledge and skill.

Copper is a refractory metal, which melts at from 2200 to 2600 degrees Fahrenheit - a temperature that can be reached only in a furnace, assisted by some form of coal, and an artificial blast. We must have good evidence before we assert that these dwellers by the Lakes possessed these indispensable auxiliaries to successful working in metals. Copper, when melted, is thick and pasty, and without the addition of some other metal, will not run into the cavities and sinuosities of the mould. Even now there is no article smaller than a three pound hammer cast in pure copper. In casting in copper, it is positively necessary to put the materials in a crucible, and that the surface of the melting mass be covered with a flux in order to protect the melting metal from the oxidizing action of the atmosphere. The manufacturing of good crucibles, such as will withstand the heat necessary to melt the more refractory metals, requires such a degree of knowledge, that for many generations the entire civilized world was dependent on a small section of Germany, and even now Hessian crucibles are unsurpassed. It will sufficiently indicate difficulties and scarcity of the materials used, when it is known that America today is dependent upon Europe for the immense number of crucibles used in this country.

A large majority of these copper implements have specks or points of pure silver scattered over their surfaces. Now I am prepared to prove that one single particle of pure silver, visible even with the aid of a microscope is evidence positive that the specimen was never melted. A fibrous texture is another evidence that these implements were hammered or rolled out. This fibrous quality is well exhibited by the stria of hard bands found in all specimens. We certainly would expect to find some evidence of a sprue - the point where the metal is poured into the mould, more especially if they were so carelessly finished as to leave the imprint of the mould visible, as erroneously supposed by some. Surely if these slight elevations and ridges are the imprint of the moulds, then such specimens are of recent casting, for it is evident that these delicate marks would be the first to be corroded by the tooth of time.

I make here a short extract from a paper entitled "The Ancient Men of the Great Lakes," read by Henry Gillman at the Detroit meeting of the American Association for the Advancement of Science. Mr. Gillman is a close observer, and an accomplished archaeologist, and has made the ancient mines of Lake Superior a specialty. He says: "I cannot close, however, without expressing my wondering admiration of a relic, which, taken in connection with our former discoveries, affords some of the most important evidences of the character of the ancient miners, the nature of their work, and the richness of the mineral field selected for their labors at Isle Royale. On cleaning out of the pit the accumulating debris, this mass was found at the bottom, at the depth of sixteen and one-half feet. It is of a crescent shape, and weighs nearly three tons, exactly 5,720 pounds. Such a huge mass was evidently beyond the ability of the ancient men to remove. They could only deal with it the best they knew how. And as to their mode of procedure, the surroundings in the pit, and the corrugated surface of the mass itself, hear ample testimony - the large quantities of ashes and coals lying around it; a great number of the stone hammers or mauls, were also found nearby, many of them fractured by use. With these the surface of the mass had evidently been beaten up into the projecting ridges, and broken off. The entire upper face and sides of the relic presented repeated instances of this; the depressions several inches deep, and the intervening elevations with their fractured summits covering every part of the exposed superficies. How much of the original mass was removed in the manner described, it is impossible to say. Innumerable fragments of copper chips lay strewn on all sides, and even the scales of fish, evidently the remains of the meals of the miners, were recovered from the pit." Mr. Gillman was asked if there were in or about any of these ancient mines, any indications of the copper having been melted. His reply was, "not the least." And now, were not these innumerable copper chips that were strewn on every side additional evidence that these ancient men knew nothing about casting in copper? Those fragments would have been the most suitable to melt, as in all metals the smaller the fragments the more easily they melt. It is evident that those chips, being too small to make any form of their implements, were abandoned as useless.

Finally; how were they made if not cast? I believe that I have the key, and can fabricate any form of these so called ancient implements, so exactly as to deceive good judges. These ancient Indians, for I believe they were Indians, (and I think I have accumulated facts enough to prove them Indians,) used fire in their mining operations. The vein-rock was made hot by building a fire on or against it; then by dashing on water, the rock could not only be fractured, but the exposed pieces of copper be softened, so that it could be beaten into shape. When the metal became condensed and hard, in consequence of its being pounded, it was again heated and plunged into cold water; for copper is, in this particular respect, the opposite of steel; the one is softened, while the other is rendered hard. In this way copper was fashioned simply by pounding. In addition to the hammering process, cylindrical articles were evidently rolled between two flat rocks, which is the manner in which several of the articles in the collection of the State Historical Society might have been made. Some of those implements that have been supposed to be cast were swedged; that is a matrix was excavated in stone, into which the rudely fashioned copper was placed, and then by repeated blows the article was made to assume the exact shape of the mould. Many of those plano-convex articles were undoubtedly made in this manner. Of twenty axes taken from mounds near Davenport, nearly three-fourths were of this pattern. I will quote a few lines from R. H. Farquharson on Recent Explorations of Mounds near Davenport, Iowa.

"The Davenport collection of copper implements consists at present of twenty axes, six of which were more or less covered with cloth, four copper awls or borers, over one hundred beads, and a curiously spoon-shaped implement. The axes are all of two forms; one plano-convex, the other with flat sides. They are all cold wrought by hammering; some retaining the original scales or laminae on the surface; none of them shows signs of use."

All of these interesting implements are figured in the proceedings of the American Association, Detroit meeting, page 304. We can learn more from this Davenport collection than from any other, for the reason of the perfect condition of the specimens, having never been used, and, in some degree, protected by their covering. Besides, his half-swedging process, I am persuaded that, in a few instances at least, there was a complete mould worked out in halves on the face of two flat stones, so that by placing a suitable piece of copper between them, and given repeated heavy blows, the copper was made to fill the mould accurately. I was so fortunate to discover a matrix on the face of a large granite boulder. I made a pattern of this, and the beautiful axe, deposited in the collection of your Historical Society, were made by me of float copper, cold swedged, first having been partly fashioned with a stone axe. I have cylindrical implements tapering regularly from the center to the points, as well as the beautiful hatchet referred to, made to illustrate in evidence of my position. (Racine, November 12, 1879.)

THE MOUND-BUILDERS IN MICHIGAN
By Henry Gillman of Detroit

Michigan Pioneer Collections; The Mound-Builders in Michigan
Vol. 3, 1879-80 - pp. 202-213

Throughout the region of the Great Lakes abundant evidence, often of the most interesting character, of the presence in bygone ages of that peculiar race known as the mound-builders, is constantly being brought to light. And our own State of Michigan, from the low monotonous shores of Lake Erie to the rocky cliffs of Lake Superior, has contributed, in many directions, some of the most remarkable relics and monuments of a people whose cranial affinities and evidently advanced civilization totally separate them from the North American Indian, and ally them to the ancient race of men who inhabited Brazil in the remote past.

Along the Detroit and Rouge rivers those monuments, in the shape of the well-known mounds, were at one time not infrequent; but in numerous instances, and even within our present city limits, they have been destroyed, often without their true character being recognized, and thus large amounts of valuable relics have fallen into their ignorant hands, and have finally been forever lost. Even those works which remain are fast disappearing before the march of modern improvement.

Indian tradition says that these mounds along our river were built in ancient times by a people of whom they (the Indians) know nothing, and for whom they have no name; that the mounds were occupied by the Tuetle Indians, and subsequently by the Wyandottes, but were constructed long before their time. These facts were ascertained by me in the course of some investigations which I made several years ago, and at that time I further learned that the Tuetle Indians had been absorbed by the Six Nations, and if any survive it is there they must be looked for.

In this connection it is proper to state that I have lately been informed, through the instrumentality of Prof. Henry, of the Smithsonian Institution, of the result of some inquiries made at my suggestion in regard to the name Tuetle. The conclusion arrived at is that the word Tuetle is probably a corruption of Tutelo, a tribe "admitted as a younger member of the confederacy of the Six Nations, about the middle of the last century;" and that the Tuteloes "are believed to have migrated from Virginia northward, to lands assigned them on the Susquehanna by the Six Nations; but very little is known of their early history and migrations." An interesting paper on the Tuteloes was read by the Rev. J. Anderson, before the American Philological Association, in July, 1871. Reporting Mr. H. Hale's discoveries, this assigns the Tuteloes to the Dakotan and not the Iroquois stock, and gives an account of Mr. Hale's visit to Nikungha, the last survivor of the tribe of the Tuteloes, and who has since died at the age of 106 years.

The establishment of the identity of the Tuetles with the Tuteloes, and their residence on these mounds and along the Detroit river, is not only an interesting addition to our local history, but is of special value in view of its tending to sustain Mr. Hale's opinion (opposed to the conclusions of others regarding the Dakotan migration) that "in former times the whole of what is now the central part of the United States, from the Mississippi nearly to the Atlantic, was occupied by Dakotan tribes, who have been cut up and gradually exterminated by the intrusive and more energetic Algonquins and Iroquois."

The relics exhumed from the mounds consist of stone implements, such as axes, chisels, scrapers, arrow-heads, spear-points and knives, fragments of pottery of a great variety of pattern, including the favorite cord pattern so frequently seen in such connection, from the Northern Lakes to the Gulf of Mexico; and the bones of man, generally much decayed, and exhibiting other indications of antiquity. From the fragments of burned bones and charcoal found, it would appear that in the earlier interments cremation was practised.

The tibiae present, in an extreme degree, the peculiar flattening of compression pertaining to platycnemic men. In the fourth annual report of the Peabody Museum of Archaeology and Ethnology, attention is called to this, some of the relics which I collected here having been donated to the museum by the Hon. Robert C. Winthrop, to whom I had presented them. The curator, Prof. Wyman, says: "Of the tibiae of forty individuals from the mounds of Kentucky, one-third presented this flattening to the extent that the transverse did not exceed 0.60 of the fore and aft diameter. The most extreme case was from the mound on the River Rouge, in Michigan, in which the transverse was only 0.48. In the most marked case mentioned by Broca, viz: In the old man from the Cro-Magnon (France), it was, as deduced from his figures, 0.60." Prof. Wyman draws attention to certain resemblances in this bone to the same bone in the ape, adding: "In some of the tibiae the amount of flattening surpasses that of the gorilla and chimpanzee, in each of which we found the short 0.67 of the long diameter, while in the tibiae from Michigan it was only 0.48."

Subsequent to this (in 1870), I discovered in adjacent mounds several instances in which the compression of the tibiae was developed to even a greater extreme. Two remarkable cases of this peculiarity were afforded by tibiae taken by me from a mound on the Detroit river. In one of these unique specimens the transverse diameter of the shaft is 0.42, and in the other 0.40 of the anteroposterior diameter, exceeding, I believe, any platycnemism which has been observed before or since in any part of the world. In communicating these facts to the American Naturalist, not long afterwards, I claimed that the last mentioned case "may be considered as the flattest tibia on record." (See American Naturalist, October, 1871). Both of these bones are strongly marked with the saber-like curvature, also a characteristic of the chimpanzee, as are likewise many others of the tibiae from the vicinity. The majority of the tibiae present the flattening, which is an exception to the facts as noted in other sections of the United States, where it is supposed to pertain to "only about one-third of all the individuals observed." In fact it is an exception to find a tibiae from our mounds along the Detroit destitute of this peculiarity; and where one is found it is generally of later burial and consequently of less ancient origin.

A few years ago the greater part of the large circular mound in the vicinity of Fort Wayne was removed and most important results were obtained. Eleven human skeletons were exhumed; a large number of burial vases; stone implements in great variety and of superior workmanship, consisting chiefly of axes, fleshers, spear-points, arrow heads, chisels, drillers and sinkers, pipes; a peculiar implement of unknown use, formed of an antler, with duplicate perforations at its thickest end; and two articles manufactured from copper, - one the remains of a necklace, formed of a number of beads strung on a two-stranded cord, a few fragments of which remained sufficiently preserved to satisfy me that it was made from vegetable fiber, probably from the basswood (Tilia Americana, L.); the other article of copper consisted of a needle, or borer, several inches in length, quadrangular at the base, and well-wrought. One of the skulls is remarkable for its diminutive size, though adult, its capacity being only 56 cubic inches, or less than 76 per cent of that of the average Indian cramium, which is given as 84 cubic inches by Morton & Meigs, the minimum observed by them being 69 cubic inches. The measurement by Morton of 155 Peruvian crania gives 75 cubic inches for the average bulk of the brain (no greater than that of the Hottentot or New Hollander), the maximum being 101 cubic inches, while the minimum sinks to 58, the smallest in a series of 641 measured crania; and yet you will perceive this is exceeded in diminutiveness by this crania from the Detroit river. The average volume of the brain in the

Mexican is 79 cubic inches, while in a series of measurements of 24 crania from the Kentucky mounds it is found to be 84. The teutonic crania gives the average of 92 cubic inches. Thus it is seen that while the great volume of the brain is indicative of power of some sort, the opposite is not always to be regarded as proof of a degraded condition. In short, quality may here, as in other instances, compensate for deficiency in quantity. Do we find the cranium of the Peruvian, who possessed a high degree of civilization and refinement, equaled in capacity by that of the New Hollander or Hottentot, while it **is** exceeded by that of the degraded, brutal North American Indian to the extent of nine cubic inches. Still the crania of the mound-builders, it must be acknowledged, present characteristics which, in the language of Foster, "indicate a low intellectual organization, little removed from that of the idiot." And this skull from the Detroit river mound must be placed in the same category. Prof. Wyman, in the sixth annual report of the Peabody Museum, in referring to this skull, goes on to say: "In ordinary skulls the ridges of the temporal muscles on the two sides of the head are separated by a space of from three to four inches, seldom less than two, while in the Detroit mound skull this space measures only three-quarters of an inch; and in this respect it presents the same conditions as the skull of a chimpanzee." It is interesting to remember that the flattest tibiae on record," already referred to, were taken by me from this mound; and all the tibiae had more or less sabre-like curvature associated with the platycnemism.

It remains for me in this connection to call attention to the fact that the perforation of the humerus is another remarkable characteristic which I have observed to pertain to those platycnemic men of our region. I refer to the communication of two fossae situated at the lower end of the humerus. This is of great interest, as this peculiarity is most frequently met with in the Negro race; it has also been observed in the Indian, and, though not always present, is quite general in the apes, while it is very seldom seen in the white races.

One of the most remarkable and extensive series of tumuli which are known to exist in this part of the lake region, it was my good fortune to discover in the year 1872. I refer to the mounds situated at the head of the St. Clair river, and at the foot of Lake Huron. They extend in continuous succession for about one mile and one-half northward, as I have satisfactorily determined. Strange to say, those who lived in their immediate vicinity knew nothing of their character. A paper which I wrote on the subject, embodying the principal facts, subsequently formed a part of the sixth annual report of the Peabody Museum of Archaeology and Ethnology, and was afterward copied into several of the leading periodicals of the country, including the American Journal of Science. The general publicity thus given the discoveries precludes the necessity of more than a passing notice here. The numerous mounds, with few exceptions, are of similar character, having been largely used for burial purposes. One of them presented some features distinctive of the "refuse heaps" of our Atlantic coast, and of the north of Europe, a wide area at one end being covered with a solid crust of black ashes from eighteen inches to two feet thick, containing the bones of various animals used for food, broken pottery and stone implements. The relics from the burial mounds in addition to those usually found, consisted of an extraordinarily large number of broken stone hammers of the rudest kind, a plate of mica five by four inches, and two necklaces, one made of small bones, mostly cervical vertebrae, stained a beautiful green color resembling enamel, the other composed of the teeth of the moose, finely perforated at the roots, alternating with well-wrought beads of copper, and the bones of birds stained green as in the first instance. In the mound containing the last mentioned ornaments several interments had been made, and the decayed stump of a scarlet oak (Querous occinea Wang.) two feet in diameter

surmounted the summit, the roots spreading above the contents in all directions.
All the tibiae noticed by me exhibited the compression characterizing platycnemic men. In dwelling on this circumstance, in connection with my previous
discoveries in the same direction, I made the remark, "I cannot but believe,
from what I have seen that future investigation will extend the area in which
this type of bone is predominant to the entire region of the Great Lakes, if not
of the Great West; or, in other words, that at least our northern mound-builders
will be found to have possessed this trait in the degree and to the extent denoted,"
which prediction recent discoveries in Wisconsin and Iowa would seem in a fair
way of fulfilling.

On the west bank of the Balck river, a tributary of the St. Clair, is a burial
mound, which contributed some unusual features. A road having been cut
through the easterly slope of this mound, the consequent excavation revealed
a large number of human bones, pottery, stone implements and other relics.
Stone lance or spear heads of great length were taken out, two of them being
each over a foot long, and one sixteen inches in length. But the most interesting feature of this repository of relics was a grave, the interior of which was
described to me as being lined with pottery similar to that of which the vases,
pots. etc., are formed. This was so peculiar a circumstance, no other
instance of the kind having come to my knowledge, that, at first, I considered
the statement highly improbable. But I availed myself of an opportunity of
visiting the locality, not long after, to make a special examination. Though
the construction of the road through the mound had destroyed most of the
original features, and scattered a multitude of valuable remains, further excavation revealed a considerable quantity of fragments of the pottery above referred to as having been said to have lined the grave. This certainly appeared
to confirm the statement. I found this pottery to be of rather a coarser description than usual, and marked abundantly with the cord pattern, known to be
of such frequent employment, but in this instance made with a large cord or
small rope. The side so ornamented was invariably concave, while the other
side was convex, and unsmoothed, different from any other specimens I have
seen elsewhere. So rough and unfinished was the unornamented side that it
had every appearance of having been pressed upon the ground while yet plastic,
and sand, and even gravel, adhering to it, confirmed this impression. After
having viewed the evidences I had no longer any great difficulty in receiving
the statements previously made. My chief informant was perfectly uneducated
in such matters, and even attributed the peculiar formation lining the sides of
the grave to the coagulation and final hardening of blood, accounting for its
presence in such large quantity by presuming a battle to have been fought in the
vicinity. The few fragments of human bones, which, on this occasion were
exhumed with the pottery, were in the last stages of decay.

Time will not permit me to speak of a number of other mounds which have
come under my observation. A remarkable series of those works occurs at
Beaver harbor, on Beaver island, in Lake Michigan. A very limited and
hurried examination which I made of the group in 1871, sufficiently satisfied
me as to their ancient origin. They appeared to be of the same character as
the mounds on the Detroit river and those at the foot of Lake Huron. They were
probably largely used for purposes of sepulture. From the success attending
my brief labors it would appear that the more valued relics of the mound-
builders have been here deposited in unusual abundance. Highly wrought stone
implements, many of them being of uncommonly skillful workmanship, are
frequently encountered. They are formed of a great variety of stone, such as
diorite, or greenstone, sienite, shale and chert, many of them being finely
polished. One of the handsomest stone axes I ever saw was taken out of this
place. It is made from sienite, a favorite material for this implement, and

the handicraft displayed in its construction is of the highest order.

I shall close with a short account of the recent discoveries of ANCIENT MINING AT ISLE ROYALE, LAKE SUPERIOR.

In the year 1872 some of the most remarkable of the ancient works yet encountered were brought to light by a party of explorers on Isle Royale. Some idea of their extent may be arrived at from the statement of a gentleman well known in mining interest, who is at present engaged in developing the mineral sections of land toward the north side of the island, the amount of labor performed by those ancient workmen far exceeds that of one of our oldest copper mines on the south shore of Lake Superior, a mine which has now been constantly worked with a large force for over twenty years. This may well appear almost incredible when we take into account the disadvantages under which these primitive miners must have labored, and all the advantages comprehended by our present civilization, including the various improvements in mining appliances and the vast resources of modern science.

Isle Royale is situated about fifty miles from the south shore of Lake Superior, and from fifteen to twenty miles from its north shore, and lies off Ontario, Canada, to which geographically it would seemingly belong; or one might suppose that belonging to the United States, it pertained to Minnesota rather than to Michigan. Consequently, the mistake of supposing it to belong to Canada is frequently made. The island is nearly fifty miles in length, varying from five to nine in breadth, having, in most parts of the coast line, and exceedingly ragged, rocky shore, abounding in deep inlets and small harbors or coves. A large number of islands and rocky inlets lie off the main island, particularly in a northeast and southwest direction - the line of its greater axis - to which direction the rocky elevations of the island, in some places rising more than 700 feet above the level of Lake Superior, correspond in a remarkable degree. Nearly the entire of the island is covered with a growth of timber, more or less dense, consisting of the species usually composing our northern forest.

The works, generally pits of from ten to thirty feet in diameter, and from twenty to sixty feet in depth, are found scattered throughout the island, wherever examined being sunk through the few feet of superincumbent drift, where it exists, into the amygdaloid copper-bearing rock. They invariably are on the richest veins; and the intelligence displayed in the tracing and following of the veins; and the intelligence displayed in the tracing and following of the veins when interrupted, etc., has elicited the astonishment of all who have witnessed it - no mistakes having apparently been made in this respect. These excavations are connected underground, drains being cut in the rock to carry off the water. Stops 100 feet in length are found. A drain sixty feet long presented some interesting features; having been cut through the surface drift into the rock, it had evidently been covered for its entire length by timbers felled and laid across. When opened, the timbers had mostly decayed, and the center portions had sunk into the cavity, filling it for nearly its entire length with the rotted wood.

At a deep inlet known as McCargoe's Cove, on the north side of the island, excavations such as are described extend in almost a continuous line for more than two miles, in most instances the pits being so close together as barely to permit their convenient working. Even the rocky islets off the coast have not escaped the observation of these ancient miners, and where bearing veins of copper are generally worked. The stone hammers, or mauls, weighing from ten to even thirty pounds, the chief tool with which the labor was performed, have been found by cart-loads. They are either perfect or are broken from use, and the fragments of large numbers of them are found intermingled with the debris on the edge of the pits, or at their bottom. These mauls are occasionally found grooved for the affixture of the handle, but are oftener without this adaptation. Tools made of copper, and consisting principally of chisels and knives, have been taken from such of the pits as have been explored. Arrowheads of copper have also been picked up, both in the vicinity of the pits and scattered over the island, at the surface, as if lost in the chase. The tools, though injured from oxidation, appear to have been of fair workmanship, and were evidently hardened, apparently through the agency of fire. With the exception of the stone hammers, no other tools formed of stone have been observed. A large portion of a wooden utensil, shaped like a bowl, was taken from the debris, charcoal, etc., at the bottom of a pit. This vessel had possibly been used in bailing water from the excavation. It must originally have been about three feet in diameter, and from its appearance something of the rude character of the tool employed in shaping it could be gathered. A fragment was not of uniform thickness throughout; the wood having been more easily removed when working in certain directions, e.g., when cutting with the grain, the vessel was thinner in those portions.

Having seen the remark that the copper tools of the ancient miners are of rough and not polished exterior, inferences being drawn therefrom as to their rude construction, I wish to say that, having examined a large number of those tools, I believe this roughness to have been caused mostly by corrosion. In many cases this is quite palpable, the original surface being apparent in places, and evidently confirming the fact that at least the external faces of the tool were originally approximately smooth, if not polished.

Excellent arguments have been advanced by Mr. Foster to prove that the mound-builders understood the art of fusing copper, and that, at least, some of their copper tools were made by being cast or moulded. From the method pursued by this people in mining, in which the agency of fire bore so prominent a part, it would seem improbable they could have long remained ignorant of the fusibility of the metal; yet in most cases the evidence appears conclusive that the rudely-fashioned tool was simply wrought by being beaten into the desired form, often in the roughest manner. It is possible the two classes of tools here referred to may mark two distinct eras in the history of this manufacture, and that the moulded tool designates an advance from the primitive method of hammering the metal into shape. Some of the copper heads taken from the "mounds" in Michigan display a wonderful degree of neatness in the manipulation of the metal, the junction of the bead being in many cases almost imperceptible; yet the agency of fire was here evidently not employed.

The pits which have been examined, by being cleaned out, invariably had on top a large deposit, mostly of vegetable matter, the accumulations of many a fall of the leaf, beneath which lay a thick bed of charcoal and mud mingled with fragments of copper-bearing rock. Besides this, they were partly filled with water. The removal of the contents was consequently very dirty work. The method of mining pursued by those people was evidently, on turning back the overlying drift, to heat the rock through the aid of fire; then, when by the application of water the rock was sufficiently disintegrated, to attack and separate it with their great stone mauls. What a slow, wearisome process! Even with a large force constantly engaged in this labor, it must have taken a long series of years to accomplish the work exhibited; and, if those people withdrew during the lengthy winter season, as had been supposed, it would more than double the period required. An experienced mining captain computed that two hundred of those men, with their rude methods, could barely be equivalent to two of our skilled miners. Though no exact estimate can now be made as to the length of time occupied in the prosecution of those extensive works, more or less interrupted as they undoubtedly must have been, yet it does not seem too much to estimate hundreds of years for their accomplishment.

As to the time which has elapsed since the mines have ceased to be worked by this by-gone race, a more definite approximation can be reached. Various careful estimates have placed this period from seven hundred to eight hundred years. I cannot but conclude that since the last work was done on those pits, several generations of trees have arisen and disappeared. The remains of trees older by hundreds of years than the oldest of our present timber are found in and on the sides of the pits. The present growth of forest covers, unbroken, those excavations and the debris surrounding them; all the timber now growing on them being of the same character as that covering the adjacent land, and which is not in process of supplanting by what is known as our "second growth." The late General Harrison, President of the United States, acknowledged to have been remarkably skilled in woodcraft as well as in warfare, in his notes on the Ohio mounds, has made some valuable and suggestive remarks on the relation observed by the different species of forest growth. Lyell, in his "Antiquity of Man," quotes the passage with further and approving remarks. As at Isle Royale, therefore, the species of the present forest covers equally the excavations and the adjoining land, no difference being observable in the growth, we may form some slight conception of the period which must have elapsed before, through the regular rotation, the present condition of things was brought to pass. Trees, from two to four feet in diameter, are now growing in the pits, on their sides, and on the tumuli formed of the excavated debris which surround them. In one case, the partially decayed stump of a red oak (probably Quercus coccinea, Linn.) was found on the tumulus at the edge of a pit. This tree had not been blown down, but had grown and decayed where the stump stood. A large proportion of the rotted wood surrounded it, only the red, interior portion of the stump remaining sound. A careful enumeration of the annual rings composing this red, undecayed center of the tree, gave as the result the number of 384. If to this be added 200 rings, as representing the decayed outer portion of the stump, and not considered an overestimate, we have 584 years as the period of its growth. To this will have to be added the number of years which a tree with the durability of the wood of this species takes to reach the stage of decay here exhibited; and some years may also be allowed for the time which may have elapsed before it commenced growing on its peculiar site. So that the placing this period at from 700 to 800 years, as already given, may not be far from the truth. But it must be remembered that this does not prevent the period of the desertion of the works being placed back at twice or even three times that distance. In other words it only proves that the pits had not been worked within the time mentioned. On removing this stump the debris underlying it was found to consist of the usual angular fragments of copper-bearing rock, thrown out from the adjoining pit, and with which were intermingled a large number of stone hammers, some perfect, others fractured from use, and more interesting still, a knife, made of copper. Pine-trees (Pinus strobus) of the present forest, in which 380 annual rings have been counted, have frequently been cut on the tumuli.

From another pit, beneath a third deposit of vegetable matter, the remains of the skeleton of a deer were exhumed. The bones were so decayed, however, that they crumbled to pieces, and it was only through the undecayed portions of an antler that the animal was recognized. It had evidently fallen into the pit long after it had been deserted, and, unable to escape had perished. Another interesting relic consists of a sheet-like piece of copper, which had apparently been exposed to the action of fire and then had been partially hammered into a shape approximating to a bowl-like utensil. This, too, exhibits the character of the copper generally sought by those men. It is manifest from the working of the veins, that those miners followed the deposits of sheet-like copper, which varied from a quarter of an inch to an inch in thickness, rejecting as unmanageable the fragments of rock which contained even large-sized nuggets of the metal. The latter are found in large quantities in the rubbish forming the tumuli at the mouths of the pits, as well as in the excavations themselves, where, mingled with considerable amounts of charcoal, they seemingly had been pushed behind those miners as they advanced in the exploration of the vein, the walls of which were generally left unbroken.

At an indentation of the coast on the south side of the island, where a stream about forty feet in width had cut a channel through the rocks and formed quite a fall of water, was discovered what is taken to be the site of the town, or the habitations of these people. It occupies an elevated slope, giving an extensive view of Lake Superior and overlooking the intervening point of land which makes the little bay an excellent harbor. The remains consist of a series of shallow excavations, generally about four feet in depth, and occupying the successive terraces of the slope. Some of these pits are circular, others are quadrangular, and they vary from ten to thirty feet in diameter. Indications suggest that timber or bark was used in their construction, the soil being thrown up around them to a sufficient height. But time did not permit a satisfactory examination of this interesting locality, which, with other points on the island, it is hoped will afford, on a thorough examination, many valuable facts connected with the life of this remarkable people. They doubtless shipped the copper, the object of their toil, to the south shore of Lake Superior, the wonderful metal finding its way thence to other parts of the country, as is testified by the articles of copper found in the burial places of the mound-builders. This point, therefore, was well selected as a town site. The good landing, the admirable harbor, the abundant stream and fall of water, the sheltered and yet commanding hillside, which enabled them to watch the return and departure of their copper-laden flotillas, were all strong recommendations even to those semi-savage inhabitants.

Singular to say, up to this time the bones of man have not been met with on the island. Some contend that during so long a lapse of time they have completely disappeared through decay. But this conclusion will hardly be accepted as satisfactory. It is difficult to believe that of a population so crowded, as is implied by the extensive excavations on Isle Royale, some were not buried there who must have died during even the periodic occupation of the island, and it is to be hoped that the explorations in process of being made will result in the discovery of human remains. These will doubtless identify this people with the mound-builders whose monuments are so widely distributed through our country. The conformation of the bones of this race, and especially the cranium, as has already been remarked, widely separate them from the North American Indian, and ally them rather with the ancient inhabitants of Brazil; the skull being orthocephalic, i.e., occupies a position between the Indian cranium, which is brachycephalic, and the Teutonic, which is dolicocephalic. Their characteristics suggest a people who, though not of any great intellectual development, are yet capable of patient endeavor and the unremitting toil which is devoted to the amelioration of life through the improvement of its surroundings, and are not devoid of an ambition which, however humble, places them above the Indian in the scale of humanity.

It is also remarkable that the discoveries of the remains at the settlements on the south shore of Lake Superior have never included human bones - so far as I am aware - but have been confined chiefly to excavations, copper tools, and stone hammers. It is possible those men may have had some superstitious belief which led to the removal of their dead to the burial mounds further south.

Of the excavations on the small islands lying off Isle Royale an interesting example was discovered by me on the rocky islet which, for the purpose of distinguishing it, I have named, from its general outline, Triangle Island, it being hitherto unnamed on any of the maps. This island lies off the south-west end of Isle Royale, and is a sandstone rock with very little soil on any part of it, and only a few small trees or brushes at one end. The sides of the island rise abruptly and there is no landing for even small boats, except for a short space on the northeast side, and also in a cleft-like indentation on the south side. This last mentioned landing has much the appearance of its natural conditions having been improved by artificial means; a gradual slope sixty feet in length by about twenty feet wide leads down to the lake, the rock being generally smooth throughout. Small boats could easily be hauled out here, particularly with the aid of timbers laid for the purpose. Near this, and all along it, wherever there are indications of copper mines, are the circular pits of the ancient miners. Though of small size, from two to five feet in diameter and about as many feet deep, they are remarkably distinct. At this place the rock is mostly as level as the floor of a room, and the well-like pits are immediately perceived to be the work of human agency. Though careful search was made, no relics were met with other than the angular fragments of the rock broken off by the usual methods pursued by these rude miners. The fragments occasionally contained copper.

One of the smaller pits, a little over two feet in diameter and nearly two feet deep, had a large slab or rock covering its mouth. It required two men to remove this. We found this pit more than half full of the angular fragments above alluded to, but though emptied of its contents nothing further was encountered, to our disappointment, as from indications we hoped to find this the repository of some valuable relics. Had any tools or other utensils been deposited here, as a place of safety, they had long since disappeared; probably decaying through the lapse of ages. From appearances, and the isolated character of the island, I am inclined to think that mine were the first hands to rest on those objects since the departure of the primitive workmen.

At two places, at each end of the circular pits, the copper veins in the wall-like cliff had been attacked and partly excavated. The rock is discolored as if from the action of fire, and at the base of the more central point the sandstone is considerably hollowed. All those works exhibit the same roughish surface, totally unlike that produced by the action of water.

Immediately at the inner end of the southern landing already described is a marked depression occupying nearly the center of the island, and presenting some indications of artificial origin, but about thirty-five feet northwestward of the head of the landing occurs a more remarkable excavation. This is of rectangular form, twenty-five feet long by twenty feet wide. It is filled with water, as are most of the pits. It may not be uninteresting to state in this connection that I found the rare fern Botrychium lunaria (Swartz) flourishing, and rather abundant on the exposed rock of this island. It grows in tufts of Potentilla tridentata (Ait.), grass, and other dwarfed plants.

The discoveries on Isle Royale throw a new light on the character of the mound-builders, giving us a totally different conception of them, and dignifying them with something of the prowess and spirit of adventure which we associate with the higher races of man. The copper, the object of the mining, to be available, must, in all probability, have been conveyed in vessels, great or small, across a stormy and treacerous sea, whose dangers are formidable to us now, being dreaded by even our largest craft and often proving their destruction. Leaving their homes these men dared to face the unknown to brave the hardships and perils of the deep and of the wilderness, actuated by an ambition which we today would not be ashamed to acknowledge.

In contemplating the facts involved many questions are naturally suggested. How did this people become aware of those mineral deposits at so isolated a point? How did these men become present in such large numbers as is implied by the extent of the works discovered? What was the character of their vessels or sailing craft, if such were employed? How did so great a population support life in such circumscribed limits while still carrying on their mining operations? Did they make a permanent settlement, their families abiding with them, or were they simply migratory, visiting the island and returning as occasion offered? Did any or all of them remain throughout the severe northern winter, or was the work prosecuted during the summer months only? These are questions not easily answered.

It is evident that such extensive operations as are here described required a system and an organization of no mean order for those days. The vast extent, and the method of their labors, would seem to imply that they were of no desultory or intermittent character. The island probably abounded in game. The deer, caribou, bear, and smaller mammals, were doubtless not scarce, while the waters were alive with many varieties of fish, thus affording food in considerable quantity. The caribou, long extinct here, gives evidence of his former presence in the horns which are sometimes found; and I have now in my possession two interesting relics - the larger portions of the antlers of this animal, much decayed and gnawed by rodents - which were picked up at two separate points on the island. However, we have hitherto supposed that the mound-builders were essentially an agricultural people, largely dependent on cereals for subsistence. If grain food was used by them, as is probable, it was most likely transported to the island

The question will not fail to suggest itself: Were these vast operations accomplished through slave labor? That a conquered people were kept at this isolated place by their victors, and in this thraldom obliged to work the copper mines, is an opinion, however, which cannot be received without further confirmation. That a central government, situated at the south, ruled with patriarchal if not autocratic sway over the entire region, from Mexico to Lake Superior, many circumstances more than hint at. If the ancient miners were not identical with the mound-builders, that commercial transactions, at least, existed between them, the constant finding in the burial places of the latter of ornaments and utensils made of Lake Superior copper would warrant. The apparent similarity of their characteristics and habits is further testimony in this direction.

Standing on the rocky eminences of the island, and looking down on the surrounding features, in presence of the remarkable disclosures here detailed, it was not difficult for the imagination to re-people the solitudes once more with those primitive men. The past rises and recreates itself. Again they swarm along the rocky beaches with those ragged shores, even then torn with the storms of thousands of winters; landing on the precipitous islets, baptized in the silvery spray of Lake Superior, the rude boats or vessels pass to and fro in busy traffic; some, disappearing in the distance, are bound with their valued freight for the main land far to the south; the half-naked savages, begrimed from their toil, delve in the slowly-deepening pits which lie scattered along the pleasant indentations of the coast, or by the banks of the beautiful lakes of the interior; the voice of an unknown language falls upon the air with a strange rhythm; the overhanging cliffs echo and resound with the clang of their stone hammers; the forest falls beneath the blows of their rude axes; the curling smoke rises from their excavations or their dwellings, softly ascending to the same blue heaven which still bends over all with its eternal benediction.

ANCIENT COPPER MINES OF ISLE ROYALE
By
Professor N. H. Winchell
From THE ENGINEERING AND MINING JOURNAL, Volume XXXII,
July to December 1881, Scientific Publishing Company, New York

These mines are rude, irregularly disposed, shallow pits in the general surface, which, on being cleared of rubbish, are found rarely to exceed the depth of ten feet, but in some instances reach the depth of twenty. They seem to have been located by the accidental outcropping of native copper, over large areas the rock being entirely bare. In other cases, the mining seems to have been systematically prosecuted along the strike of a known copper-bearing belt of rock. In this case, it is a rock of marked lithological characters, being of a red color; and when once its trend was established by a series of pits, it was followed under the drift-materials, that were thrown off into heaps, in which are found, mingled with charred wood and other relics, a great many stone hammers. In one instance, a cross-drift ran under a rude archway from one red belt to another, through a thin partition of darker rock; but in general, no planning for easy excavation or skillful and prolonged effort in the operations of the miners can be discovered. So far as can be ascertained, they resorted to the very simplest and most laborious methods of excavation in the rock, using their stone hammers, wielded in the hands alone, sometimes aided, perhaps, by the application of heat, and by repeated blows battered and broke away the rock surrounding the copper masses. When once a mass was detached or sufficiently uncovered, it was parted into smaller pieces by the same means. Some of the masses found, being too large for removal from the pits, show the marks of long-continued pounding, and about them in the pits are a great many small, thin chips of metallic copper, of irregular shapes, with concavo-convex surfaces, exactly such as would be produced by battering a small nugget of copper to a thin layer by pounding it continuously on the same side. The finding of these thin chips of copper is the first indication to the present miners of the proximity of a large mass. In the summer of 1874, the first of these large masses was discovered. It was sixteen and one half feet below the surface, and under it were poles, as if it had been entirely detached, but it had not been much displaced. This mass was exhibited publicly in the yard of the courthouse at Detroit, and was also on exhibition at the Centenniel Exposition in 1876. It was subsequently fused and sold as commercial copper. It weighed 5720 pounds, and has been described by Mr. Henry Gillman in the annual volume of the American Association for the Advancement of Science for 1875. In the summer of 1879, two other large masses that had been wrought by the ancients were found at the minong Mine, which is at the head of McCargoe's Cove. One had a weight of 3317 pounds, and the other 4175 pounds, the latter being about nine feet long. The largest mass yet found at that place was taken out the previous summer, weighing six tons; but the ancients had not discovered it, though one of their drifts ran within two feet of it. The large masses discovered by the ancients show the labor that has been spent on them in their hammer-marked and pitted surfaces. They seem to have been beaten up into ridges and points, by hammering alone, for the easier removal of parts. One of those found in 1879 was not detached from the inclosing rock, although it was wholly uncovered and undermined.

Various articles have been found in these old pits or in their neighborhood. Several copper implements, such as a gad, a chisel, knives, and arrow-heads, have been discovered, both on Isle Royale, and in the vicinity of similar old mines on the south shore of Lake Superior. Mr. Gillman reports that a large part of a "wooden bowl" originally about three feet in diameter, which had been used probably for boiling water, was taken from one of these pits. The timber found in some of these excavations bore the marks of an ax, the bit of which must have been about two inches in width. Fragments of charcoal and partially consumed sticks abound. The bark of the white birch is still preserved, though the interior woody portion is wholly rott ed. At McCargoe's Cove, Captain William Jacka discovered a wooden shovel, or paddle, which showed by its worn and battered side that it had been used in moving dirt. It had a blade four and three quarters inches wide, and about twelve inches long. The handle had been broken, but still showed the length of about a foot. It was all perfectly wrought and smooth, and very true in form. A rounded ridge on the upper and lower sides of the blade extended along its middle, tapering off along the same sides of the shaft or handle upward. It was wet and swollen when found, but on drying, it shrank to a width of three fourths of an inch, and curled out of shape. A restoration of this ancient paddle or shovel is seen in Fig. 2, as drawn under the direction of Captain William Jacka, and a cross-section of the blade in Fig. 3: "a" represents the upper side of the blade, and the ridge evidently designed to strengthen the instrument, extends to within an inch or two of the end, and gradually and smoothly sinks to the level of the surface. This shovel was found within a few feet of one of the large masses of copper, in the summer of 1879.

Dr. G. K. Gailey also discovered a piece of string about a foot long, made of some raw-hide, supposed to be of the caribou, tied in the middle by "a square knot and a half-hitch." This lay under one corner of the copper mass found in Maylast (1879), and seemed to break on being pulled out, but the remainder could not be secured. When examined, this string seemed to possess the fiber and much of the strength of dried rawhide, a circumstance that will not allow the assignment of a very great antiquity to the date of the last mining. Caribou were on the island till a few years ago, and are now common on the shore directly north of the island.

In regard to the main implements of the mines, the stone hammers, they seem not to have been made for the purpose for which they were used. Great numbers of them have been found in moving the dirt which the miners handled. They are of various sizes and forms, but generally about five inches in diameter, though some are eight and even ten inches, and of a rounded oval outline. They were certainly gathered as pebbles along the shore of the lake, north from the island, where there are still others of the same shapes and sizes, and of the same varieties of rock, formed on the beach by the action of the waves. The great profusion in which they are scattered among the debris of the pits would itself indicate the ease with which they were obtained. They are not grooved for the reception of a withe, like those found on the south shore, near Ontonagon; but they were apparently used for the most part by simply swinging them in the hand, or probably in both hands clasped, thus by repeated blows breaking away the surrounding rock or hammering the desired metals into such shapes as to facilitate its separation in smaller pieces. The rock of which they are composed does not occur as pebbles on Isle Royale, and indeed it is doubtful if it exists at all on the island. It forms the coast of the mainland for several miles opposite the island. It is an igneous rock, usually a diabase, as shown in thin sections under the microscope, consisting essentially of a triclinic feldspar and augite, more properly be styled a dolerite or a gabbro. They belong to the formation designated by Sir Wm. Logan THE LOWER VOLCANIC GROUP, but since styled ANIMIKIE GROUP, by Professor T. S. Hunt. Occasionally, however, the workmen seem to have gathered rounded stones of other varieties of rock, though nothing equaling the firmness of the above, and so fit for the purpose of a rude hammer in simple mining, can be selected among all the rocks of the region. One or two, of a granite containing red orthoclase, were seen at the mine, and a few of other granites are reported to have been found. These other varieties are also seen mingled sparsely with the diabase stones along the Canadian shore, and are referable to the drift forces which transported them from farther north and east in Canadian territory.

Although these hammers, as a rule, are not withed, it is still true that occasionally one is found that is withed--that is, grooved for the reception of a withe handle. One seen at the time of this visit was owned by Dr. Gailey, and was not well wrought. The groove was evidently made by an unskilled hand, and was unfinished. This allies these miners with those of the south shore of the lake. The absence of these hard, rounded stones on the shores of the south side of Lake Superior, owing to the strike of the formation producing them across the interior of the States of Michigan and Wisconsin, made it necessary for the miners on that side to manufacture their hammers, which they did with greater perfection and symmetry than are seen in the beach-wrought hammers of the Isle Royale miners; and they almost invariably grooved them for a withe. These found on Isle Royale are generally broken with use on one end or on both, a fact which probably caused their abandonment. Fig. 5 shows the imperfectly grooved hammer belonging to Dr. Gailey. Fig. 6 shows the outline and irregularity of three others, also found at the Minong mine. These are a fair average for form of the most of those found. They are also evidently such as would result from the constant attrition of angular fragments on the beach, and show no evidence of designed shaping. Their battered and even fractured extremities are the only sign of the agency of man in giving them shape.

If we inquire now who were the men, and when did they live, who did this work, we enter on a very interesting question, but one on which we are not in total darkness. A single observation at the pits at once places them later than the last glacial epoch. The dirt that they removed lies on the drift-clay. This is shown by the subjoined diagrammatic sketch taken on the spot (Fig. 7). It is also shown by the fact that some of the pits are but a few feet above the present lake level (about thirty feet); since during the period of the drift, and particularly toward its close, the interior lakes of the North American continent were much higher than they are now.

It has been agreed for some years, by American archaeologists that the ancient miners of Lake Superior were identical with the mysterious race known as the mound-builders. The evidence of this, first partially elucidated by Messrs. Squier and Davis, has multiplied by subsequent observations, so that there is now a concurrent series of facts pointing to that conclusion. It consists largely in the discovery of many copper implements in the mounds that have been opened. These implements sometimes contain small nuggets of metallic silver closely welded to the copper. At no other place in the United States are copper and silver found thus naturally combined. They must have been pounded into shape, since the melting of the copper for casting would certainly have produced an alloy, in which the appearance of the silver would be entirely lost. This, taken in connection with the well-established mining methods of the Isle Royale miners, undeniably identified them with the mound-builders.

If we inquire further what relation the mound-builders bore to the aborigines found here by Columbus, we shall be compelled to admit from the evidence that the aborigines themselves were the mound-builders and the ancient miners. As this conclusion is at variance with the generally accepted opinion, it will be necessary to consider some of the characteristics of the mound-builders, as stated by the highest authorities, and to compare them with the known peculiar habits and customs of the Indians.

106

1. Squier and Davis state that "there probably existed among the mound-builders a state of society something like that which prevailed among the Indians. Each tribe had its separate seat, maintaining, with its own independence, an almost constant warfare against its neighbors" (<u>Smithsonian Contributions,</u> vol. i., p. 44).

2. The mound-builders occupied the entire country from Lake Superior, at least, on the north, to the Gulf of Mexico on the south, and from the Alleghanies, at least, on the east, to the Sierras, on the west. This is demonstrated not so much by the distribution of the mounds--though they are said by Lewis and Clark to occur on the upper waters of the Missouri, and, by Mr. A. Barrandt, in the valley of the Yellowstone--as by the existence of copper implements from Lake Superior in the same mounds with mica from the Alleghanies, pearls from the Gulf shores and from the Carolinas, and sharks' teeth from the cretaceous beds of the South and West.

3. They were an agricultural people, of generally homogeneous customs, habits, religion, and government, each tribe carrying on a trade with surrounding tribes, and some of them with distant tribes.

4. They worked copper in a cold state having no knowledge of iron, nor of the methods of smelting any of the ores of the metals by the aid of fire.

5. They built extensive earthworks and mounds, both for purposes of warfare and for sepulture.

6. They exhibited very frequently a remarkable flattening of the shinbone (platycnemism).

7. They made a coarse kind of cloth, by twisting and weaving the fibers and bast of various plants.

8. They made pottery of clay, which they hardened by burning, and rudely ornamented with figures of animals, or by simpler lining.

9. They wrought stone, making axes, arrows, and spear-heads, knives, wedges, pestles, discoidal stones, tubes, pipes, beads; and they had a high regard for mirrors of mica.

10. They made rude sculptures, in stone and burned clay, of animals and of the human face.

11. They had no knowledge of writing by the use of an alphabet, nor hieroglyphics; but sometimes resorted to pictures to convey information.

12. They employed shells, pearls, sharks' teeth, obsidian, copper, silver, steatite, black and mottled slate, mica, coralline limestone, and bones of some animals, and some other minerals, especially galena and hematite, for making articles of personal adornment.

13. Besides rude sculptures of most of the present animals of the larger types, the elephant (or mastodon) was known to them, as evidenced by the "elephant mound" in Western Wisconsin, by the discoveries of Dr. Koch in Missouri, and by the "elephant pipe" lately brought to light in Louisa County, Iowa. (John T. Short, <u>The North Americans of Antiquity,</u> p. 530.)

Some of these characteristics it is only necessary to name, to enable any one to recognize also their belonging to the red men who were here when Columbus discovered America, and who probably are identical with the Skrellings, seen by the Norse adventurer, Thorwald Ericson, in 1002, described as having sallow-colored, ill-looking faces, ugly heads of hair, large eyes, and broad cheeks, coming to his ship in canoes for purposes of trade, but becoming hostiles and treacherous. The various tribes into which the red men were, and still are, divided, extended over the whole territory that is known to have been occupied by the mound-builders.

That they were an agricultural people, although given to warlike expeditions, and to long journeys for the purpose of trade and for rice-gathering and hunting, is also abundantly attested by the journals of the earliest explorers. Of these it is only necessary to refer to those of Hudson and Juet in the

Half-Moon, who mention in several places the existence of extensive cultivated fields along the banks of the Hudson, and to the historians of De Soto's expi- dition, who speak frequently of Indian villages containing from fifty to six hundred dwellings, substantially constructed of wood, in which must have dwelt upward of two thousand persons. They frequently mention, also, extensive fields of corn, beans, pumpkins, and other vegetables. In one in- stance, De Soto's army traveled two leagues through fields of corn, and sometimes large quantities of corn and of meal were obtained from the houses (vide Irvings's Conquest of Florida.)

The fact that the aborigines worked stone, using stone axes, arrow-heads, disks, wedges, hammers, pestles, and scraper, not only is authenticated by the testimony of early writers, but also by the continuance of the same custom nearly if not quite up to the present time among some of the most inaccessible tribes of North America, though they have almost wholly ceased to be used, in consequence of the metallic implements furnished them by the whites.

The manner of making pottery among the Mandan Indians is described by Catlin, who states that "earthen dishes are made by the Mandan women in great quantities, and modeled in a thousand forms, and tastes," and that they are nearly equal in hardness to our own manufactured pottery, though they knew not the art of glazing. Fragments of pottery, evidently made by these Indians, are found about Bismarck, in Dakota, and on the Heart River, and in various parts of Northern Minnesota, where it was doubtless made by the Chippewas; and they greatly resemble the pottery taken from the mounds, being unglazed, gray slightly baked or unbaked, and somewhat ornamented by lines and figures.

The articles of cloth that have been found in the mounds are made of the bast-fibers of certain plants, and have been preserved by the antiseptic action of the salts of copper, "the cloth having been wrapped about copper axes and nuggets prior to being placed in the mounds." (R. J. Farquharson, "Recent Explorations of Mounds Near Davenport, Iowa," Proceedings of the American Association for the Advancement of Science, vol. xxiv, p. 305.) It appears to be "a kind of hemp, possibly the Apocynum cannabinum, formerly used by the Aztecs," or perhaps, as suggested by Colonel D. A. Robertson, of St. Paul, the fibers of Urtica gracilis. Cloth of equal fineness is still made by several of the Indian tribes, particularly by the Navajoes of New Mexico; and nearly all of the tribes are known to have had mats and even carpets, woven of various sedges or of bast-fibers. They are still made by the Chippewa Indians in Northern Minnesota.

The sculptured objects taken from the mounds, even those of the human face, are generally cut in some very soft stone, or are made of clay. They are equaled in skill and design by the sculptured pipes and hatchets the Indians have been known to make ever since the Columbian discovery, and particularly by those made of the famous red pipestone or Catlinite of Minnesota. (Mr. Farquharson, American Association for the Advancement of Science, vol. xxiv, p. 306, speaks of a green variety of Catlinite, which, on the contrary, is always red. Other American archaeologists have in the same way spoken of Catlinite (?) pipes found in the mounds, which by the descriptions given are precluded from being Catlinite. The Chippewa Indians of Minnesota make pipes of a greenish argillitic slate, obtained near the international boundary; but the Sioux use the Catlinite of the celebrated pipestone region in Southwestern Minnesota. By trade the Catlinite sometimes finds its way into the northern part of the State, and is employed as inlaid ornaments in the dark slate, in the same manner as lead is used for a similar purpose.) As illustrative of the sculpture of the mound-builders, Fig. 8 is here presented. This is from a photograph of a representation of the human face taken from a mound lately opened at Lanesboro' in Fillmore County, Minnesota. For this I am indebted to the kindness of Mr. H. G. Day, who states that the image was found in the same mound with stone arrowheads, one copper arrowhead; clay-burned pipes and the remains of a large number of human skeletons. This piece of burned clay, about three inches in height, represents the human face, and is certainly not evidence of greater skill than the Mandan pottery made by the women of that tribe, but shows that the burning of clay was a practice common to both peoples.

There was a time, recently, when the flattening of the shin-bone was claimed to be a striking peculiarity of the mound-builders. This view was very fully set forth by Mr. Henry Gillman, in his papers on the contents of several Michigan mounds, particularly those on the Rouge and Detroit rivers, explored by him in 1869 and 1870 (Smithsonian Report, 1873). This view has also been advocated by Dr. A. E. Johnson, before the Minnesota Academy of Sciences, in a description of bones taken from a mound at Palmer Lake, near Minneapolis. If this distinction could be fully established, it would be one of the most valuable and one of the most remarkable ethnological discoveries of American scientists, and would form a basis for future investigations that might fully establish the distinctness of the mound-builder among the dynasties of North America. But, according to Mr. Gillman's own observations, made at a later date, this peculiarity is not uniform or constant in the tibiae taken from the Michigan mounds, and in some mounds it is wanting. The same is true of the perforation of the humerus, which has also been regarded as peculiar to the mound-builder. Of six humeri taken by the writer from mounds at Big Stone Lake, Minnesota, but one was perforated. Both these osteological variations are found occasionally in the present Indian, and the former is very common in the negro and in the ape. Dr. Jeffries Wyman informs us, according to Professor J. D. Dana, that the playcnemic tibia is a common fact among the American Indians, as well as in the prehistoric remains of Europe. More lately, a platycnemic tibia from the Lainesboro' mound was submitted to Professor Leidy, of Philadelphia, who, in reply to a question as to its significance, stated that it was now regarded as of no special significance, but was a common occurrence in the early races.

We come now to consider the most interesting as well as the most difficult points in the genetic relationship of the Indian and the mound-builder. These are the existence of the mounds, the mining of copper, and the use of copper implements. The Indian, it is said, knows nothing of the mound--that is, nothing of its origin. He also avers, at the present time, that he knows nothing about the copper knives, axes, and arrow-points that are shown him. This fact, taken with a sentiment that has exalted the builders of the mounds to a stage of civilization far in advance of that evinced by the commonalty of the savage races of North America as they exist in the 18th and 19th centuries, has erected a barrier between the Indian and the Mound-builder, which, though wholly imaginary when subjected to close analysis, is so great that they have been regarded as either misinformed or rash who have ventered to question its validity. Messrs. Squier and Davis, who first systematically explored and described the remarkable mounds of the Ohio Valley, were led to regard the mound-builders as a race wholly distinct from the Indian (Smithsonian Contributions to Knowledge, vol. i., 1848) and this view is also maintained by the beautiful and able work of Mr. John T. Short (The North Americans of Antiquity, 1880). Mr. Squier, however, in his work on the "Aboriginal Monuments of the State of New York" (Smithsonian Contributions, vol. ii,) in 1849, mentions many points of resemblance between the mound-builder and the Indian, though he does not specifically state that the Ohio Valley earthworks are probably of Indian origin, while he does conclude that the mounds and earthworks of Western New York, as well as their contents, are the product of the Iroquois. Mr. Lapham, in vol. vii of the <u>Smithsonian Contributions</u>, unhesitatingly ascribes the mounds and the copper mining to the Indians, but his opinion has been generally ignored. Colonel J. W. Foster, in <u>Prehistoric Races of the United States</u>, makes light of Mr. Lapham's views.

Upon consulting a number of works in the library of the Minnesota Historical Society that bear on this subject, it is found that there are a great many more references to the use of copper by the Indians, and to their knowledge of its origin, than has generally been supposed. They are too numerous and circumstantial, and are spread over too wide a stretch of time, to be supposed to be exceptional.

Following are a few quotations from early journals and histories that seem to demonstrate that not only did the Indians use and mine native copper but that they also erected mounds of earth, or of stones, in commemoration of their honored dead and for sepulture. The Indian is a dull utilitarian. He is but little given to sentiment. As he knows nothing of the future, so he re-members little of the past. Hope and history are alike feeble in his mental garniture. His traditions are worthless, and "his chronology of moons and cycles is an incoherent and contradictory jumble." (Short, <u>The North Americans of Antiquity</u>, p. 22.) If he says he knows nothing of these relics, his testimony can apply only to himself personally; for his ancestors, on the most undeniable evidence, did know all about them.

In regard to the use of copper, and the mining of it by the American aboriginies, may be made the following quotations and references:

In the Collections of the New York Historical Society, second series, vol. i, is given a translation of the Italian account of the voyage of John de Varrazano along the coast of North America, from Carolina to Newfoundland, A.D. 1524. When about at Narragansett Bay and Harbor, he makes these notes: "We saw upon them (the aborigines) several pieces of wrought copper, which is more esteemed by them than gold, as this is not valued on account of its color, but is considered by them as the most ordinary of the metals, yellow being the color especially disliked by them; azure and red are those in highest esteem by them." Further on he says of another tribe: "In this region we found nothing extraordinary except vast forests and some metalliferous hills, as we infer, from seeing that many of the people wore copper ear-rings."

Henry Hudson's ascent of the river that bears his name is given in the same volume, in the form of a journal kept by Robert Juet, a mate. Speaking of the natives, on page 323, Juet says, "They had red copper tobacco-pipes, and other things of copper they did wear about their necks; also, "They have great tobacco-pipes of yellow copper," also, on page 300, Hudson himself says, "The people had copper tobacco-pipes, from which I infered that copper might naturally exist there."

Raleigh observed copper ornaments among the Indians on the coast of the Carolinas; Granville, in his voyage in 1580, observed copper in the hands of the natives of Virginia, and made an effort to reach the place where they said it was obtained. After a toilsome journey into the interior, of some days' duration, the attempt was abandoned. Heriot's "Voyage," in Pinkerton, vol. Xii., p. 594, gives an account of copper found "in two towns one hundred and fifty miles from the main, in the form of diverse small copper plates, that are made, we are told by the inhabitants, by people who dwell farther in the country, where they say are mountains and rivers which yield white grains of metal, which are deemed to be silver. For confirmation whereof, at the time of our first arrival in the country, I saw two small pieces of silver, grossly beaten, about the weight of a tester (an old coin about the weight of a dime), hanging in the ears of a Wiroance. The aforesaid copper we found to contain silver." McKenzie found copper in use among some of the extreme northern tribes, on the borders of the Arctic Sea, according to his "Second Voyage," page 333, as quoted by Squier. (Smithsonian Contributions, vol. ii, p. 117). "They point their arrows and spears with it, and work it up into personal ornaments, such as collars, ear-rings, and bracelets, which they wear on their wrists, arms, and legs. They have it in great abundance, and hold it in high estimation." Alexander Henry, in his "Travels," page 195, states that the Indians obtained copper at Lake Superior, which "they made into bracelets, spoons, etc." De Soto found copper hatchets in possession of some of the tribes along the coast of the Gulf of Mexico, which they stated they obtained from a province called Chisca, far to the north. Claude Allouez, in 1666, visited Lake Superior, and states that "it happens frequently that pieces of native copper are found, weighing from ten to twenty pounds. I have seen several such pieces in the hands of savages; and since they are very super-stitious, they esteem them as divinities given them to promote their happi-ness, by the gods who dwell beneath the water. For this reason they pre-serve these pieces of copper, wrapped up with their precious articles. In some families, they have been kept for more than fifty years. In others, they have descended from time out of mind, being cherished as domestic gods. For some time, there was seen near the shore a large rock of copper, with its top rising above the water, which gave an opportunity for those passing by to cut pieces from it; but when I passed that vicinity, it had disappeared. I believe that the gales, which are frequent, like those of the sea, had covered it with sand. Our savages tried to persuade me that it was a divinity who had disappeared, but for what cause they were unwilling to tell." (Foster and Whitney's Report on Lake Superior, Part I, page 7). Dablon, in his "Relation" for 1669-70, states that "the savages did not agree as to the course of the copper. Some say that it is where the river (Ontonagon) begins, others that it is close to the lake, in the clay, and others at the forks and along the eastern branch of the river." Again, Dablon gives an account of its being reputed to occur on an island about forty or fifty leagues from the Saut toward the north shore, opposite a place called Missippicoatong (Michipicoten?). The savages related that the island was a floating island, sometimes near and at other times far off. These statements, with other particulars, make it very probably that the Indians of Lake Superior were familiar with the localities prior to their acquaintance with the French, and that the place here described can be no other than the even then celebrated Isle Royale.

Jacques Cartier in 1535 spent the winter at or near Quebec, and learned several facts concerning copper that were in possession of the Indians, which he has given in his Brief Recital. They made an effort to explain to him where the copper came from. They gave Cartier to understand that there were large quantities where they obtained it, situated on a bank of a river near a lake. One of the chiefs drew from a sack a piece of copper a foot long and gave it to Champlain. "This was quite pure and very handsome." He said they had "gathered it in lumps, and, having melted it, spread it out in sheets, smoothing it with stones." The Indians at Montreal and Quebec, in 1535, were familiar with the fact that Sanguenay was a copper-bearing region. John Gilmary Shea, LL. D., says (Shea's Charlevoix): "The Saguenay of the St. Lawrence Indians was evidently the Lake Superior region, and possibly the ports accessible by the Mississippi. The river Saguenay was not so called from being in, but leading in to Saguenay." Thus, at a distance of from eight hundred to one thousand miles from its origin, Cartier, in 1535, and Champlain, in 1610, encountered Indians who informed them of the man-ner of mining and of manufacturing copper implements, Champlain stating that the copper was melted.

It is not presumed that this is a complete list of historic references to the use of copper and copper mining by the Indians; but it is amply sufficient to show that it is not necessary to invoke a strange race, prior to the Indian, to account for the copper implements and the nuggets of copper that have been found in the mounds, as well as those found on the surface of the ground throughout the Northwest.

The term mound-builders is distinctively applied to the race that constructed the remarkable earthworks of the valley of the Ohio and of the interior of the United States in general; but it is true that in nearly all parts of the world the practice of mound-building has prevailed, sometimes among nations that come within historical epochs. Mounds are found among the Celts and the Scythians, in the Sandwich Islands and in New Zealand, in Japan and India, and throughout the central parts of the Eastern continent, as well as in both Americas, from the country of the Esquimaux to Chili and Fuegia. The earliest of human records refer distinclty to this method of honoring the dead. The heroic age of Greece, as sung by Homer, abounded with ceremonies and curious details relating to the tumulus erected over the bones of the slain hero. The burial of Patroclus, as related in the twenty-third book of the Iliad, is an illustration of the practice of mound-building by the ancient Greeks:

"The sacred relics to the tent they bore,
The urn a veil of linen covered o'er.
That done, they bid the sepulcher aspier,
And cast the deep foundations round the pyre;
High in the midst they heap the swelling bed
Of rising earth, memorial of the dead."

At the burial of Hector, the Trojans erect a pile of large stones over the urn containing his remains, and upon that pile up the tumulus. When AEneas buried the pilot of his fleet, Misenus, he

"...piously heaped a mighty mound sepulchral;"

Artachaeas, superintendent of the canal at Athos, was honored by Xerxes with a memorial mound which still remains, in remembrance of the skill of that engineer, and an evidence of the custom of the Persians. The Scythian kings are entombed in tumuli along the banks of the Dnieper. Orestes, bewailing his father, Agamemnon, says:

"If but some Lycian spear 'neath Ilium's walls
        Had lowly laid thee,
A mighty name in the Atridan halls
        Thou wouldst have made thee.
Then hadst thou pitched thy fortunes like a star,
To son and daughter shining from afar,
Beyond the wide-waved sea the high-heaped mound
        Had told forever
Thy feats of battle, and with glory crowned
        Thy high endeavor."

In Asia Minor, the tome of Alyattes, the Lydian king, has a circumference of nearly a mile, requiring ten minutes to ride round its base. In the same neighborhood, near the Lake Bygaea, are numerous other circular mounds.

The same practice was continued into the later days of Grecian history. Alexander raised a mound over Demaratus, which, Plutarch says, was "eighty cubits high and of vast circumference." The tumulus erected on the plain of Marathon, in commemoration of the one hundred and ninety-two Athenians, who fell in the battle, is near the sea, and is to be seen by all travelers. It is about one hundred feet in circumference, and about twenty-five feet high. Finally, coming within the scope of modern history, the construction, at the order of the English government, of a mound of earth on the plains of Waterloo, attests the tenacity of that sentiment of veneration for the dead who die in the service of their country, and the persistence of a practice, which seems to be common to all mankind, and to have survived from prehistoric times, of resorting to the mound of earth, as being at once the easiest made and the most enduring monument in memory of the departed.

The practice of mound-building not being distinctive of any race, tribe, or epoch of the human family, it may be considered not at all unlikely that the aboriginal tribes of America, perhaps without exception, had their ceremonies and habits of burial, if not other sacred rites, in one way and another associated with the erection of mounds of earth. Indeed, it would be a remarkable exception if the native Americans did not erect mounds. They possessed the land without molestation prior to the discovery by Columbus. They had the necessary elements of perpetuity and stability, at least so far as these can be predicated by savage tribes. They cultivated the soil and conducted a considerable trade with their neighbors. They exhibited all other characteristics common to mankind in an uncivilized state. The denial of their resort to mound-building, for the same purposes as other tribes in similar circumstances, carries with it the necessity to account for such an anomalous exception.

It is often stated that the Indian, when interrogated concerning the mounds and earthworks of the country, shakes his head in ignorance, affirming that he knows not their origin. The fact is carried further than it should be when it is invoked to prove the non-Indian origin of the mounds. Admitting, with some reservation, that the Indian at present knows nothing of the origin of the mounds, still it may be true that his immediate ancestors were familiar with the facts of their erection. The Indian has been driven from the home where he was born, and where his ancestral traditions and customs have centered and exhibited their unconstrained development, and has been a fugitive for several generations, from the cupidity and the bayonet of the white man. When it is remembered that the erection of a mound, similar to those seen all over the Northwest, was not the act of a day, nor of a year, but of many years, and perhaps generations, it is easy enough to understand why the custom has become so nearly extinct. The Indian has become modified by contact with the European. He has gradually been compelled to forsake many customs and abandon arts which came into competition with the customs and the acts of the stronger race. The semi-nomadic life which he has been compelled to accept has not been favorable to the erection of mounds, which required the quiet of permanent and peaceful residence.

We are not, moreover, without testimony to the fact that the present Indians did build mounds. Lewis and Clark mention the custom among the Omahas, saying that "one of the great chiefs was buried on a hill, and a mound twelve feet in diameter and six feet high was erected over him." Bertram states that the Choctaws covered the pyramid of coffins taken from the bone-house with earth, thus raising a conical hill or mound. Tomochichi pointed out to General Oglethorpe a large conical mound near Savannah, in which he said the Yamacraw chief was interred, who had, many years before, entertained a great white man with the red beard, who entered the Savannah River in a large vessel, and in his barge came up to the Yamacraw bluff. Featherstonhaugh, in his "Travels," speaks of the custom among the Osages, referring to a mound built over the body of a chief, called Jean Defoe by the French, who unexpectedly died while his warriors were absent on a hunting expedition. Upon their return, they heaped a mound over his remains, enlarging it at intervals for a long period, until it reached its present height. Bradford says that many of the tumuli formed of earth, and occasionally of stones, are of Indian origin. They are generally sepulchral mounds--either the general cemetery of a village or tribe, or funeral monuments over the graves of illustrious chiefs, or upon a battle-field, commemorating the event and entombing the fallen, or the result of a custom, prevalent among some of the tribes, of collecting at stated intervals the bones of the dead, and interring them in a common repository. (American Antiquities and Researches into the History of the Red Race. 1841, p. 17.) A mound of the latter description was formerly situated on the low grounds of the Rivanna River, in Virginia, opposite the site of an old Indian village (Jefferson's Notes on Virginia, pp. 100, 103.) It was forty feet in diameter and twelve feet in height, of a spheroidal form, and surrounded by a trench, whence the earth employed in its erection had been excavated. The circumstances attending the custom alluded to were the great number of skeletons, their confused position, their situation in distinct strata, exhibiting different stages of decomposition, and the appearance of bones of infants. A mound of similar character, and constructed in layers of strata at successive periods, existed near the south branch of the Shenandoah, in the same state. A tumulus of stones, in New York State, is said to have marked the grave of a distinguished warrior (McCauley's History of New York, vol. ii., p. 239). Beck's Gazetteer (p. 308), states that "a mound of the largest dimensions has been thrown up, within a few years, in Illinois, over the remains of an eminent chief." The Natchez Indians, when expelled from Louisiana in 1728 erected a mound "of considerable size" near Natchitoches, as stated in the documents accompanying the President's message for 1806. C. C. Jones, referring to plate xl. of the Brevis Narratio says that "here we have a spirited representation of the ceremonies observed by the Florida Indians upon the occasion of the sepulture of their kings and priests. Located in the vicinity of a village appears a small conical mound, surmounted by the shell drinking-cup of the deceased, and surrounded by a row of arrows stuck in the ground. Gathered in a circle about this sepulchral tumulus, the bereaved members of the tribe, upon bended knees, are bewailing the death of him in whose honor this grave-mound has been heaped up." Jones also mentions an instance of a primary burial under a mound erected in honor of the dead, on the coast a few miles below Savannah, in which, along with an earthen pot, several arrowheads, a stone celt, and bones of a human skeleton, was found the immediate association, a portion of an old-fashioned sword. This tumulus, thus proved to have been erected since the advent of the Europeans, was seven feet high and about twenty feet in diameter at the base. Of the sword, the parts preserved were the oak handle, most of the guard, and about seven inches of the blade. The rest had perished from rust. The Mandans, according to Catlin (North American Indians, vol. i., p. 90), constructed mounds in commemoration of their dead; and the same is said of the Arickarees by Prof. Lewis H. Morgan (Twenty-First Report of the New York State Cabinet). The mounds at Lanesboro' in the state of Minnesota are said by the old Winnebago chief Winneshiek to have been erected by the Sioux in commemoration of a great victory won there over the Winnebagoes many generations ago. The same old chief, when shown a clay pipe taken from the Lanesboro' mounds, said it was like those made by the Sioux, and, pointing to an earthen spitoon for illustration, said the Sioux made many like it. In the Proceedings of the American Association for the Advancement of Science, for 1875, Dr. Sternberg, of the United States Army, critically analyzes the contents of certain mounds near Pensacola, Florida, and concludes that they were built by different but contemporaneous tribes of Indians, one probably being the Natchez. In these mounds were found pottery, red hematite for pigment, fling weapons, and shell ornaments in the shape of beads and perforated disks, in conjunction with blue-glass beads and fragments of iron. The latter show that these mounds were still used, or in process of erection, later than the advent of Europeans.

Mr. E. G. Squier, in the second volume of the Smithsonian Contributions to Knowledge, has described in detail many mounds and earthworks of Western and Central New York, remarking that they extend down to Susquehanna as far as the valley of the Wyoming northward into Canada, along the upper tributaries of the Ohio, and westward along the shores of Lake Erie and Ontario. These mounds and earthworks are said generally to be smaller than those in the Ohio Valley. They were found to contain ornamented pottery, pipes of clay regularly and often fancifully molded, or bearing the forms of animals, stone axes and hammers, stone disks and implements which the author remarks are almost identical in shape and material with some described by him from the mounds of the Ohio Valley, and spear-points and bodkins of bone. In connection with these are described articles of European manufacture, such as cast copper and axes, and kettles of copper, iron and brass. Although Mr. Squier had previously expressed the opinion that the earthworks of Western New York were of like nature and origin with those of the Ohio Valley, when confronted with the fact of articles of European manufacture, such as cast copper and iron axes, commingled with the aboriginal, discovered by his own investigation, was forced to assign the New York mounds to the Iroquois. It seems not unreasonable to assume that the New York series of mounds will be found undistinguishable from those of Northern Ohio and Eastern Michigan, which have unquestioningly been regarded as of the same age as those of the Ohio Valley, as well as synchronous with those of Wisconsin, which, while possessing all the essential characters of the Ohio Valley mounds, have been assigned as unhesitatingly to the existing races of Indians by the late J. A. Lapham of Milwaukee.

It hence seems demonstrable, as well as admitted by some of the best American ethnologists, that the existing Indian races formerly carried on extensively and methodically the practice of mound-building. The mounds of sepulture are often referred to by historians and travelers. They were built by slow accretions. Not to mention the veneration which impelled the untutored savage to cast a handful of earth on a mound every time that he passed it, in testimony of his remembrance of the departed, it may be well to refer to what has been called the feast of the dead. This is asserted to have been common to many tribes, although conducted with some variation of detail. Gathering the bones of the dead from their temporary resting-places, the tribe assembled at a chosen spot, and with solemn ceremonies performed the last rites of sepulture. Sometimes they were placed in coffins separately, and buried in a pit over which was erected a mound of earth, and sometimes they were arranged serially, and simple buried under a mound. More frequently the bones were burned, the cremation being accompanied with lamentation and followed with feasting. The ashes and the unconsumed fragments were then covered with earth. For many generations, this feast of the dead, which occurred sometimes every eight years, or every ten, or when the accumulated bones made it necessary, was doubtless performed on the same spot; and in course of time a mound of considerable dimensions was the result, which, while containing human bones, or fragments of them, and much evidence of fire in the form of ashes and charcoal and reddened stones, yet discloses, on exhumation, no perfect skeletons.

As further testimony to the erection of mounds by the present Indians, the statements and opinions of a few who have investigated the subject, and have dwelt long with them, may be referred to.

Mr. Jones, in his review of the Antiquities of the Southern Indians, remarks: "During the progress of this investigation, it will be perceived that mound-building, which seems to have fallen into disuse prior to the dawn of the historic period, was entirely abandoned very shortly after intercourse was established between Europeans and the red man." Again, in summing up the evidence, **Mr.** Jones says in conclusion: "In a word, we do not concur in the opinion so often expressed, that the mound-builders were a race distinct from and superior in art, government, and religion to the Southern Indians of the fifteenth and sixteenth centuries." Bradford, in <u>American Antiquities and Researches,</u> affirms that "from very respectable authority it appears that many tribes still continue to this day to raise a tumulus over the grave, the magnitude of which is proportioned to the rank and celebrity of the deceased."

From the foregoing it appears that every known trait of the mound-builder was possessed also by the Indians at the time of the discovery of America. It hence becomes unnecessary to appeal to any other agency than the Indian. It is poor philosophy and poor science that resort to hypothetical causes when those already known are sufficient to produce the known effects. The Indian is a known adequate cause. The assignment of the mounds to any other dynasty was born of that common reverence for the past and for the unexplainable, which not only unconsciously augments the actual, but revolts at the reduction of these works to the level of the existing red man.

ANNUAL REPORT OF THE COMMISSIONER OF MINERAL STATISTICS
OF THE STATE OF MICHIGAN, FOR 1880.
Lansing: W. S. George & Co. 1881.
"Early History," pp. 7-8.

The occurrence of copper was one of the objects that early attracted the
attention of the Jesuits, and its presence, so frequently met with among the
Indians, naturally excited their curiosity and wonder. Frequent mention of it
is made, and in some instances the descriptions relate to masses of considerable size. But long prior to this period, the metal that attracted the
attention of the missionaries and early voyageurs, and which now forms the
basis of a great and growing industry, had been sought and mined for by a
people who have left no record but the implements which they used and the
excavations which they made. These excavations, obscured from view by the
slow accumulation of debris during the years which have since elapsed, and
the Indians, whom the good fathers labored to christianize, had no knowledge
whatever of the matter. No suspicion that any such work had ever been performed occurred until within a recent period, after the country was thrown
open to settlement and actual mining had begun. Then it became known that
this ground had been previously occupied, and that these metalliferous veins
had been long ago extensively worked and apparently large amounts of copper
obtained; but when and by whom is a mystery. But that this mining work is of
a high antiquity is evident from many facts; the pits and tunnels which had
been made had become filled up with rubbish and with decayed vegetation and
grown over with forest trees. If the depressions were ever observed they
were naturally regarded as those made by overturned trees or as hollows in
the rocks, and it was not suspected until the discovery was actually made, so
late as 1847-48, that here, too, men had formerly delved in search of metals.
These ancient excavations are found in all portions of the Mineral Range and
in Isle Royale. So general is this fact, that there is scarcely a vein or outcrop of mineral in the whole copper district but the evidences are found of
their ancient workings, extending into the solid rock from a few feet to sixty
feet in depth. In these pits, when cleared of the accumulated dirt and rubbish,
have sometimes been found large masses of copper which these primitive
seekers had unsuccessfully endeavored to remove. Masses of copper or many
tons weight have thus been discovered surrounded with stone hammers in
great numbers, pieces of burnt wood and other evidences of former labor.
The method of mining which these people apparently pursued was to heat the
rock with fire and then by pouring on water and pounding the rock with their
stone hammers to disintegrate and separate it.
Quantities of these stone hammers are nearly always obtained from the
bottoms of these ancient pits. They consist of small boulders of hard trap
rock of from three to thirty pounds in weight, around which a groove has
sometimes been made for the purpose of holding a withe which fastened on the
handle. Copper tools and other utensils and materials have also been found,
but no indications that would lead to the identification of the race to which
these miners belonged, have been, as yet, discovered.
These ancient "diggings," as they are locally called, are everywhere so
abundant and have now become so well known and familiar to those engaged
here in mining as to be no longer a matter of surprise or wonder. In one
respect they have undoubtedly been of great service, serving as guides which
have led to the discovery of lodes, which were thus shown to have been previously worked and as indicative of the value of such lodes. As in the iron
region, the magnetic needle has guided to the discovery of many valuable deposits of ore, so in the copper district these pits of the ancient miners extending along the surface outcrop of the copper bearing veins, have silently

betokened to the eager explorer where was hidden the object of his search. But to the Indians who roamed the country at the time of its discovery, to the Jesuits, and to the early voyageurs and explorers this fact of ancient mining was wholly unknown. The evidence of the existence of copper in this region - a knowledge which had already become widespread - was derived from the specimens in the possession of the Indians and from seeing the erratic boulders of that metal which were sometimes found in traversing the country, and from observing the copper bearing veins which outcropped along the streams and near the shores of the lake.

PREHISTORIC MINES OF LAKE SUPERIOR
By J. H. Lathrop
From THE AMERICAN ANTIQUARIAN AND ORIENTAL JOURNAL
Vol. XXIII, Jan-Nov., 1901 Chicago, 1901

The first information given to the civilized world of the existence of copper on the shores of Lake Superior was contained in a book published at Paris, by one Lagarde, in 1636, in which he says, speaking of the Lake Superior Country: "There are mines of copper which might be made profitable if there were inhabitants and workmen who would labor faithfully. That would be done if colonies were established." His information concerning the existence of copper in this region was derived from the Indians then inhabiting the country.

Pierre Boucher, in his book published in 1640, also at Paris, states: "There are mines of copper, tin, antimony, and lead. In Lake Superior there is a great island, which is fifty leagues in circuit, in which there is a very beautiful mine of copper; it is found, also, in various places in large pieces, all refined."

The "beautiful mine of copper" referred to by this writer undoubtedly was the ancient workings reopened by the Minong Company in 1874, and referred to more fully later in this article. It is not improbable that the exodus of the ancient miners at that time may have been so recent that the masses of native copper, later taken out by the Minong Company from the ancient pits, were then fully exposed. If their work on Isle Royale was so plainly defined more than two hundred and thirty years later, it is not unreasonable to suppose that, at the time Boucher speaks of, these openings were more like a recently opened mine than of one long since abandoned.

From 1660 to 1665, and later, the Jesuits made several visits to Lake Superior, establishing missions at various points; and the memories of Fathers Allouez and Mesnard have been perpetuated in those mines of Houghton County which were named for them. The Jesuits were keen observers, not only for the spiritual welfare of their charges, but also of the geography of the country and its minerals, and their writings gave further information as to the deposits of copper along the shores of the lake. M. Charlevoix visited Lake Superior in the course of his extensive explorations, and wrote intelligently and with truth concerning the native copper which he saw along the shore and in the hands of the Indians, who, however, made no practical use of the metal, but hoarded it, regarding the nuggets with superstitious reverence.

In 1765 Captain Jonathan Carver says he discovered "mines of virgin copper which was as fine as that found in any other country," and also that the Ontonagon River is "remarkable for the abundance of virgin copper that is found on and near its banks." A few years later, on returning to England, Carver formed a company in London to work the proposed mine in Ontonagon. In 1771 a party of miners came over from England to establish the mine, but their efforts were fruitless, owing to wrong methods adopted in their mining.

The traces which the ancient miners have left of their work in the Lake Superior copper country indicate that they were a most industrious and intelligent race, and that their manual labors must have extended through centuries of time, as they cover an area in Michigan, known as the trap-range, having a length of nearly one hundred miles through Keweenaw, Houghton, and Ontonagon counties, and with a width varying from two to seven miles. Their works were also very extensive on the island in Lake Superior, some forty miles from the Michigan shore, known as Isle Royale. This island is about forty miles in length, by an average of five miles in width. Their works here will be spoken of more in detail later.

From examination of their ancient pits we can get a fair idea of their methods of mining, which are crude and primitive to our eyes, but which show

5720 POUND MASS OF PURE COPPER

5720 pound mass of pure copper found on the Minong Mine
Property near McCargo's Cove, Isle Royale. The prehistoric
miners had raised this part way to the surface.

wonderful perseverance on their part. The process was to heat the rock containing the embedded copper by building fires along the outcrop of the vein, and then, removing the coals, to dash water on the heated rock, thus cracking it, and afterwards taking out the broken pieces of rock; then by breaking away the remaining rock with stone hammers, they released the copper. This method is shown plainly, in all the ancient workings, by the presence of quantities of charcoal and of stone hammers. In some places remains of birchbark baskets have been found. These were used to carry water to the fires, or the pieces of copper to the boats. It is assumed that the ancient miners had no knowledge of raising water otherwise than by hand, for the pits have only been sunk to a depth where water could be baled out with comparative ease by sets of men.

All along the trap-range the vestiges of ancient mining works are very numerous. As far back as 1771, a large mass of native copper weighing about four tons was found near the bank of the Ontonagon River. It is supposed that this mass was moved from its native resting place to the place near the river where found. In 1845 it was floated on a raft down the river by James K. Paull, who thus became the first shipper of modern times of a large amount of copper from the Lake Superior District. Unfortunately for Mr. Paull, this mass of copper was appropriated by an agent of the United States Government, by him shipped to Detroit, and later to Washington, where it now reposes in the Smithsonian Institute.

The earliest record in detail of the work of the ancient miners was the discovery in 1846 by the prospector, Albert Hughes, on the Minnesota mine location in Ontonagon county, and thus described by Samuel O. Knapp, then agent of the Minnesota mine:

"When he had penetrated to a depth of eighteen feet, he came to a mass of a native copper, ten feet long, three feet wide, nearly two feet thick, and weighing over six tons. On digging around the mass it was found to rest on billets of oak, supported on sleepers of the same material. The wood, from its long exposure to moisture, was dark-colored and had lost its consistency. It opposed no more resistance to a knife blade than so much peat. The earth was so firmly packed as to support the mass of copper. The ancient miners had evidently raised it about five feet, and then abandoned the work as too laborious. The number of ancient hammers he took from this and other excavations exceeded ten carloads. They were made of greenstone or porphyry boulders."

From further explorations in this pit, it appeared that the original work was about thirty feet in depth. On the debris outside the mouth of the pit were trees showing three hundred and ninety-five rings of annual growth.

In 1857, while exploring on the lands of the North Cliff Company at Keweenaw Point, west of Eagle River, Edwin J. Hulbert and Amos H. Scott discovered evidence of the work of ancient miners which was described by Mr. Hulbert as follows:

"The opening was a perfectly-formed underhand slope. The vein was rather in the form of a large cross course. The ancient miners had excavated between the walls of this vein, a width varying from two to three and one-half feet, almost the entire matrix for a distance of some thirty feet in length, and in some places six feet in depth. They carried away with them the entire product of their copper, the excavation containing only decomposed leaves."

A large mass of float-copper was found in the woods on the land of the Mesnard Mining Company, located to the northeast of the Franklin mine. This mass had been worked at by the ancient miners, as much charcoal was found around it, and the top and sides had been beaten smooth by stone hammers, the marks of which were plainly visible. All projections, and every particle of copper which could be beaten off, had been carried away. The ancient miners must have felt much regret at having to abandon such a treasure. This mass weighed about eighteen tons, and was cut up under direction of Mr. Jacob Houghton, agent of the Mesnard Company.

The most extensive series of continuous workings as yet discovered were those found on Isle Royale, on what is known as the Minong Belt. Here, for a distance of about one and three-quarter miles in length and for an average width of nearly four hundred feet, successive pits indicating the mining out of the belt of solid rock to a depth of from twelve to thirty feet. Between the rows of pits are ridges of rock and soil, taken from successive pits, and indicating that they were left as dams to prevent the passage of water from one pit to another while the latter was being wrought. In another place a drain sixty feet long had been dug and covered with timbers, felled and laid across. In one place the vein had been followed on an incline to a depth of more than thirty feet, and some thirty inches in width, with large boulders rolled and wedged to keep the rock above from falling in on the miners, thus taking the place of timbering, as in our modern mines.

These discoveries on the Minong Belt, first noted in 1867, and more extensively explored in 1871 and 1872, led to the formation of the Minong Mining Company in 1874; and in the work of clearing out the old pits much barrel-work and stamp copper was found, also a mass weighing nearly three tons, which had been detached from its bed by the ancient miners, as it showed the marks of stone hammers, but was evidently too heavy to be carried away. From the extent of these workings on Isle Royale, it would indicate that a large number of men must have been employed for a long series of years, and as Lake Superior is a treacherous sheet of water, the crossing of the intervening forty miles between Isle Royale and Michigan must have been risky work for small boats or canoes.

Nothing has ever been found on either Isle Royale or in the Lake Superior region, to indicate that the ancient miners were permanent dwellers in the copper country. The climate is severe, and the best of protection has to be given to the people at the mines. When one considers the length of time which had to be taken in making the long journey from even Southern Michigan to the copper region, unless the seasons were different in those ancient days than at the present, it is safe to infer that the actual mining in the Lake Superior Country, and particularly on Isle Royale, could not have been exceeding three months in the year. These ancient miners were doubtless well posted as to the advantages of the organization of labor, particularly in these extensive works at Isle Royale. There were probably parties who were expert in the extraction of copper from the rock, others whose time was occupied in bailing water from the pits, or carrying it to the heated rocks, and still others who were engaged in the manufacture of stone hammers, sledges, and other implements from the water-born boulders from the beach. Other parties, also, were busy in procuring food from the lake, and from the woods surrounding the workings.

A peculiarity of the immense numbers of stone hammers which were found in and about the Isle Royale workings, and which has often been commented upon, was the absence of a groove around the stone. This groove was for the purpose of bending a piece of flexible wood around it and then holding it firmly in place by thongs of deerskin, thus providing a handle which could be reinforced by stiffer pieces of wood. The stone hammers found on the mainland of Michigan almost invariably have the grooves. In some explorations made during the summer of 1899 on the Ontonagon Range, one of these hammers was found with a part of the handle still intact, held in place by the thongs of skin. It may be that the miners at Isle Royale found the stones on the beaches so well shaped by nature and the attrition of the waves that they made excellent hammers just as they were picked up, so that no time was taken to fit them with handles. On the mainland, near the Ontonagon River there was found quite an area of ground which was strewn with stone chips and pieces of broken porphyry, showing that at some time in the distant past it had been a sort of workshop for the purpose of preparing the stone hammers and other implements for transportation inland.

The articles and tools into which the pieces of native copper were made, were arrowheads, bracelets, awls, needles, knives, spears, chisels, wedges, fleshers, axes, and various other things. Articles made of copper are found scattered from Lower Michigan to Central America, and from Pennsylvania to Arizona, but the greatest numbers have been found furied in the works of the Mound-Builders throughout Wisconsin, Lower Michigan, Ohio, Indiana, Illinois, Iowa, Kentucky, and Tennessee. That the copper from which many of these tools were made came from the Lake Superior District cannot be questioned, though the tools and implements were scattered over a vast area of country. Copper ore exists in vast deposits over Arizona, New Mexico, and Central America, but nothing has ever been discovered which would lead any one to imagine that the ancient miners were sufficiently skilled in metallurgy, as to be able to reduce the ores to refined copper. In all the relics of the Mound-Builders there is no evidence of any vessels which would indicate that they had ever been used for crucibles, nor is there any evidence of furnaces.

In the Lake Superior Country are the only known extensive deposits of native copper in the world. This virgin copper, of almost absolute purity, was of great value to the ancient miners, owing to its extreme ductility and the comparative ease with which it could be manufactured into their necessary implements. They seem to have known how to harden copper, so as to give it a cutting edge. This is shown by the edges of many of their axes which have been found, the points of spears, etc. A peculiarity of Lake Superior copper is that silver is often found in direct connection with copper, by nature's welding and with the line of impact clearly defined. Implements of copper, showing the same characteristics, have been found in the works of the Mound-Builders.

How these strange people came to the Lake Superior region can only be a matter of inference, but from the traces they have left, there is but little question that their migrations were made by water. Traces of their storage-pits have been found along the shore of St. Mary's River below Sault Ste. Marie, locally and generally known as the "Soo." Another series of storage-pits was along the north shore of Portage Lake, just below the town of Hancock, and these were doubtless used to store the copper taken from the range now occupied by the Quincy and Franklin mines. That the pits along Portage Lake were used for the storage of copper there is no doubt; for the native rock at this place is a sandstone, carrying no copper. The storage-pits on the St. Mary's River were used for the same purpose, for there is no native copper in that vicinity. On the other side of the river, in Canada, many exploration pits of the ancient miners have been found, but no extensive workings, for the Canadian copper is in the form of copper ore, and there is no evidence that it was ever worked. It would seem as though many canoes or boats must have been employed during the summer months in conveying copper from the Lake Superior storage-pits to the "Soo," thence to be transported either to the south shore of Lake Erie or by way of Lake Michigan to more interior portions of the country.

By far the most interesting of these storage pits was that discovered by

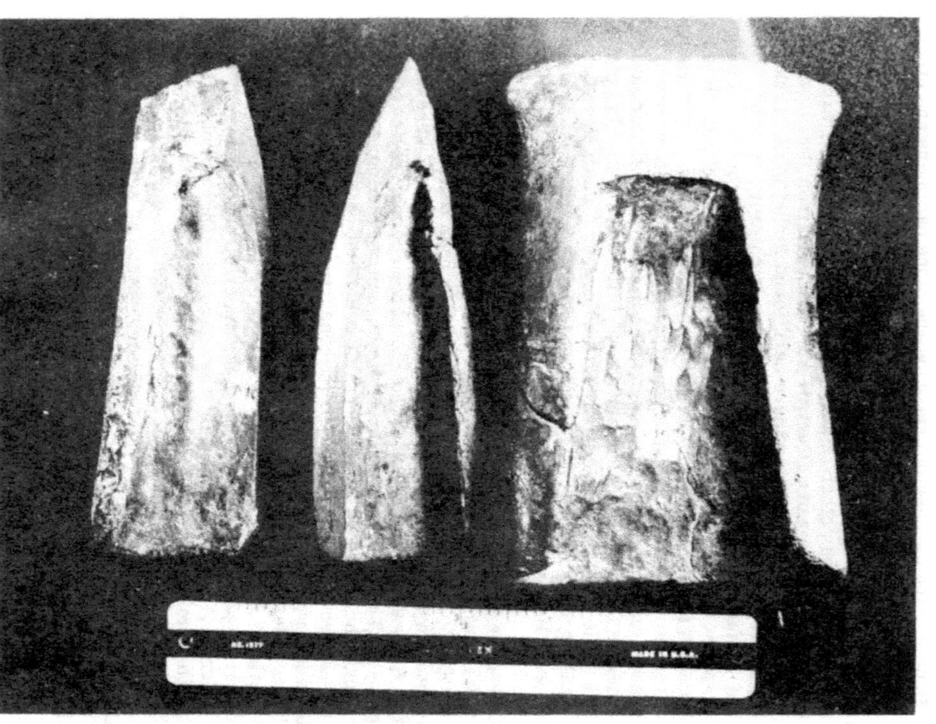

SOCKETED COPPER AXES

One axe has been cut in two for metallurgical examination.
Hardness indentations can be seen on one cut surface.
One-half size. Michigan College of Mining & Technology
collection.

Edwin J. Hulbert in 1858, and opened by him in February, 1865. This pit was situated on the crest of the hill about midway between the head of Torch Lake, where the Calument and Hecla stamp-mills are now located, and Lake Superior. The position on the hill is now a part of the Calument and Hecla location, and No. 1 shaft of the Calument mine was sunk through this ancient pit. It is a generally accepted theory that one route of the ancient miners was through Torch Lake in their canoes, then a carry of nine miles over the hills to Lake Superior, and thence to Isle Royale. This would cut off the long journey of some eighty miles by water around Keweenaw Point. By a singular coincidence, this storage-pit was dug by the ancient miners directly above the famous Calument lode, but there is no evidence to show that the men who dug it originally ever knew of the richness below, for the lode lay beneath a heavy over-burden of earth, and the ancient miners did not go down deep enough to uncover the rock below. It was not an exploration pit, but a storage-pit, pure and simple.

This pit was about fifty feet in diameter, practically nearly circular in shape, and presented the appearance of a huge bowl-shaped depression in the earth. The burrow, formed of the earth taken out, extended for a distance of some twenty feet all around the depression, and on this burrow, with smaller trees around it, was an enormous hemlock tree on one side of the pit, and an equally huge black birch on the other. This birch on being cut down showed wood rings to a number of nearly two hundred, indicating a good number of years since the pit was abandoned. The pit was evidently filled and emptied on successive occasions with copper obtained from sources other than the conglomerate lode; for the character of this lode, on which the Calument and Hecla mine has its principal workings, is that of extreme hardness, and it is doubtful if the primitive implements of the ancient miners could have made any impression on it. Moreover, the copper in the conglomerate rock is mostly in small particles, and thus valueless to those who were searching for the larger pieces, such as are found in the softer rock of the fissure-veins and the amygdaloid lodes.

Therefore it is absolutely certain that this pit was used for the storage of copper from some foreign source, most probably the workings on Isle Royale.

When the pit was opened it showed a covering of earth nearly four feet in thickness, well laid, and free from stones or rock. Under this was a vast deposit of green carbonate of copper, nearly twenty tons of which was taken out and sent to the smelting-works at Hancock, fourteen miles away. Thus the Calument stockholders of 1865 reaped the benefit of the labors of the ancient miners centuries before. Everything found in the pit tended to show that it had been partially filled with pieces of native copper for storage purposes. There was not found a single tool or implement of any kind, such as were employed by the ancient miners in the extraction of copper from the rock, or such as were invariably found in all the ancient workings by explorers in the counties of Keweenaw, Houghton, Ontonagon, and on Isle Royale. The men who took out the carbonate of copper found oblong birch baskets, used for carrying the copper to the pit; skeins of narrow, flat threads of spruce roots used for binding the bark to the bale of the basket; sheets of birch-bark, used for repairs; and pieces of tanned deerskin for mending or making moccasins. These articles were all in a fair state of preservation, due to the carbonate of copper. Centuries of time must have elapsed to have changed the native copper, which the miners placed in the pit, into the carbonate form. No better proof can be offered of the great antiquity of the working of these ancient miners than that presented by the opening of this ancient storage pit, showing the changing of this great deposit from native copper to the green carbonate. Probably more than two hundred of the pits and workings of the ancient miners were opened by explorers from 1843 to 1890, but in the history of the copper country this pit stands unique. With the exception of the small deposit found at the Winthrop mine in 1852, nothing like it had been discovered before, and nothing since.

The route taken by the ancient miners to their workings in what is now Ontonagon county, was doubtless through Portage Lake, thence by a small stream connecting Portage Lake with Lake Superior. This stream was obliterated when the present ship canal, one hundred feet wide and two and one-quarter miles in length, was cut through in the years 1866 to 1873. At the western end of this canal is a high-sandy bluff, now mostly covered with a spare growth of trees of small size. That this location was occupied as an intermediary camping-place there is not much doubt, for when the canal was cut through this bluff, large numbers of copper tools, axes, spears, and arrowheads were found. It may be that here was the workingplace of the ancients in the manufacture of tools, etc., from the copper found on the Ontonagon Range; for the long, gently sloping ground toward the east, and the waters in Portage Lake, would make an ideal camp - sheltered as it would be from the western winds blowing across Lake Superior.

What calamity befell the ancient miners, who can tell? That they left the country at the close of the season, expecting to return at the opening of the next, is reasonably certain. The pits, the charcoal, the stone hammers, the implements and tools of copper, are the only relics left of the race which discovered and worked the Lake Superior mines. Not the vestige of a dwelling, a skeleton, or a bone has been found. From the earliest acquaintance of the white man with the Indians inhabiting the copper country, not one legend or tradition is extant of these ancient miners.

When we consider the extent of country over which this mining work was done, and the slow and crude process of labor, and the immense amount of work done, we are forced to believe that the time thus spent extended through many, many years of time, and was carried on by vast numbers of people who were as active and enterprising in their way as those who, centuries later, have made the copper country of Lake Superior the wonder of the world.

ABORIGINAL COPPER MINES OF ISLE ROYALE, LAKE SUPERIOR
By William H. Holmes
From <u>American Anthropologist</u> New Series, Vol. 3 (1901)
New York, G. P. Putnam's Sons

INTRODUCTION

In the spring of 1892 the writer was engaged in gathering material for the anthropological exhibit of the Smithsonian Institution at the World's Columbian Exposition in Chicago. It was intended that a leading feature of the exhibit in the Archeological Section should be a display illustrating the ancient mining and quarrying industries of the American aborigines, and in carrying out the plan visits were made to a number of important sites in the Middle West - to the flint quarries of Ohio, Arkansas, and Indian Territory; to the site of the quartz shops at Little Falls, Minnesota; to the pipestone quarries of Minnesota; and to the ancient copper mines of Isle Royale, in Lake Superior.

Although exhibits of the collections procured through these explorations were made in due course of time, full reports of the work done and the observations made at some of the points have never been published. Papers were prepared describing the flint quarries of Arkansas and Indian Territory, and the re-markable deposits of the refuse of implement-making left upon the associated shop sites. A brief report was also published describing the excavations made on the site of the ancient quartz shops at Little Falls.

In the vast area drained by the Great Lakes and the upper Mississippi lived and labored the native peoples encountered by the early French voyagers, and later by English and Americans. In gathering material for their stone imple-ments these enterprising tribes discovered and sought to utilize lumps of a peculiar material, heavier and tougher than any stone with which they had been acquainted. Experiment showed that the ordinary processes by means of which stone was shaped were entirely incompetent to treat it. It could not be flaked, pecked, nor ground into shape, but in time the discovery was made that by hammering with stone sledges remarkable results could be achieved and valued ornaments and very superior implements could be shaped. These were the small masses of native copper, known as float copper, that had been torn from the massive trappean formations of the Lake Superior region by the ice-sheets and carried far down over the vast area now comprised in the states of Wiscon-sin, Michigan, Indiana, Illinois, and Iowa. The beginning of the use of copper by the native tribes of the Mississippi Valley and the Great Lakes was due, in all probability, to the presence of these transported fragments, often folded, scratched, and rounded off, and in cases reduced, by the irresistible move-ments of the ice-sheet, to shapes that might be utilized to some extent as im-plements. We may surmise that, little by little, the aberrant fragments were traced northward to the region of their origin, where, instead of loose abraded lumps of metal, ragged masses were found fixed in the rock in place, and with the removal of these began the new and vastly important industry of copper mining in the Great Lakes Region.

When the French pioneers came into the country, this work of freeing the copper bodies from the enclosing rock had gone on for a long time, - hundreds or many hundreds of years, and really wonderful progress had been made in mining the copper, in transporting it to far-away districts, and in shaping it into implements, utensils, and ornaments.

VISIT TO ISLE ROYALE

Desiring to examine for myself the existing traces of a great native indus-try, I resolved to undertake a trip to Isle Royale, since there modern mining had not so completely destroyed traces of the ancient work as on the southern shores of Lake Superior, where extensive mining operations have been carried on for many years. A very good account of the old mines has been published by Prof. N. H. Winchell, who visited Isle Royale some twenty years ago; and other men of scientific attainments - especially mining engineers - have visited the island, giving the mines some attention, but maps and photographic illustrations are entirely wanting, and the collections of artifacts made have not found their way into the larger museums.

Availing myself of the generous hospitality of officers of the Booth Packing Company, at Duluth, I took the company's steamer at that point and, sailing by way of Port Arthur, Canada, landed at a little fishing station on the rocky northwest shore of the island. This was a mile north of the mouth of McCargoe's cove a small bay or inlet extending two or three miles into the land in a southwesterly direction. It was at the head of this inlet that the mining company had located its shipping station, and the mines, now entirely deserted, lie still a mile or two to the south. Having taken with me from Duluth one laborer and a supply of provisions and tools, I obtained a second man and the necessary rowboat from fishermen at the station, and rowing into the little cove, found comfortable lodging in one of the deserted buildings of the mining company.

At the time of my visit there were no permanent inhabitants on this part of the island, the fishermen, who are concerned entirely with the waters of the open lake, living in improvised and temporary shelters along the shore. To all appearances no one had occupied the place for many years. When headquarters were established and our housekeeping arrangements in good shape, we set out by way of an old tramway line, now completely hidden by undergrowth, to find the site of the mines. The shallow valley up which we made our way is meandered by a small stream draining into McCargoe's cove. On the right, a gentle slope rises to a low ridge, which, at most, is not more than three or four hundred feet in height, while on the left is a low, abrupt bluff, as indicated in the section (figure 73).

Approaching the mines we found ourselves passing the ends of lofty ridges of excavated material, - the dumps of the mining company, - and continuing in among these we encountered the remnants of workshops, engine houses, and elevated tramways, and on the right saw extensive excavations and the mouths of deserted tunnels penetrating the slope.

Topographically, this little valley and its bo rdering ridges are a part of a system of ridges and troughs, extending, I believe, over a large portion of the island. The glacial ice-sheets pressed forward apparently along the strike of the strata, leaving the harder masses in bold relief, and, where the formations were less compact, excavating shallow valleys and depressions connecting one with another along the trend of the island, which is northeast and southwest. The deeper portions of these depressions are now occupied by ponds and swamps, and these with their alternating ridges, the fallen timber and dense undergrowth, make a country most difficult to traverse and wholly without scenic interest. Post-glacial drainage has not been active enough to modify the glacial sculpture, and the elevated portions present today the abraded and channeled surfaces left by the retreating ice. It was probably on some of these exposed masses of rock that the Indians first discovered the copper in place, since the ice, as it pared away the rock, caught the irregular masses of metal and tore them bit by bit from their firm anchorage, leaving half-detached fragments and ragged masses exposed. But the removal of these bits of metal was no easy task. They could not be broken off nor cut by any primitive device, and the only effective means of securing them was by crushing the enclosing rock with heavy sledges and shattering it by fire until the masses were freed. When the supply thus obtained was exhausted, the tedious work of uncovering the soil-hidden surface began, and the search was continued until a large part of the superficial formations of the little valley were worked over.

The overplaced deposits appear to consist largely of vegetal mold and other finely comminuted materials, but they have been so fully worked over by the ancient miners that their original character is not readily determined. In the valleys their extent is probably considerable, but at no point where excavations have been made is a thickness of more than a few feet exposed. In ascending the slope higher up we find that the overplaced deposits occupy only the depressions between the glaciated ribs of the hill.

The operations of our modern times, although extensive, have by no means obliterated the ancient work. All over the slopes, above and between the recent excavations, are traces of the ancient diggings, and the extent of this work was a matter of great surprise to me. As in the flint quarries previously examined, I found myself wandering over the wilderness of pits and their accompanying mounds of excavated material, marveling at the enterprise and perserverance of the aborigines. For a people with only primitive tools, the work seems colossal. A long, narrow area amounting to at least half a mile square of the surface has been worked over, pit connecting with pit, the impression given being hardly a square rod of ground within that particular area has been left unexplored. The pits are neither so deep nor so wide as those of the flint quarries, but they do not afford a good index of the work accomplished. The earlier pits were often filled up as the work advanced, and the crumbling debris has gradually been leveled by gravitation and the growth of forests.

From the surface indications it is hard to say how far the ancient excavators penetrated the rock in place. It is apparent, however, that there was little tunneling. The rock was too massive and refractory, save where somewhat decomposed near the surface, to permit of successful manipulation by men having only stone tools. The work of the miner consisted in uncovering the rock surface with a view of discovering protruding masses of the metal, and these, when found, were removed by crushing the enclosing rock with sledges. The deeper and larger pits probably often mark the spots where important masses of the metal were found and removed, while the smaller openings are those resulting from general and, probably in many cases, bootless exploitation. It is said that in some of the old excavations bodies of copper were found by our own miners only partially liberated from the enclosing rock, while in other cases the masses encountered were so large that native devices were not equal to their removal. Indeed, some of the masses uncovered by the white miners defied for a long time the most advanced breaking-up and transporting contrivances of a civilized age.

The pit depressions are rounded or irregular in outline and seldom are more than three or four feet in depth. Numerous examples of the battered stone sledges are in sight. The plenitude of these sledges is everywhere apparent, and it was not unusual to see them turned up among the roots of the fallen forest trees. The battered, truncated ends of the originally symmetrical water-worn forms clearly tell the story of their use by ancient men.

A very good idea of the conditions under which the native quarrying work was carried on can be obtained by studying the margins of the modern excavations. These expose the entire thickness of the superficial and generally worked-over deposits, as well as much of the solid rock beneath.

EXCAVATIONS IN AN ANCIENT PIT

Wishing to examine the ancient pittings more in detail, I searched the walls of the modern mines for a favorable exposure in which to begin excavation, and finally selected a spot where the complete section of an ancient mine, some ten feet in depth and probably twenty feet in diameter, was exposed in a steep slope. The ancient pit was filled nearly to the top with well-compacted material, mainly crushed trap-rock and earth, the debris of excavation from this and neighboring pits. The most notable feature of these excavations was the ever-recurring sledge-hammers. Plate XXIII shows these implements projecting from the excavation face and clearly defined because of their light-colored smooth surface and entire unlikeness to the other material in the pit. The work of excavation continued until a large part of the contents of the mine was removed and complete vertical sections were exposed to view and photographed. In the plate upward of a dozen of the sledges are seen in place in the evenly-dressed front wall, and others already removed appear to the right and left in the bottom of the excavation. A silver dollar placed near the base of the front wall serves as a scale, as does also a pick resting on the bed-rock. It is seen that the rocky walls rise from the floor of the pit at an angle of about forty-five degrees, extending almost to the surface. How much of the excavated space was originally solid rock, removed by the ancient workmen, no one can say; but judging from the very large percentage of shattered trap found in the filling, and the multitude of sledges broken in the work, it is fair to assume that a considerable body of the rock in place was crushed and moved.

The discovery of considerable quantities of charcoal scattered through the mass indicates pretty clearly that fire was used to aid the sledge in breaking up the rock. I was not so fortunate as to encounter any copper nuggets or masses in this excavation. If such were found by the miners they were not too large to be disposed of, but there were many fragments of rock impregnated with the green oxide, indicating the copper-bearing nature of the formation.

The question of the disposal of the larger masses of copper encountered was no doubt a very serious one with the native miners, and when they were too large to be carried away to the shops or to distant settlements, efforts were made to break them up. All protruding parts were belabored with hammers and if possible removed, as shown by the appearance of several masses deserted by the old miners because they were too large to be in any way utilized. They bore evidence of long-continued battering with sledges. Professor Winchell who seems to have had excellent opportunities to observe the phenomena of the pits, remarks:

"Some of the masses found, being too large for removal from the pits, show the marks of long-continued pounding, and about them in the pits are a great many small, thin chips of metallic copper, of irregular shapes, with concavo-convex surfaces exactly such as would be produced by battering a small nugget of copper to a thin layer by pounding it continuously on the same side. The finding of these thin chips of copper is the first indication to the present miners of the proximity of a large mass. In the summer of 1874, the first of these large masses was discovered. It was sixteen and one half feet below the surface, and under it were poles, as if it had been entirely detached, but it had not been much displaced. This mass was exhibited publicly in the yard of the Court-house at Detroit, and was also on exhibition at the Centennial Exposition in 1876. It was subsequently fused and sold as commercial copper. It weighed 5720 pounds, and has been described by Mr. Henry Gillman in the annual volume of the American Association for the Advancement of Science for 1875. In the summer of 1879, two other large masses that had been wrought by the ancients were found at the Minong mine, which is at the head of Mc Cargoe's cove. One had a weight of 3317 pounds, and the other 4175 pounds, the latter being about nine feet long. The largest mass yet found at that place was taken out the previous summer, weighing six tons; but the ancients had not discovered it, though one of their drifts ran within two feet of it. The large masses discovered by the ancients show the labor that has been spent on them in their hammer-marked and pitted surfaces. They seem to have been beaten up into ridges and points, by hammering along, for the easier removal of parts. One of those found in 1879 was not detached from the enclosing rock, though it was wholly uncovered and undermined."

Perhaps the most constantly present and remarkable feature of these sites is the stone quarrying sledges, varying from three to twelve inches in length and from an inch to eight inches in diameter, a few specimens reaching a weight of perhaps sixty pounds. They occur in countless numbers upon the surface and in and about the pits, proclaiming the aboriginal character of the work. The bruised and shattered remnants of these sledges literally fill the ancient mining debris, as already shown, and in sections of the deposits made by recent mining operations they are seen protruding at all points, being rendered distinctly visible by their smooth surfaces and general bluish or light-gray colors contrasting with the dark earth. In places cascades of sledge-charged refuse descend into the recent mines, as shown in some of the views taken. Upward of twenty specimens had fallen into a little heap of gravel from an ancient pit at the top of the wall in front of the entrance to one of the modern mines.

The presence of multitudes of stone sledges in and about the mines tells a clear story of the character of the aboriginal work. Wooden implements would have served to loosen and remove the superficial materials, laying bare the rock surfaces and exposing extruding masses of copper, but the globular boulder-sledge could have served no purpose in the work save that of breaking up the enclosing rock and freeing the lumps of metal. Although these sledges are natural boulders rarely modified by art, they are by no means rude affairs, or mean makeshifts. They are as perfectly adapted to the rock-crushing work as if shaped for the purpose. Doubtless they were carefully selected, and it is believed that they were brought from the beach several miles away, or, more likely, from deposits of water-polished boulders along the northern shore of the lake. Professor Winchell says:

"They were certainly gathered as pebbles along the shore of the lake, north from the island, where there are still others of the same shapes and sizes, and of the same varieties of rock, formed on the beach by the action of the waves. The great profusion in which they are scattered among the debris of the pits would itself indicate the ease with which they were obtained.... The rock of which they are composed does not occur as pebbles on Isle Royale, and indeed it is doubtful if it exists at all on the island. It is an igneous rock, usually a diabase, as shown in thin sections under the microscope, consisting essentially of a triclinic feldspar and augite, with magnetite. Sometimes the grains are coarser, and the rock would more properly be styled a diorite or a gabbro. They belong to the formation designated by Sir William Logan The Lower Volcanic Group, but since styled Animikie Group by Prof. T. S. Hunt. Occasionally, however, the workmen seem to have gathered rounded stones of other varieties of rock, although nothing equaling the firmness of the above, and so fit for the purpose of a rude hammer in simple mining, can be selected among all the rocks of the region. One or two, of a granite containing red orthoclase, were seen at the mine, and a few of other granites are reported to have been found. These other varieties are also seen mingled sparsely with the diabase stones along the Canadian shore, and are referable to the drift forces which transported them from farther north and east in Canadian territory."

PREHISTORIC COPPER TOOLS

Split in wedge indicates forming by forging.

Note ridge in middle of socketed spear head.
An excellent method of strengthening the tool.
(Roy W. Drier collection)

If the theory that the boulders used in the mines came from the northern shore of the lake, ten or fifteen miles by water and perhaps two miles by land, is well founded, the question of transportation must have been a very serious one for a savage people. The number of pieces packed in from McCargoe's cove, perhaps on the backs of women, was very great, and may be estimated not by thousands but by hundred of thousands. If the worked-over ground is as much as half a mile square and averages one yard in depth, we have upward of seven hundred thousand square yards of implement-bearing material. An examination of the exposed pit-sections often shows as many as two or three sledges to the square yard, and this would give perhaps four times that many to the cubic yard, and some three million for the mines as a whole. A million does not, therefore, seem an excessive estimate. Allowing three pounds each for these boulders, the material transported would amount to upward of a thousand tons.

It has been stated by a number of authors that the stone sledges were probably used in the hand without hafting. This view is due to the fact that on Isle Royale very few specimens are grooved, while on the southern side of the lake grooving is the rule. It would seem, however, that these stones held in one or even in both hands would make very ineffective tools with which to crush the solid masses of living rock. I conceive it to the fact that in many cases there is a polished band around the implement at the point where the withe would encircle it, seems to warrant the conclusion that hafting was common. It would look like a waste of energy to undertake the tedious task of pecking a groove in these boulders when the first blow struck in the quarry work might shatter the instrument, making it entirely useless. We observe that the boulders chosen were generally ovoid in shape and often with the sides approximately parallel, so that withe shafting would be easy. Two typical examples are shown in plate XXIV, the upper specimen being much battered at one end and the other at both ends. A polished band extends around the middle of the implement.

Among the stone implements found are a few forms that may properly be classed with the flaking hammers of the flint quarries. All are small and somewhat discoidal, and are flaked and battered more or less completely all around the periphery. They could have been used in grooving sledges and in shaping or repairing other stone tools.

COPPER AND OTHER WOODEN IMPLEMENTS

Professor Winchell mentions the finding of several forms of copper tools, including a gad or bodkin, a chisel, knives, and arrowheads. He states that Captain Jacka discovered a wooden shovel or paddle which was battered on the edges as if from use in moving dirt. It is not improbable that a canoe paddle may have been devoted to this work, the form being well suited for the purpose.

DISPOSAL OF THE PRODUCT

The question of the utilization of the quarry product is a very interesting one. I was extremely anxious to discover traces of the workshops of the ancient miners and smiths, but the sites likely to have been occupied were buried in a dense growth of grass, weeds, and underbrush, and nothing could be seen. It is unlikely, however, that any considerable amount of the shaping work was conducted on the island. It seems to me more likely that the pieces of metal obtained were carried away to distant centers of population to be worked up by skilled artisans, and we may fairly assume that a considerable trade existed in the raw material. A knotted rawhide string also was found, preserved possibly by contact with copper oxide. The articles mentioned are just such as would be used and lost or abandoned by aboriginal workmen, and serve to connect the known tribes of the lake region with the working of these mines.

MINES OF THE ONTONAGON DISTRICT

Subsequent   to my visit to the Isle Royale mines I have had the opportunity of seeing something of the ancient work on the southern side of Lake Superior. At Rockland, near Ontonagon, where a vast amount of modern mining has been done, I found the aboriginal evidences quite plentiful, and apparently identical in character with those of the more northern district. The sledges differ in being more frequently grooved, but this need not be attributed to the usages of a different people, but to the fact that the shapes of the available stones were not well adapted to hafting and had to be more or less completely remodeled to make them available; besides, the material is less brittle, making them better worth the trouble of groove-hafting.   The area worked over by the ancient miners is very great, a series of sites extending all along the Copper range, and it is said by those most observant of the ancient traces that hardly a site that has yielded native copper to the modern miner was missed by the aboriginal workmen. Here, as in many other parts of the county, the remarkable enterprise and acumen of the natives are made apparent, as nothing in the way of available resources seems to have escaped them. It was in this region, no doubt, that most of the copper distributed over the Mississippi valley and the Atlantic slope originated, and here we are in the midst of the district in which copper implements are found today in greatest plenty.

EVIDENCES OF PREHISTORIC MAN ON LAKE SUPERIOR
MICHIGAN PIONEER AND HISTORICAL SOCIETY
By John T. Reeder
Vol 30, 1903
Pages 110-118

<u>Prehistoric.</u> --Belonging to a period antecedent to that covered by written history.

For a number of years as opportunity offered, I have visited the several known localities in this Portage Lake District of ours, where copper implements have been found, and the old Indian "pits" or "diggings" as locally called, along the mineral belts in Keweenaw and Ontonagon Counties, where the metal from which these copper implements were made, was obtained. I have read much on this subject and queried often, to learn if possible, by whom, when, and under what conditions was this work done. I learn from reading University of New York publications, "Metallic Implements by W. M. Beauchamp," that, "copper occurs in mines and in scattered fragments," (undoubtedly referring to what is called "Float copper," which is frequently found in beds of gravel in Connecticut, New Jersey, and several other states; and very frequently in this part of Michigan, very large masses of copper have been discovered, one piece in particular weighing eighteen thousand pounds, was found in a gravel bank near Lake Linden). "Farther north there is little doubt that all articles came from Lake Superior at an early date, and they have such marked peculiarities as to make it probable that they were commonly wrought into shape in that vicinity." "Rude implements have occasionally been found in New York state which were not made in Michigan." Mr. Beauchamp further states that "implements of native copper have not been made in the interior of New York within four hundred or five hundred years and further explains that this conjecture about date, is good opinion now, but later may be changed."

Soon after Quebec was founded, Champlain mentions a piece of native copper which was given him by an Algonquin Indian who said "there were large quantities where he had taken this piece from" "It came from the banks of a River near a big lake," probably referring to the Ontonagon River which empties into Lake Superior. Schoolcraft mentions this river and a large piece of native copper for which the Indians of his day had veneration, and further says: "The Indian tribes constitute an anomalous feature in our history. Recognized as a strongly marked variety of mankind, they appear to be branches of oriental stock, who relapsed into nomadic state at primeval periods, and of whom no records, either oral or written, can now be found to guide the labors of the historian."

Father Claude Allouez, who visited Lake Superior in September, 1666, speaks of the Indians as savages. "They respect Lake Superior as a divinity and offer sacrifices to it because of its size and its furnishing them with food. It happens frequently that pieces of copper are found weighing ten to twenty pounds. I have seen several such pieces in the hands of savages and since they are superstitious they esteem them as divinities or as presents given them to promote their happiness. For this reason they consider the pieces of copper very precious and protect and preserve them by carefully wrapping them up. In some families they have been thus kept for more than fifty years; in others they have descended from family to family for a much longer period," but nowhere does he speak of the Indians or savages having copper weapons such as arrows, spears or knives, or such implements as we find in our cabinets. Radisson wintered on Lake Superior in 1658 and mentions copper several times. The Jesuit Priests' report of Lake Superior in 1660 speaks of "copper so excellent and refined and in large lumps." Dr. J. D. Baldwin, in his Ancient America, says "The Mound Builders used large quantities of copper such as that taken from the copper beds of Lake Superior, where the extensive mines

TWO SOCKETED POINTS
ONE EAR SPOOL
ONE-HALF EAR SPOOL
ONE AWL OR HOOK

Full size.   (Roy W. Drier Collection)

SOCKETED SPEAR HEADS

ARROW OR SPEAR POINTS (NOT SOCKETED)
About one-half size. (Keweenaw Club Collection)

yield copper not in ore, but as pure metal. It exists in these beds in immense masses, in small veins and in separated lumps of various sizes." The mound builders worked the copper without smelting it. "One characteristic of the Lake Superior copper is the frequency of small spots of silver appearing as if welded on to the copper, not alloyed with it. No other copper has this peculiarity. Copper with small particles of silver has been dug from the mounds. It was naturally inferred from this fact that the ancient people represented by these antiquities had some knowledge of the art of mining copper, which had been used in the copper region of Lake Superior, this inference finally became an ascertained fact."

Foster and Whitney report of 1850 says:--"That the Lake Superior region was resorted to by an uncivilized race for the purpose of procuring copper, long before the white man's time, is evident from numerous memorials scattered throughout its entire extent. Whether they were the race who built the mounds or the forefathers of the present generation of Indians is a matter undecided."

"The evidence of early mining consists of numerous excavations in the solid rock, of heaps of rubble and earth along courses of the veins,--of the remains of copper utensils fashioned into form of knives and chisels, of stone hammers, some of which are of immense size and weight, of wooden bowls for bailing water out of the mines or pits, and numerous levers of wood used in raising the masses of copper to the surface." "The high antiquity of this rude mining is inferred from the fact that the existing race of Indians have no traditions by what people or at what time it was done, the places even were unknown to the oldest of the band until pointed out by white men. It is inferred from the character of the trees growing upon the piles of rubbish, between which and those forming the surrounding forest no perceptible difference can be seen: further, says copper rings designed for bracelets are frequently met with in the western mounds. Are these rings not a strong link in the chain of evidence to connect the ancient mining of this region with the earthworks of the Mississippi Valley? Evidences of the antiquity of these diggings may be based upon the age of the trees growing upon the debris thrown out. On the Minnesota Mine location a pine stump broken fifteen feet from ground was ten feet in circumference, and a large hemlock growing upon the same ground had 395 annular rings by actual count of the Agent of the Minnesota Mining Co., Mr. Knapp. Thus it would appear that these explorations were made before Columbus started on his voyage of discovery."

"The amount of work done by these ancient miners must have been very extensive, their diggings extend for miles, (extending from Ontonagon County on the West to the end of Keweenaw Point on the East, a distance of about eighty to ninety miles. This does not include pits or diggings on the Island of Isle Royale) on the outcrop of the veins, and their pits by the thousand. Mr. Knapp estimates the stone hammers found on his, the Minnesota Mine location, at more than ten carloads. Mr. Knapp used the hammers to wall up a spring. They are nearly all made of greenstone of porphyry pebbles with a groove single or double cut around by which a withe was attached."

Henry Gilman in his "ancient works on Isle Royale," says--"The works referred to are generally pits of a few feet to thirty feet in diameter, some being quite shallow, while many are from twenty to sixty feet deep. They are scattered throughout the island, wherever the Amygdaloid copper-bearing rock is found and are invariably on the richest veins." "The amount of mining on three sections of land at a point on the north side of the island is estimated to exceed that of one of our oldest mines on the south shore of Lake Superior, a mine which has been constantly worked with a large force of men for over twenty years. When we compare the tedious methods of the primitive miners with our modern improvements in mining appliances, this may well appear incredible.

At another point the excavations extend in a continuous line for over two miles, the pits being often so close together as to hardly permit their being worked. The tools found consist of chisels and knives. Arrowheads of some material are frequently found. As to the time when this work was done, Mr. Gilman says that the latter period may extend from 700 to 800 years. Mr. Gilman cites an oak tree growing on the debris at the mouth of an old pit on which he counted 584 annular rings, and further says a copper knife and other implements were found underneath the stump."

Since the above was written, the following article, by S. E. Moffett, appears in the April Cosmopolitan: "Five hundred years ago when the forest stretched unbroken from sea to prairie, and no smudge of coal smoke defiled the sapphire sky, the finger of land pointing from Northern Michigan into Lake Superior, with Isle Royale beyond, was a center of American industry. The Indians prized copper as we prized gold, and there were but two places on the continent where they could get it. One was on the Copper Mine River, on the bleak Arctic confines of Canadian Northwest and the other was on Lake Superior."

From the reading of the authorities here cited, and from personal knowledge I conclude:

First.--That the Lake Superior district has the largest deposits of native copper now known, or that were known to ancient man, and are in fact practically the only merchantable deposits of native copper today known and worked in the civilized world.

Second.--Lake Superior native copper was mined and worked into metallic implements by an ancient race of people and was practically the only source of supply known to them, and that (about) all the native copper implements found in the States bordering on the chain of Lakes, consisting of Lakes Superior, Michigan, Huron, Erie, St. Clair, and Ontario with the connecting rivers, were made from Lake Superior native copper, and by means of barter or trade said Lake Superior native copper and finished implements made from it were carried hundreds of miles East, South and West.

Third.--Many hundreds of years have gone past since the first workmen opened the native copper deposits of Lake Superior: just how many years, is and always will be, a mooted question. From data at hand I should say that as early as 700 to 800 years ago, and as recent a date as 400 years ago. The earlier date can be better estimated than the more recent one, as the growth of trees on the debris thrown out, establishes to a very close certainty the years of life of the trees. The second date by the apparent age of the relics found and place where found. Many relics I have are very heavily coated with, first, a red oxide of copper, and then by a green carbonate, showing that a slow process of oxidization had been going on for years,--while other relics I have found at same locality under exactly same conditions, show a nice green carbonate, but have not the depth of color and lack the deep red oxidization of the much older specimens. Many of the older pieces I have, are turned into oxide almost completely, but a tissue sheet of native copper in centre of implement remaining.

Fourth.--That mining was carried on to a large extent by a prehistoric race who came to this district of ours in the early spring, worked at mining all summer, until late in the fall, and then went south in their boats, carrying implements and copper in bulk. Nowhere in this section can I learn of any remains indicating a permanent village having been found. No burial places nor skeletons exhumed with the implements, nor can I find any trace of village sites. At the Lake Superior Ship Canal where nearly all travel, to and from Ontonagon on the West, Eagle River on the East, and Isle Royale on the Northwest, stopped, (Portage Lake at its West end, until about 1867, was closed by a bank of sand, where the present Lake Superior Ship canal now stands, and all canoes were portaged over this mile of sand bank.) Here occasionally in

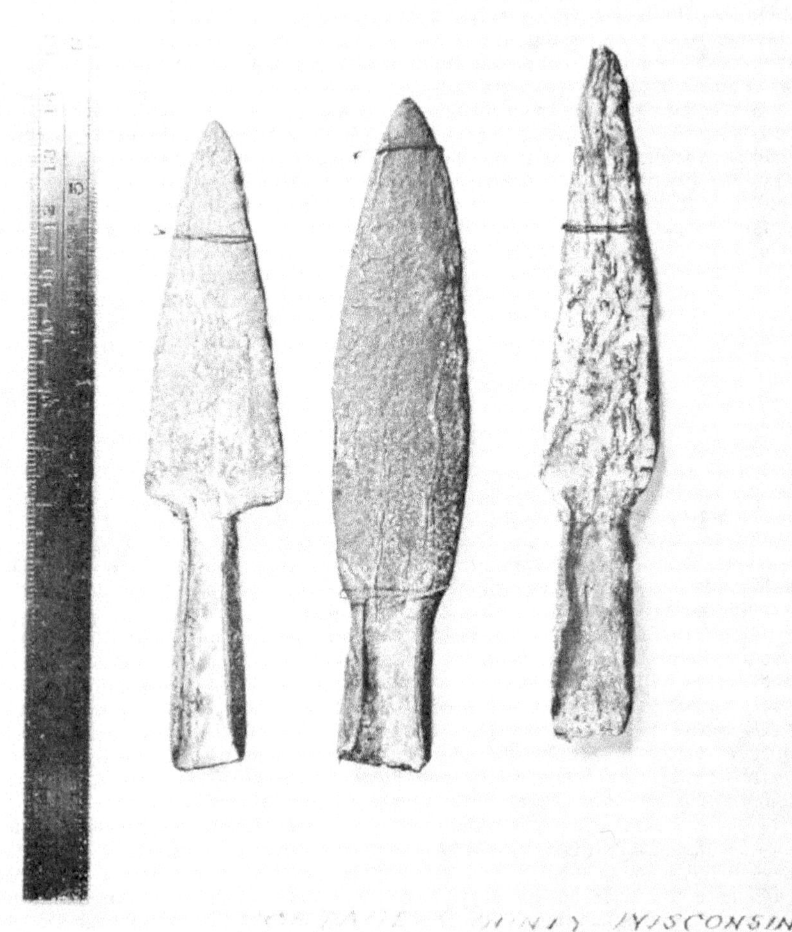

SOCKETED SPEAR HEADS
(Keweenaw Club Collection)

digging for relics, pieces of charred wood have been found and probably one or two dozen small flint arrow points. These articles, with many copper implements and fragments, thus far, complete the evidence of this place having been used as a temporary stopping place, not a permanent one.

Fifth.--From the great number of pits found, extending over three counties on Keweenaw Point, and on Isle Royale,--on Keweenaw Point for a distance of 80 to 90 miles and sometimes so close together that one could step from one pit into the next, leads me to conclude that hundreds of years were consumed in making these extensive diggings, and that an army of men must have spent these same years in order to have done this work.

From what I have learned of mining methods in vogue today, and of what I learn of mining methods in practice in Cornwall, one hundred years ago, or even on Lake Superior fifty years ago, I can consistently say that some of the ancient shafts described later on, would require a lifetime, and a good long one at that, to reach the depths in which they were found by our first white settlers. I believe I would be consistent as well within truthful boundaries were I to say that the work actually performed by the ancient miners took a thousand years of time and the work of at least one thousand men. Practically all the copper implements, in our collections here that I have seen, or that I can learn the history of, came from territory lying adjacent to Portage Lake, either from one side or the other, and have been found between the Canal on the West side of Keweenaw Point and the "Entry" on the East side of said Point, a distance of about twenty-seven miles. By reference to the general maps, you can see the position of Keweenaw Point, running out into Lake Superior about 65 to 70 miles (in a North Easterly direction), Portage Lake dividing the said Keweenaw Point, at about fifty miles from its North Eastern terminus, in fact, cuts the point in two, said Portage Lake being a navigable body of water for its entire length, for the largest Lake steamers. Keweenaw Point has been known historically for 250 years at least for its native copper deposits. This point with its continuation into Ontonagon County on the West and Isle Royale, an island Northwest of Keweenaw Point about forty-five miles contain the known native copper deposits of Lake Superior, now worked, or worked by Ancient Man. I use this name because it has not been settled who these ancient miners were, Mound Builders, Aztecs or Toltecs, or Forefathers of our present Indians. Suffice to know, that previous to any known white men's working of these deposits of copper, they were very extensively worked and by a class or race of men who used nothing but fire and water, and rock hammers to break and dislodge the copper veins treasures.

Many wagon loads of grooved stone hammers have been taken out of pits say sixty to thirty feet deep in Houghton, Keweenaw and Ontonagon Counties and on Isle Royale, these pits in all cases being located on copper veins, in many of which copper still remained when discovered by white men. A case in point, at the old Minnesota location. At the bottom of an old pit or shaft a large mass was found evidently too large or solid to be broken up with materials then at hand. Again on Isle Royale at the Minong Mine Location, a mass was found which weighed over five thousand pounds. This mass has been hammered until every projecting point had been pounded off, showing unmistakable evidences of stone hammer pounding. I have examined this mass many times myself while it lay in Detroit. This mass was at the bottom of a pit, 20 to 25 feet deep and was propped or raised from the bottom of the pit by cedar poles or blocks. Underneath the mass was a great quantity of ashes and charcoal, showing an attempt to reduce by means of heat or for purposes of removing rock every vestige of which had been removed when the said mass was discovered by the owners of the mine. I would like here to state that at least four hundred years had elapsed between the time the ancients worked at the shaft and the time of taking it out by white men in 1870, or thereabouts,

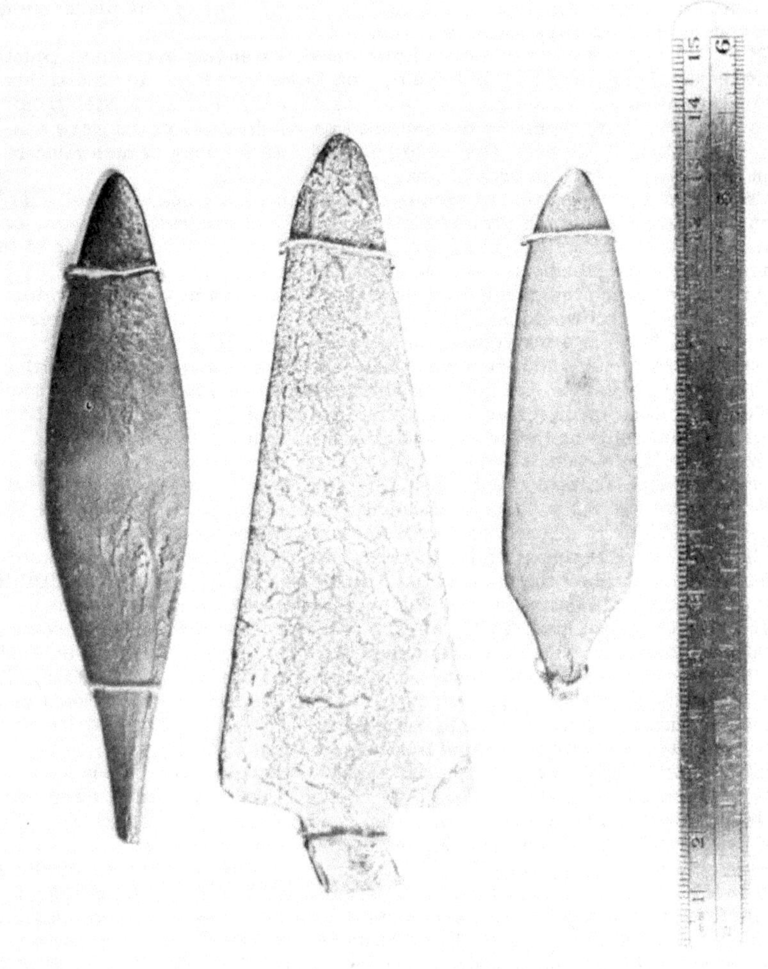

ARROW OR SPEAR POINTS (NOT SOCKETED)
(Keweenaw Club Collection)
About one-half size.

as pine trees were growing on the refuse thrown out by these ancient miners, which by actual count showed 350 annular rings.

Many copper implements have been found at the West or Canal end of Portage Lake, at Pilgrim River, midway between West and East or "Entry" end, and Dollar Bay where the Rolling Mills and smelting works now stand. I have two crescent-shaped objects, and one spear in my collection, which were found at Dollar Bay. Nearly all the implements found have been of copper, a few flints, one old slate and one sandstone pipe of recent small pattern, and stone hammers without number, constitute the many finds from this Portage Lake District. At the Canal end of Portage Lake on the north side of Canal many implements have been found, more in fact than at any other point along the Lake. Up from the Canal and near the shore of Lake Superior, as well as back from the Lake Shore, say two thousand feet, copper implements, finished and unfinished, and hundreds of pieces of copper or small fragments have been found. Many implements of superior workmanship, such as adzes or spuds, spears, knives, chisels and gouges, arrow points, needles with eye and without, ornamental pins and ceremonial trinkets, and many bits not easily recognized, have been discovered. The writer has hundreds of fragments of copper many showing the effects of fire and pounding but no recognized forms or designs. I consider the adze or spud the best implement found in this district and think more adzes or spuds have been found here than in any other one locality. I can now recall eleven which were found along Portage Lake. Probably the making and repairing of canoes for which the adze was admirably adapted, required very careful attention.

A few words at this time about the finding of so many of these copper relics at the Canal might be in place. For years the United States Government has maintained a lighthouse and life saving crew at the Canal, the members of which, when off duty, amuse themselves by looking over the sand, and scraping the surface slightly, many times picking up a bit or two of copper, at other times nothing. Years ago finds were quite common, but today finds are very few and far between. A little digging was done the past summer on a ridge about two thousand feet from Lake Superior and parallel with its shore, and at right angles to Portage Lake Canal. A few implements, a small knife, arrow points, two ceremonial objects and a number of needles and pins were found at a depth of four to six feet. Several old pine stumps stand on this little rise of ground, and under one of these stumps, which must have been two hundred years old at least, two fine spuds were found in the fall of 1901. From all the evidence I can obtain it looks as though the ancient searcher after copper, whoever he may have been, came up from the south in canoes, following the south shore of Lake Superior until Portage Entry was reached, when he entered Portage Lake, and followed its course until he reached the place where the United States Government has cut the present United States or Portage Lake Canal. At this point the boatman must needs portage his canoe over half a mile or more of sandy hill to reach Lake Superior on the West side. In coming to Lake Superior copper deposits and returning home again the ancient voyagers crossed Keweenaw Point by passing through Portage Lake. Hence it was most convenient to make a camping ground at the West end of Portage Lake now known as Portage Lake Canal. All travel to the copper deposits at Isle Royale was started from the camp at the Canal, also in going West to the Ontonagon fields or East to deposits near Eagle River in Keweenaw County. This, to my mind, explains the finding of so many fragments as well as completed implements at this point. The rough material was carefully sorted over at this point before the long boat trip down the shore of Lake Superior in the fall of the year was begun.

The "Entry," or East end of the Portage Lake, distant about twenty-seven miles from the West or Canal end, was also a stopping place for the ancient

travellers. A good many copper relics and a few flints have been found there.
Near the Entry End is an island called Battle Island, on which tradition says
a big battle between Indians was fought, quite a few copper relics have been
unearthed, also a few flints on this island. I hardly think the Indians who
fought on this island and from which battle the name was given it, were the
makers or owners of these copper relics, in fact I am sure they know nothing
about the relics or copper mining. This battle was fought a little over one
hundred years ago. In all my investigations I have not found nor seen any
tempered copper. I have been told that several spears were found a few years
ago at the Canal that were tempered and would bend and spring like steel. I
did not see them. All the copper tools I have seen were cold hammered,
showing no marks of having been melted. All the hardening that appears in
many implements I think due to the cold pounding or hammering, and the
apparent hardness on the edges to silicious particles of sand adhering to the
oxidized metal. I have eight copper implements on which are small spots of
native silver, six of these pieces were found in Wisconsin. A knife found in
Johnstown, Wisconsin, and a spear point and knife from Washington County,
Wisconsin, also a spear and knife from Door and Calumet Counties, Wisconsin. The silver spots are natural, have not been put on by artificial means.
This confirms what Dr. Baldwin says about Lake Superior copper being the
only copper which contained particles of native silver, and that copper implements showing particles of native silver were without doubt made from copper
mined on Lake Superior. My own experience confirms this theory.

Since the above was written I have received from Fox River lighthouse,
Wisconsin, and from Sheboygan, Wisconsin, several copper fish hooks and
arrow points, which are identical in workmanship, shape, size and material
with those found along Portage Lake. This, to my mind, is a strong argu-
ment that Lake Superior copper was the material, and the same family or
ancient copper-smiths hammered these articles into shape, either at the camp
at the Lake Superior Canal or while sojourning along Fox River, or at Sheboygan.

PREHISTORIC COPPER MINES OF THE LAKE SUPERIOR REGION
J. C. Gannon
(1953)

"By the shores of Gitcha Gumee
By the shining Big Sea Water." -- Hiawatha

The ice that for untold ages had covered the North American continent, had disappeared when a people of unknown origin arrived, discovered, worked, and distributed the native copper of the Lake Superior region.

The scene of their labors was the Keeweenaw Peninsula for a distance of one hundred and fifty miles, and Isle Royale lying to the north and west some fifty miles in Lake Superior.

That they were industrious, persistent and hard working is apparent in the silent record they left behind. In the counties Ontanagon, Houghton and Keeweenaw, hundreds of their pits or diggings have been found and on Isle Royale an area some five miles long by one and a half miles wide, hundreds of their workings have been located. When one considers the crude and primitive methods used by these people, it is to marvel.

Colonel Whittlesly writing for the Smithsonian Institute in 1856 in a letter dated Eagle River, Mich. says, "They had only the simplest mechanical contrivances, and consequently penetrated the earth but a short distance. They do not appear to have acquired any skill in the art of metallurgy or of cutting masses of copper. For cutting tools they had chisels, and probably adzes or axes of copper. These tools were of pure copper, and hardened only by condensation or beating when cold. They sought chiefly small masses or lumps and not for large masses.

"No sepulchral mounds, defenses, roads, or canals are known to have been made by them. No evidences have been discovered of the cultivation of the soil. They had weapons of defense or the chase, such as darts, spears and daggers of copper. They must have been numerous, industrious and have occupied the country for a long time."

When for some unknown reason the workings were abandoned, other people whom we call Indians inhabited the country. The Indians knew nothing whatever of the ancient workings. It is true they had lumps of copper in their possession, but to them it was a gift of the Gods.

Father Allouez, who visited Lake Superior in 1666 says of the Indians, "They respect Lake Superior as a divinity and offer sacrifices to it because of its size and its furnishing them with food. It happens frequently that pieces of copper are found weighing ten to twenty pounds. I have seen several such pieces in the hands of savages and since they are superstitious, they esteem them as divinities or as presents given them to promote their happiness."

Whittlesly reporting to the Smithsonian in 1862 writes, "Although the Jesuit fathers mention the existence of copper, and even use the term 'mines,' it is clear, from the general tenor of their narratives, that they neither saw nor knew of any actual mining in the technical sense of the word. They announced as early as 1636 the presence of the native copper and refer to it as having been taken from the 'mines.' This was prior to the time when they had themselves visited the Great Lakes, and their information was derived from Indians. If the Chippewas had known of the ancient workings, they would have communicated the fact to their spiritual fathers, who would not have suffered so interesting a fact to be lost."

"It will appear that they were abandoned several hundred years before the French became acquainted with the northern tribes; no mines have been found that could have been wrought as late as the earliest Jesuit."

From the abandonment of the workings, and their discovery in modern times, centuries passed as is evident in the accumulation of earth, leaves and decayed vegetable matter within them. Forest trees were growing in them and upon the waste thrown out of them, so that it was difficult to distinguish them from natural depressions. Some of these trees, as shown by ring growth, were four to five hundred years old at the time of their fall.

Lake Superior native copper is easily distinguishable from smelted copper, and its distribution can be traced to the finding of copper artifacts and ornaments which have been found from British Columbia on the west to New Hampshire on the east. To the south the trail is more easily followed. Throughout Wisconsin thousands of their products have been found. Continuing southward we find them in the mounds by those people known as the Mound Builders, thence through Illinois, Ohio, Tennessee, Louisiana, Mexico, Central America, the islands of the Carribean.

The first mention of copper in the New World occurs in Columbus' "First Letter" written in 1493, in describing what he found on his voyage of discovery in 1492. After mentioning the various Islands so far discovered, he mentions the island of Quaris whose people are very fierce. He then goes on to say, "They are very ferocious among these people, who are very cowardly to an excessive degree, but I make no more of them than the rest. They are those who have intercourse with the women of Matinio, which is the first island met on the way from Spain to the Indies, in which there is not a man. These women engage in no feminine occupations, but use bows and arrows of cane like those already mentioned, and they arm and protect themselves with plates of copper, of which they have much."

In describing Drake's attack on City San Domingo, Island of San Domingo (Hispznola) goes on to say, "The gold and silver mines of this Island are wholly given over and thereby they are found in this Island to use copper money, whereof we found very great quantity."

Discovery of Virginia: July 1584 states, "The rest of the women of the better sort had pendants of copper hanging in either ear, and some of the King's brothers and other noblemen have five or six in either ear. He himself had upon his head a band of gold or copper, for being unpolished we knew not which it should be, but when the King's brother was present, none dared trade but himself except such as wore pieces of Copper on their heads like himself for that is the difference between the noblemen and governors of countries and the meanor sort."

"Copper seems to have been the only metal in common use among the Mound Builders. Two well authenticated discoveries of gold are known, silver was rare, and that found must have come from Lake Superior, where it was found associated with native copper in a metallic state. Iron was unknown- not a scrap of it has been found, but meteoric iron was discovered by Putnam and Metz in the Little Miami Mound was considered very valuable, since copper ornaments were plated with it as others were with gold or silver."

"There is no evidence that metal was ever obtained from ore by smelting. The Mount Builders were ignorant of the arts of casting, welding and alloying."

In a letter, Putnam states, "Were ancient implements hammered or moulded into shape?"

"Besides beating," adds Putnam, "these men employed one other process; the metal was rolled between two flat sones, by which means the required form was obtained."

"And lastly they must have been traders, for beneath the same mounds we find the copper of Lake Superior, the mica of the Alleghenies, the obsidan of Mexico, and the pearls and shells of the Gulf."

(This paper not published before.)

DUG FOR COPPER IN PREHISTORIC DAYS
Banks of Streams Yield Tablets with Queer Characters
Which Defy Interpretation

(The following is the second of the series of articles on
supposedly prehistoric relics found in Michigan and is a
contribution of Dean James Savage's statement in the
American Antiquarian.)

Sunday Mining Gazette
May 7, 1911

"In the year 1885 Capt. Henry Reaney, who then was chief clerk of the
lighthouse department of the great lakes, told me of a find made when digging
for the foundation of a lighthouse built by the United States government at the
head of Lake Michigan west of St. Ignace. He stated that when the workmen
had excavated four feet deep for the foundation of the lighthouse they unearthed
a cedar box three and one-half feet long by 18 x 18 inches and dovetailed. The
box contained chisels, saws, axes, knives, etc., which he stated would re-
mind one of a carpenter's kit and tray.
"These tools were all chilled copper, he stated. He spoke of one saw in
particular, some twenty inches long, that had several teeth broken out, showing its high temper and hard usage. I asked him 'What became of this box
and its contents?' He stated that he did not know. This is only a sample of
the estimate in which such valuables were held by those who found them.
On Mainland, too. - The prehistoric mines on the mainland showed similar
conditions as described by Mr. Greusel when discovered by the white man,
i.e., 'tools lay around in groups as though the workman,' one old man related
to me, 'had left them down, gone to dinner and never returned.' And why?
Another instance of man's cruelty to man.
"We find a similar condition of things around the Ontonagon river. Mining
tools and implements of various kinds lay around, showing the confusion and
precipitation in which the miners left and never returned. I believe that it
was from this mine that the large nodule of copper, weighing some six tons
and which is now, or was, in the Smithsonian collection at Washington, was
taken. The prehistoric mines of Ontonagon were reopened by the white man
in 1847.
"Those who are somewhat acquainted with the Indian, as to his instincts,
habits and dealings with his fellows before the white man's conduct influenced
him, have noted the heartless ferocity that utterly exterminated entire tribes
and peoples. We can safety say that 'our people' were exterminated by the
same helpless, insane ferocity.
"There was a tradition among the Attiwanderons that their fathers utterly
exterminated a great white people, taking their cattle and their lands. These
same Attiwanderous themselves had destroyed the Hurons by the Iroquois
about the year 1650.
Chippewas Had Tradition. - "A similar tradition obtained among the Chippewa
Indians; Chief Shop-no-gun, an aged Indian who resides at Grayling, Mich.,
tells with apparent pride how his fathers 'killed off white man; way back; took
too much cattle and lands.' Mr. Soper showed him a ceremonial taken from
a mound below Grayling, and asked 'Did the Indian make that?' He answered
indignantly. 'No, Indian no make; white man make long ago, way back.' He
asked, 'Where you get?' We told him we dug it up. He looked at me indignantly, and coming forward, his hand extended and index finger pointing,
called my attention to a large bible on his desk, saying, 'See book, book says
no dig 'em up; let them rest.'

"The first war tablet we found, describing a battle between these prehistoric people and the Indian, was on Aug. 9, 1909, in one of a group of eleven mounds that we discovered on a high tableland at the juncture of the Au Sable river and a stream emptying into the Au Sable from the south, thirteen miles below Grayling, Mich.

"The next war tablet was found some two weeks later by Mr. Soper and a party of explorers in Wayne county near Detroit, two hundred miles from the first find.

"Since these first finds of war tablets we have found five more; in all seven tablets describing battles and the death of one or other of their chiefs, showing the manner of his death, the moon and quarter of the moon in which he was killed.

"Judging from the number of war tablets, the labor it must have taken to make them, the accuracy displayed in description and the distance apart where found, one would naturally conclude that these wars were many, protracted and general.

"In the year 1890 a young man of the name of James O. Scotford discovered a mound by accident while in the employ of a Mr. Stewart. James Remick owned in Montcalm county a large tract of land called 'slashings'--land on which the pine had been cut. Mr. Scotford was engaged to throw a fence around a tract of these 'slashing' for cattle range. He ran a line fence. This line ran over a hillock some thirty feet across. When digging a post hole on this hillock his auger struck something hard--too hard to be a root, and there were no stones in the place.

"His curiosity prompted him to get a spade from his companion, who was setting posts after him. He dug the object up and found it to be a large earthen casket. He had broken the cover with the auger. The casket was unbroken. This was the first discovery of these mounds in Michigan.

<u>Mounds Near Edmore.</u> - "There were many small mounds and hillocks around Edmore which were looked upon before this find as natural formation or the results of uprooting of large trees. As a result of this find a number of people dug into the hillocks and sounds around Edmore, with more or less success in finding prehistoric specimens. (See M. E. Cornell's pamphlet, published in 1892.)

"M. E. Cornell of Battle Creek, Mich., who died in 1902 or 1903, published a pamphlet regarding these finds around Edmore and Wyman. (These villages are about three miles apart.) He had made extensive excavations, finding caskets, tablets, etc., with cuneiform and hieroglyphic writing. He states in his pamphlet, page seven, regarding conditions of some of these finds:

"'On this point, take as a specimen the fact that a casket was found under the root of a pine tree, which by concentric circles was shown to be above three hundred years old, and that one of the roots of the tree had grown through the corner of the casket.'

"Three caskets have been found pierced by roots of trees growing on the mounds over them. We found one with the cover broken in by the root of a tree and the casket was filled with sand. The root was coiled up inside the box, but so decayed that it was broken with a touch. Only the decayed stump of the tree and a few rotten roots were left.

.sels, the writer and three others were present and took part in the digging. The professor lifted the casket from its ancient bed with his own hand, exclaiming: 'Gentlemen, this is no fraud.'

<u>Called Men Fakes.</u> - "A professor of the University of Michigan in an address to a scientific gathering assembled at Chicago in 1907, denounced these finds as 'fakes.' In his address the professor tells us that some other archaeologists viewed some 'photographs,' if you please, of these finds, and in their indig-

nation used 'vigorous utterances.' If these gentlemen had refrained from the 'vigorous utterances' mentioned by the professor in his address, the group of gentlemen, which the professor kindly designates as 'the syndicate,' would undoubtedly now have a collection that would astonish the world and hundreds of these specimens, if not thousands, that are now broken and thrown away, and therefore lost to the world and to science, would have been preserved and we might have a museum in Michigan worthy of the name, which we now have not.

"There seems to be a general opinion among scientists that a people whom they designated as mound builders were the original inhabitants of North America. The same opinion seems to obtain regarding the prehistoric people who mined the copper mines of Isle Royale, the mines around Houghton and of Ontonagon, namely, that these people belonged to a distinctive people called the mound builders.

"In the thirteenth annual report of the ethnology, Washington, page 45, it is there shown that after a long investigation the conclusion arrived at was that the mound builders were 'the historic Indian and his ancestors.'

Was It the Indian. - "Col. Powell of the Bureau of Ethnology wrote an able defense of this same opinion, given in another number of this same annual namely, that the mound builder was the Indian, and this from the contents of the mounds found in different parts of the country. This opinion agrees with the report of De Soto, the reports of early missionaries and also with the report of a French officer stationed at St. Ignace.

"The prehistoric mounds of Michigan which Mr. Soper and myself have opened are, as a rule, not more than ten to thirty feet in length, frequently oval in form. Some are round or nearly so. These latter are, as a rule, not more than eighteen inches in height. They are flat, with an indication of a moat around them. They are not more than two or three feet in depth.

"Where found on highlands frequently an elongated basin-shaped stria of charcoal and ashes shows the contour of the open grave when the body was laid away. The outer and upper rims of this basin-shaped stria come to within sixteen or eighteen inches of the surface of the ground. In Wayne county the country is flat and the formation of the soil is lake sand. Here the basin-shaped stria is not so marked.

"We have opened more than five hundred of these mounds in the four counties in which we have worked--a territory extending over two hundred and sixty miles. We have diligently inquired regarding the localities of other fields and have so far located sixteen counties of Michigan in which these specimens have been found. We are confident that we are only on the borderland of this great prehistoric people.

"These mounds or graves, as a rule, are found in groups. The Sylvan club owns two forty-acre tracts (minus two acres) on the Au Sable river, Crawford county, Michigan. On the west forty acres we found only one group of mounds. This group contained eleven mounds. On the east forty acres we found three groups of mounds, one of three, another of seven and another group which covered an acre or more of ground.

"In this group some were close together, others from forty to sixty feet apart. We opened every grave we found on this group and found but one speciman. It was a large, well made chilled copper point. In the group of seven mounds we found two tablets, one of copper, the other of stone, one copper knife and one medal of sandstone. In the group of three we found only one speciman, a beautiful medallion of dark, hard stone. In the group of eleven mounds, on the west forty slate tablets, three copper spear points and one very handsomely worked ceremonial. We found groups and lonely graves along the Au Sable as far as we explored. Some of these groups were half a mile or more back from the river.

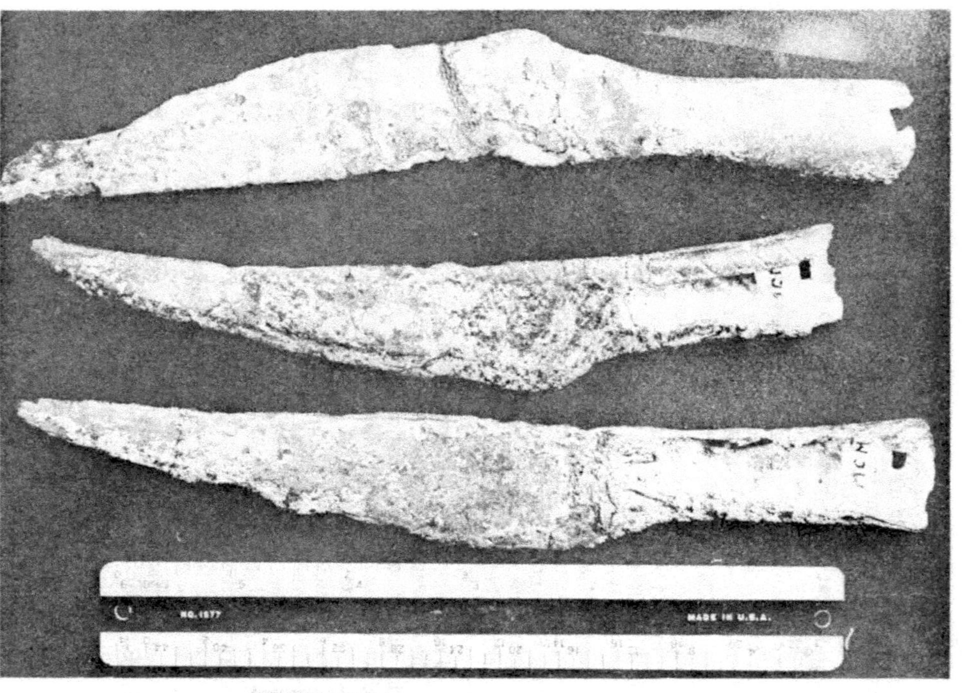

SOCKETED KNIVES.

Notice rectangular hole for a pin to attach
tool to a handle.
(Mich. College of Mining & Technology
collection).

"These prehistoric mounds of Michigan contain caskets, lamps, pipes, tablets, etc., of clay; battle axes, knives, spear, dagger and arrow points, domestic utensils, saws, chisels, spades, etc., and a variety of ornamental wearing apparel, all of chilled copper, stone tablets, medallions, medals, skinning knives, various emplements and of strange designs, the object of which we cannot imagine. One remarkable feature of these mounds they contain no flint implements of any kind, nor have I seen any stone or copper beads; other ornamental wearing apparel is frequent.

"Henry Gilman of Detroit in a paper read before the Detroit Scientific association in 1874, speaking of prehistoric mining on Isle Royale, states:

"'With the exception of stone hammers, no other tools formed of stone have been found.' (Michigan Pioneer collections, volume three, page 207.)

Stone Hammers Remain. - "On these mounds you may find large and aged trees, oak, pine and other varieties. The decayed roots of pine and other trees that grew, thrived and died on these mounds are there. They contain another peculiarity: There is a stria of charcoal and ashes in each mound.

"This stria often shows the basin-shaped contour of the interior of the mound when its possessor was laid away to rest. There does not appear, as a rule, sufficient charcoal and ashes for cremation, only enough for purification. In some mounds, however, there is a heavy stria."

PRE-HISTORIC AND MODERN COPPER MINES OF LAKE SUPERIOR
Paper read by S. L. Smith before the State Historical Society at Lansing
Circa 1915

In preparing this paper on the Copper Mines of Lake Superior I find myself beset with many difficulties. In the first place the subject is intensely interesting to me, due, no doubt, to personal associations in the pioneer days of the modern mining epoch; but it does not follow that my readers will share this interest any more than the parents and sisters shared the enthusiasm of the small boy whose fondest desire was for a hammer and who presented one to each of them as his Christmas offering.

Again, in this age of specialization, it seems almost ridiculous to attempt to boil down into one article the tremendous amount of statistics and literature on the subject. How thoroughly the ground has been gone over may be seen from Brinto who, in his excellent volume on "The American Race," refers to a list of over 300 authorities. It would seem that the last word has been written, and I certainly do not expect to add anything new; - all I can hope for is to be able to dress the subject up differently - with a slit skirt perhaps - to hold your attention for the moment.

Four hundred and twenty-two years have elapsed since America was discovered, or rediscovered, as some writers would have it. In the records of the first voyagers, mention is repeatedly made of the fact that the natives possessed copper implements, copper hatchets, copper ear ornaments and copper bracelets. In the second voyage of Cortez it is stated that the savages had copper hatchets. The Spaniards, believing these tools to be some form of impure gold, eagerly exchanged their cheap glass beads for the relatively valueless hatchets, and were greatly chagrined when they found out that the hatchets were only copper.

As these first landings of the Spaniards were in Mexico and Central America, and as it is known that the inhabitants of that section were possessed of a crude working knowledge of metallurgy, the copper they had in their possession was of local origin, and is not to be confused with copper of Lake Superior. In regard to the early metallurgy on the Pacific coast, Pinelo, an early Spanish chronicler, wrote: - "They built little abode furnaces, called guayras, and therein deposited the ore, sufficiently wetted and incorporated with others that facilitated their smelting and filled them up with fuel, when the whole began to burn by means of the natural blowing of the wind, which gave better results than the artificial draught of a bellows such as the Spaniards used. This method of smelting was continued at night, and upon the heights of Potosi the lights of more than 15,000 little furnaces were seen. Potosi, now a part of Bolivia, was a by-word for mining wealth."

On the North American continent, I believe that the source of all the copper noted in the earliest days can be traced to Lake Superior. In Cabot's voyage in 1497 mention is made that the natives had copper ornaments. Corterial, in his voyage of 1500, in which he cruised as far north as 56 degrees, speaks of the painted natives in clothing of skins of wild animals and having bracelets of copper and silver. In 1524, Verrazano, in his journey in the neighborhood of New York, tells that the natives had "many plates of wrought copper," and also that they had beadstones of copper hanging at their ears.

On Cortier's second voyage to the St. Lawrence in 1535 he kidnapped the principal Indian chief to take back to the old country. As he was held captive aboard the ship, the Indians visited the ship to say farewell, and when they were assured the chief would be returned on the next trip, they were very joyous and brought many presents of skins and "a great knife of red copper that cometh from Saguenay."

This description is interesting, as it is the first mention of copper being

154

fashioned into a knife, and from the name, Saguenay, specifically designating Lake Superior as the source of the copper.

At about this time also, the Indians described to the Franch the route to follow to find the copper, which was found to be substantially correct, when, at a later day, it was followed by the Jesuits. These Jesuit missionaries penetrated the Lake Superior region as early as 1600, and in their "relations" they made frequent mention of the occurrence of loose masses of copper on the shores of the Lake and questioned their Indian voyagers as to their origin, yet they were enabled to glean but scanty information as to their true source.

"It frequently happens," said Father Allouez, "that pieces of copper are found weighing from 10 to 20 pounds. I have seen several such pieces in the hands of the savages, and, since they are very superstitious, they esteem them as divinities or as presents given them to promote their happiness by the gods that dwell beneath the water. For this reason they preserve these pieces of copper wrapped up with their most precious articles. In some families they have been kept more than 50 years, in others they have been kept time out of mind, being cherished as domestic gods."

Father Dalton, who followed in the footsteps of Father Allouez, states that the savages did not agree as to the source of the copper. Some said that it was where the Ontonagon river began and others that it was close to the lake in the clay, and others at the forks and along the east branch of the river. He, too, dwells on the superstitious reverence with which the Indians regarded these copper masses, and in the "Relations for 1669-1670" gives the following Indian legend:

"After entering Lake Superior, the first place met with containing copper is an island about 40 to 50 leagues from the Saut, opposite a place called Michipicoten. The savages relate that it is a floating island, being sometimes near and at others far off. A long time ago, four savages landed there, having lost their way in a fog, with which the island is frequently invested. It was previous to their acquaintance with the French, and they knew nothing of the use of kettles or hatchets. In cooking their food, as is usual among savages, by heating stones and casting them into birch bark pails containing water, they found that almost all of them were copper. After having completed their feast, they hastened to re-embark, for they were afraid of the lynxes and hares, which here grow to the size of dogs. They took with them the copper stones and plates, but had hardly left before they heard a loud voice exclaiming in an angry tone, 'Who are the thieves that carry off the cradle and the toys of my children?' They were very much surprised at the sound, not knowing whence it came. One said it was thunder; another said it was a certain goblin, called Missibiai the spirit of the water, and another that it came from the Memogovissioois, who are marine men, living constantly under the water. At any rate, this extraordinary voice produces such fear, that one of them died before landing. Shortly after two others died and one alone reached home, who, after relating what happened, also died. Since that time the savages have not dared to visit the island or even to steer in that direction."

This legend is undoubtedly founded on facts, as it is easy to see how the Indians could be poisoned from the oxidized salts of copper and in the resulting delirium their imaginations could have conjured up the strange noises and voices.

The interesting feature of Allouez's and Dablon's writing is that it shows that the Indians of that period were not familiar with the use of copper; that they preserved it in its original worn boulder condition, regarded it as a strange and rare object, to which they attributed superstitious values, as the finding of horseshoes or lucky-stones is regarded by some people even at this day.

The early records of the Jesuits make frequent mention of the finding of boulders of pure metallic copper on the shores of the lake. The large size of some of these boulders and the unheard-of occurrence of pure metal gave rise to many conjectures as to their origin and source and led to a hazy belief on the part of some people that there were mountains of solid copper at some unknown place in the thickly forested section. Even some of the revered and worthy fathers let their imaginations run riot, as in the case of Isle Royale, where the finding of an extraordinary large amount of float copper on the shores so excited them that they reported that even the ledges of solid rock gave forth the sound of metallic copper when struck with a hammer. Allusions to some of these statements found their way into the prospectuses of some of the mining companies at later dates.

The first modern mining was started in 1771 by an English company. On the banks of the Ontonagon river there was a large mass of native copper. This had been frequently seen by the early Jesuits, and it was their reports that led to the formation of the English company, under the superintendence of Alexander Henry of Sault Ste. Marie. This company carried on their work at Miner's river, where the rock is the upper grey sandstone, and on the Ontonagon river, near the mass of native copper. At this point a shaft was sunk 40 feet through reddish clay, at which point red sand rock was reached. Dr. Houghton, in his report of 1841, gives the location of this isolated mass of copper as in the bed of the Ontonagon river, 26 miles by stream from its mouth.

The rugged nature of the country made it rarely visited, as is pointed out by Dr. Houghton who, in 1840, revisited the section nine years after a previous visit and found his work and tools just as he had left them. The work of this English company was a failure, and should be classed as an attempt at mining rather than as mining. They did not even recover the original mass of copper, and it now rests in the Smithsonian collection at Washington.

To Dr. Douglass Houghton, universally known in his day as the "little doctor," small in stature, but mighty in intellect, physician, and scholar, scientist and geologist, explorer, politician and, above all, indefatigable worker, the state of Michigan owes a debt of gratitude that can never be paid. By his own efforts he obtained from the legislature the small appropriation that made possible his examination and study of the copper country, which, presented in his report of 1841 turned the searchlight on the commercial possibilities of the copper deposits which was followed by the beginning of copper mining in 1844.

Until his report was made, the source of the copper was unknown. The masses and boulders of copper had been widely scattered by glacial action and had been found as far south as Illinois, Indiana and Ohio. One large piece, weighing 140 pounds, was found at Green Bay, Wisconsin. The popular belief, previous to Houghton's work, was that the copper came from the water shed between Lake Michigan and Lake Superior. Dr. Houghton traced the source of the copper to the amygdaloids, traps and conglomerates of Keweenaw Point, the South Shore and Isle Royale.

The credit of discovering or, at least, of recognizing the works of prehistoric miners is given to Samuel O. Knapp, superintendent of the Minnesota mine. In the winter of 1847-48 he noted a lone of depression which, on account of its regular course, attracted his attention. Following this indication as displayed along the southern encampment of a hill, he came to a cavern which he was convinced was an artificial excavation. In cleaning out this cavern he found numerous stone hammers, showing plainly that they had been used in mining by some former crude race. At the bottom of the excavations was found a vein with the ragged projections of copper sticking up, which the ancient miners had not detached. Later, he found another depression, 26 feet deep, filled with clay and mouldering vegetable matter. At a depth of 18 feet in this pit was found a mass of copper 10 feet long, 3 feet wide and 2 feet thick, weighing over six tons. The mass was resting on rotten billets of oak and had been raised up by the ancient workers a distance of five feet.

A short distance from this pit was another excavation into the cliff, where a portion of the vein had been left by these prehistoric workers as a pillar to support the hanging wall.

William H. Stevens discovered similar old trenches near the Forest mine that were 14 feet deep. These were in four lines, following the course of four veins. He also found the remains of a wooden bowl, probably used for bailing out water.

C. G. Shaw has called attention to like old workings on Isle Royale. In 1872, S. W. Hill wrote that he had found pits on Isle Royale fifty feet deep. Sir William Logan also reports depressions of this nature on the east shore of the lake, near Miamanse.

J. H. Forster describes the largest piece of float copper ever found as follows: "This mass of copper was found on the Mesnard location. It was so covered with moss and lichen growth that it was recognized with difficulty. It weighed 18 tons and contained very little rocky matter. It had been hammered and manipulated by ancient miners and plainly showed tool marks. Charcoal was found around the mass, the remains of fires used by the early workers to remove the gangue rock."

Mr. Forster also describes the mound that led to the celebrated Calumet find. "Here was a small mound found in the woods upon which large pine, maple and birch trees were growing. Roots of still older trees were found in the drift. After stripping off the timber, a pit, 15 feet deep, was put down reaching solid conglomerate. It was hard rock filled with stamp copper and could not be used by the ancient miners."

Other conspicuous old workings were on the sites of the present Isle Royale and Atlantic mines. The extent of these prehistoric workings was very great. In the Ontonagon district, for a distance of 30 miles, such evidences abound at intermittent intervals. On Keweenaw Point, they can be traced to Eagle river for 12 miles eastward.

As soon as their significance was realized they could be easily recognized. They showed as shallow depressions in former trenches and pits that had been put down to bed rock, and which had subsequently been filled with silt and decaying vegetation of centuries' accumulations. The waste dirt that had been thrown out formed gently curving sides. Over both the embankments and in the filled pits, trees had sprung up, lived their lives, died, and been followed by cycles of other trees.

How old these workings are cannot be determined, but there is no doubt of their great antiquity. Mr. Knapp cut down a hemlock tree that was growing on one of the ancient workings of the old Minnesota mine that had 395 rings of annual growth. There is nothing to prove that this tree may not have been but the survivor of several generations of similar trees that grew in the same location. On the other hand, it does not prove that all the workings were of as great an age as represented by the life of this one tree. However, the similarity of all the explored ancient workings, bringing to light the stone hammers, the charcoal that was used to heat the rock, so that by throwing on water it would crack away from the adhering copper, is circumstantial, if not conclusive, proof that they were all made by one race of people who antedated the Indians found in possession of the continent at the time of its European discovery.

These prehistoric workings have an economic as well as historical value. There is not a mine operating today in the district that has not its prehistoric workings. This fact was so well established in the early days that the evidence of ancient work was sought as a guide to present lodes. The development of the Calument was certainly hastened by the finding of the old mound, and many of the other mines owe votes of thanks to these mysterious, unknown, prehistoric workers.

Any subject that is surrounded by mystery naturally sets up in the minds and imaginations of its investigators different and conflicting views and theories. The prehistoric workings of Lake Superior are no exception to this rule, and we find here two classes of scientists who, reasoning from the same conditions, arrived at radically different conclusions.

R. Packard in an article on "Pre-Columbian Copper Mining in North America," published in the Smithsonian Records of 1892, concludes that there is no ground for believing that the work was not done by the Indians of Columbian time and their immediate antecedents.

Warren K. Moorehead, in his elaborate works, "The Stone Age in North America," published in 1910, arrives at a similar conclusion. I herewith quote him:

"The conclusion now universally accepted among archaeologists is that there is no reason for attributing the workings of the copper deposits or fabrications of the implements to any other people than the Indians. The early explorers found both the northern and southern tribes in this country using implements and ornaments of native copper often in common with those of stone. From South America to Canada, various travelers refer to this metal being in the possession of or employed by the natives, whether the workings of the copper deposits or fabrication of copper implements in this section, thought to have been begun at least several centuries before, was discontinued before the coming of the white man or whether the industry was continued or, at least to some extent resumed by the descendants of the pre-Columbian miners and artificers during and after his intrusion is still in dispute. It is doubtful whether this matter will ever be satisfactorily settled.

The evidence of the mounds and of earlier village sites is to the effect that before the coming of the white men the use of copper had become quite general among the Indian tribes of the upper Mississippi valley. It is probable that the native metal first became known to them through the accidental discovery of small nuggets among the debris of the glaciers, and, as it quickly came into demand, was traced to its source in the Lake Superior region. These deposits they mined, cutting it into shapes convenient for transportation to their villages, where it was fashioned into articles for their own use or for the purpose of trade with distant tribes.

Nowhere in this entire valley do copper implements however, appear to have entirely replaced those of stone, the use of which was continued until quite recent times. The manufacture of copper implements doubtless extended through several centuries. The Siouan Winnebago and Dakota of Wisconsin, being nearest the source of supply, possessed, of course, the greatest quantity. Even among them the use of copper artifacts did not in prehistoric times equal the use of others. Among the outlying tribes in other states copper implements were yet probably somewhat of a luxury, when the intrusion of the Algonquian tribes into Wisconsin made more and more difficult, and finally altogether shut off access, to the Lake Superior mines. It appears certain that the Chippewa, after their occupation of the copper region, did do at least a small amount of digging for the metal which for purposes of trade, or for other uses, they found of value. This continued until the arrival of the traders laden with desirable articles caused a suspension of mining operations and diverted the attention of the Indian from mining to other pursuits."

It will be seen from the foregoing opinions that no great antiquity is ascribed to the ancient workings. I confess that it is with disappointment that I accept these deductions. Having personally seen these old works, almost obliterated by time, with their treasures of stone hammers and copper implements, the relics of a by-gone people, it was easy and natural to follow the trail blazed by Foster and others connecting these people with the mound builders. But before I present this phase of the case I wish to give a little more information about the extent of the workings themselves.

In all the literature on this subject the expression "prehistoric mines and mining" is used. In the strict sense of the word "mining" these old workings are improperly described. It is true that they were mines as metal was produced therefrom, but they were not underground mines, opened in the usual manner by shafts and drifts. Rather, they were open cuts, made to bedrock, from which the loose copper was extracted from the disintegrated vein matter. The solid rock of the veins themselves was only penetrated for a shallow distance of a few feet at the most. For this reason, in these gopherings-like operations, the linear distances covered were of great extent, probably in the aggregate amounting to 50 miles. If all these workings should be united in one continuous stretch, they would probably form a solid line of trenches five miles long. One remarkable feature of this ancient work was almost the intuitive genius displayed in following the veins, which even at this day sometimes baffles the skill of mining engineers equipped with all modern devices to aid them in such work.

If we assume that five miles of continuous workings would represent all this old work, it is possible to form a rough estimate of the total amount of copper recovered. If we assume that these old workings penetrated the solid rock for an average distance of five feet, it would give 132,000 square feet as a total of all the work done. It is known that they did not recover the very fine copper or the larger masses, but only such portions as they could break off. On the other hand, they selected the richest parts of the veins to mine. In modern mining the yield in copper per square foot mined can be taken as 40 pounds. This includes all the coarse and fine copper which would be lost by these ancient workers. Balancing the rich, selected ground of the ancient miners with the losses in their mining, we should have 132,000 square feet, yielding 40 pounds per square foot, or 5,600,000 pounds of copper. It is doubtful if they recovered over 25 per cent of this amount, so this rough calculation would give them 1,500,000 pounds. The average annual output of the Lake Superior mines in recent years has been 220,000,000 pounds, or 700,000 pounds per day on a 300 working-day year. So all the copper that was taken away by the prehistoric miners would about equal the output of two days of our present mines. Assuredly, these ancient miners did not have to worry over the conservation of their natural resources.

Insignificant as was their output of copper in the light of our present civilization, it must be borne in mind that it satisfied all their requirements, even when distributed over the vast area as is shown by the relics we have found and are still finding. Implements and ornaments of native copper are distributed commonly or sparingly throughout a large portion of the eastern half of the United States and in some states west of the Mississippi river. Outside of Wisconsin and Michigan, numbers of them have been recovered in Minnesota, Iowa, Illinois, Ohio and West Virginia, and also from the mounds and stone graves and village sites in the states of Kentucky, Tennessee, North Carolina and Georgia. Clarence B. Moore, whose explorations have been very extensive, has reported their existence in the mounds of Florida and elsewhere in the extreme south. From five mounds on the St. Johns river in Florida he obtained ornaments of sheet copper with repousse designs, beads of sheet copper, beads of wood, shell and limestone copper coated, copper effigies of the turtle and serpent and piercing implements of copper. Dr. C. C. Abbott long ago recorded the existence of copper implements in the Delaware valley.

While it is probable that many copper implements were fabricated in the vicinity of the workings, it is now perfectly clear that fragments of the native ore were also carried away to be cut up and fashioned into implements else-where. On the extensive village sites at Two River, Sheboygan, Green Lake and elsewhere, have been obtained numerous small chips, scales and frag-ments of copper, plainly indicating that the manufacture of implements was carried on there. Elsewhere in Wisconsin have been found lumps of the metal exhibiting tool marks and other indications of working.

The following quotation from Mr. Moorehead is interesting in this con-nection:

"Copper seems to have played an important part in aboriginal life in this country. As the natives possessed neither gold nor silver and because silver ornaments are extremely rare, one may say that silver was not in use; copper appealed to them in being something beyond the ordinary, if not possessing supernatural powers. There was no other substance which they could hammer into shape, or slightly anneal and work more easily. No other malleable material possessed that bright, beautiful color and was capable of such polish. Therefore, copper appealed to the aborigines, and they made general use of it more as an ornament, or a totem, than for ordinary utility; that is, save in the "copper belt," where it was so common that tools were made of it. It has occurred to me that the peoples of Indiana and Ohio, and possibly the south, made raids in the copper country, or found copper nuggets in the drift, or mined their own copper, or robbed the northern people of such copper as they wanted. If there had been any extensive aboriginal trade, we should surely find more evidence of it."

I shall now present the brief of those scientists who reached the conclusion that the prehistoric miners were the mound builders, whose monuments were scattered so profusely over our continent.

J. W. Foster was one of the ablest advocates on this side, and in his book, the "Prehistoric Races of the United States of America," published in 1873, he sums up his conclusions which I quote verbatim:

"First. That as a race their origin extends back to a remote antiquity, but all attempts to trace that origin to a common fountain of life, as with the other races not inhabiting the earth, soon involves the investigator in the mazes of conjecture.   .

"Second. That they possess a conformation of skull which would link them to the autochthones of this hemisphere, a conformation represented in the people who developed the ancient civilization of Mexico and Central America.

"Third. That whilst their manners and customs conformed in many respects to those of ancient races of the old world, they may be regarded as the result of man's contact with external nature rather than inheritance through succes-sive generations, and therefore that they are of little importance in tracing ethnic relations.

"Fourth. That during their occupancy of the Mississippi Valley, they de-veloped traits in their domestic economy and their civil relations which dis-tinguished them by a well marked line of division from the Indian who was found in possession of the continent at the time of its European discovery. Their monuments indicate that they had entered upon a career of civilization; that they lived in stationary communities, cultivating the soil and relying on its generous yield as a means of support; they clothed themselves in part, at least, in garments regularly spun and woven; they moulded clay and carved stone, even of the most obdurate character, into images representing animate objects, including even the human face and form, with a close adherence to nature; they mined and cast copper into a variety of useful forms; they quarried mica, chert and slate for personal adornment, to domestic use or to the chase; unlike Indians who were ignorant of the curative property of salt, they collected brine of the salines into earthern vessels, moulded in baskets, which they evaporated into a form adapted of transportation; they erected an elaborate line of defense, stretching for many hundred miles, to guard against sudden interruptions of enemies; they had a national religion, in which the elements were objects of supreme adoration; temples were erected upon platform mounds and watch fires lighted upon highest summits, and, in the celebration of the mysteries of their faith, human sacrifices were probably offered up. The magnitude of their structures, involving an infinitude of labor, such as only could be expended in a community where cheap food prevailed, and the great extent of their commercial relations reaching to widely separated portions of the continent, imply the existence of a stable and efficient government based on the subordination of the masses.

"As the civilization of the Old World, growing out of the peculiar conditions of sail and climate, developed certain forms of art which are original and unique, so on this continent we see the crude conception in the truncated pyramid, as displayed in Wisconsin, Ohio and Illinois and the accomplished result in the stone-faced foundations of the temples of Uxmal and Palenque. And finally the distinctive character of the mound builders' structures and also the traditions which have been preserved indicate that this people were expelled from the Mississippi valley by a fierce and barbarous race and that they found refuge in the more genial climate of Central America, where developed those germs of civilization originally planted in their northern homes into a perfection which had elicited the admiration of every modern explorer."

From Mr. Foster's deductions it is clearly seen that he believed that the mound builders were the people who carried on the prehistoric mining at Lake Superior. Such an hypothesis leaves the door open to the interesting but illusive route that has been followed by so many writers. Who were the Mound Builders? Where did they come from and where did they go? What is their relation to the Cliff Dwellers, the Aztecs, the Toltecs, Mayas, Incas and their predecessors? Did those predecessors originate on this continent, where we know man existed in the glacial epoch, or did they come from Asia by the stepping stones of the Pacific Islands, as has been suggested by C. Reginald Enock in his fascinating book, "The Secret of the Pacific"? As Mr. Foster so aptly says, "All attempts to trace that origin to a common fountain of life involves the investigator in the mazes of conjecture."

That they were here and their work well done is known. Just who they were remains for the future to answer, so we are obliged to let them rest with the old prayer of "Peace to their ashes."

It is a long jump from prehistoric mining to modern mining - just how long no man can say. It is also "some jump," to use the slang expression, from the beginning of modern mining down to the present day mining.

In this last period of 70 years, from 1844 to 1914, wonderful transformations have taken place. Modern cities have sprung up out of a primeval forest. Modern railways run over the old trails and floating palaces land their passengers at reinforced docks. Twenty thousand men find employment in the mines which hold the distinction of being the deepest mines in the world. Each day these mines turn out about 35,000 tons of copper rock, which yields 700,000 pounds of copper which is worth $105,000 when copper is selling at 15 cents per pound, as it is today. The gross annual income of the mines is about \$33,000,000. This shows what an important industry it is and how proud the state of Michigan should be of its copper country.

about \$33,000,000. This shows what an important industry it is and how proud the state of Michigan should be of its copper country.

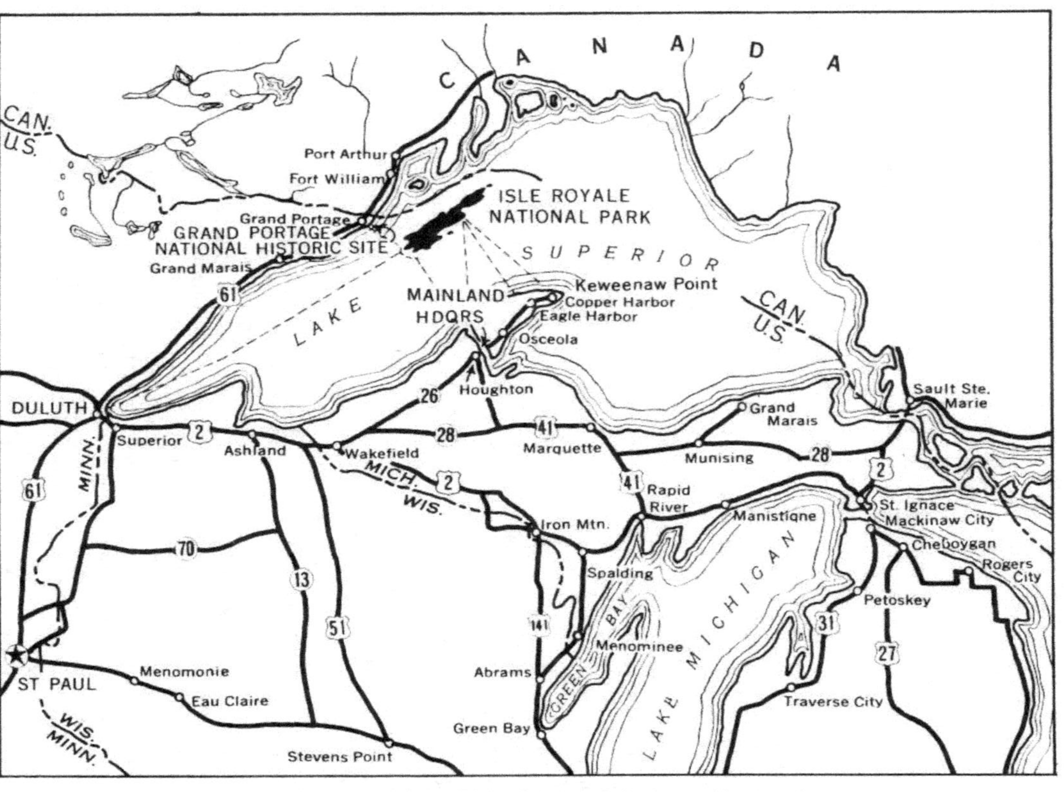

LAKE SUPERIOR REGION SHOWING ISLE ROYALE AND THE KEWEENAW PENINSULA

THE ANCIENT COPPER WORKINGS ON ISLE ROYALE
George R. Fox
Circa 1911

THE ISLAND

Isle Royale, the largest island in Lake Superior, and the second largest in the Great Lakes, lies within thirteen miles of the Canadian shore. Its greatest length is forty-four miles and, as the average breadth is five miles, it has an approximate area of one hundred and sixty thousand acres.

The surface has been fairly well explored. The ownership of the land is divided among various individuals and corporations and, as a thorough survey has been made, the allotments sometimes do not exceed forty acres.

The general direction of the island is northeast and southwest, but it is the custom of the islanders to speak of the northwest shore as the north shore and the southeast coast as the south coast, so these terms will be used hereafter.

The island is rugged and hilly, yet, as a whole, rather low, for sailors approaching Thunder Bay from the east end of the lake, say that the Sleeping Giant, the promontory to the north of the entrance to Thunder Bay, is raised long before Isle Royale can be sighted. The Sleeping Giant reaches an elevation of 1200 feet.

From end to end of the island extend chain after chain of hills; even in crossing such a small section as the long finger on the eastern end, which terminates in Blake's Point, the path is a constant climb and descent.

The island is not marshy nor swampy. On the borders of a small lake near Tobin's Harbor is a low, swampy bit of ground, yet this is said not to be characteristic of the numerous lakes and the region of the interior. Mr. Chris Anderson, who has travelled extensively throughout the island, and who has spent a winter here, says that the lakes of the central portions possess beautiful high and rocky beaches.

The eastern end of Isle Royale is indented with numerous fiords, bays, harbors or coves, and there are a number to be found on the south shore. On the west side are three, but along the shole north coast, if Todd's Harbor, as open roadstead, is excepted, there is only one, McCargoe Cove. This shore stretches for over eighteen miles without a break in the cliffs; and these slope so sharply to the water that for the greater part of the distance there is no beach.

The island is volcanic in origin and, if the lack of results produced by time and natural agencies may be taken as a criterion, its upheaval is a comparatively recent event, happening, possibly, not more than 100,000 years ago.

The basaltic rocks are the results of the usual solid lava flow, save at the mouth of Tobin's Harbor where the columnar formation is to be met with. While of neither the extent nor the impressiveness of the Giant's Causeway of North Ireland, the same structural formation is present - the many-sided prisms rising at one point to a height of twenty feet.

The entire surface of the island is covered with a dense growth of evergreen, save in a few portions where fire has swept through the forest. The evergreens are mostly hemlock, though Norway pine and a few trees of white pine, spruce and tamarack are seen. The trees fail to attain the size of those growing in the forests of Northern Wisconsin, as few trunks were observed having a greater diameter than eighteen inches. Among the evergreens were numbers of birch trees, but the oak, the elm and the other familiar friends of the Badger state seem unable to exist here. It is reported that during the winter of 1910-11 lumbering operations were carried on in the western section.

The island has no permanent inhabitants and at present outside of private launches or boats, the only means of reaching it is by the steamer America of the Booth Company, which boat leaves Duluth twice each week for a circuit of the island. A third week's end trip is made, but on this journey it only touches at Washington Harbor on its way to Port Arthur, Canada.

There are four hotels on Isle Royale, one at the eastern end near the mouth of Tobin's Harbor, two on Rock Harbor and one at the extreme western end on Washington Harbor. Aside from these resorts there are numerous fishermen's settlements. Captain Francis has his quarters on Birch Island in McCargoe Cove, there are fishermen on Fish Island six miles farther east, a small village on Tobin's Harbor, cabins near the old lighthouse at the western end of Rock Harbor, fisher stations at Chippewa Harbor, Wright Island, Fisherman's Home, Long Point, and lastly, at Washington Harbor.

The most extensive Indian workings are at McCargoe Cove and the nearest resort to this point is Capt. Smith's place on Tobin's Harbor; the distance by water is twenty-five miles. A land journey is impracticable. It is possible that anyone interested in, and desiring to be near the scene of the aboriginal diggings, could secure quarters with Captain Francis, as he sometimes accomodates sportsmen who come to enjoy the excellent fly fishing to be found in McCargoe Cove.

HISTORICAL

The Indian name for Isle Royale was Minong and under this name it must have been widely known among the tribes of the sixteenth century, for the very first maps drawn by the Franch show this island. As some of these charts were drawn long before the eye of white men rested upon this miniature continent, the knowledge of it and its position and shape could only have been obtained from the red men.

How well it was known to the aborigines is shown by the correctness with which its size, shape and position are depicted by the French cartographers. And it must have been known to the Indians because of its copper deposits, for there is nothing else found here which would attract almost universal attention among savage peoples.

There may be some doubt as to whether it is one of the islands given on the map drawn by an unknown maker between 1640 and 1650, on which the Great Lake Region is imperfectly indicated, yet the probabilities are that inasmuch as Lake Superior was shown in form somewhat approximating the real, the maker had some knowledge of what he was depicting and, as he shows four islands, quite possibly one was Isle Royale.

But Marquette's map of 1673 shows the island quite plainly. Of this chart Mr. Neill says in Vol. IV, Narrative and Critical History of America,

"Joliet marks the large island toward the extremity of Lake Superior known as Isle Royale, but gives no name and indicates four other islands on the north shore. Marquette shows the large island only but without a name."

In 1676 Joliet's maps give it the name, Minong, also written Minonk in one instance. (Same authority.)

The map of Lake Superior accompanying the Jesuit "Relation" of 1670-71 shows the island very correctly, and gives it the name Minong. Considering that no survey had been made, and that the island had never been seen by the fathers, unless Allouez had sighted it while on a mission journey to a region supposed to be near Pigeon River, the drawing is remarkable accurate.

Of the time when the French obtained knowledge of the copper found on Isle Royale there is no record, but it must have been in the years between 1665 and 1670, for Dablon, writing in the latter year, had knowledge of it, while Father Allouez, writing about the former date, knew nothing of its being found there. In describing Lake Superior he says:

"One often finds at the bottom of the water pieces of pure copper, of ten or twenty pounds' weight. I have several times seen such pieces in the Savages' hands; and, since they are superstitious, they keep them as so many divinities, or as presents which the gods dwelling beneath the water have given them, and on which their welfare depend. For this reason they preserve these pieces of copper, wrapped up, among their most precious possessions. Some have kept them for more than fifty years; others have had them in their families from time immemorial, and cherish them as household gods."

Allouez evidently intends to convey the impression that the natives made no use of copper for weapons or ornaments, yet it is known now that copper was put to such uses by the ancient Americans. Probably the pieces of which the learned Jesuit had knowledge were of odd and unusual shapes and as such might have been considered household "manitous" by the Indian just as he had made queerly shaped boulders his divinities. Allouez did not connect the coming of the Indians to the vicinity of Lake Superior with their desire for copper, for he states further:

"This lake is, furthermore, the resort of twelve or fifteen distinct nations - coming, some from the north, others from the south, and still others from the west; and they all betake themselves either to the best parts of the shore for fishing, or to the Islands, which are scattered in great numbers all over the lake. These peoples' motive in repairing hither is partly to obtain food by fishing, and partly to transact their petty trading with one another, when they meet."

But by 1670 the French had considerably increased their knowledge of copper mines in the Lake Superior region, for the Jesuit "Relations" of 1669-70 contain a long account of "The Copper Mines at Lake Superior," written by Father Claude Dablon. In his narrative he treats extensively of Michipicotan Island, yet he seems convinced that the greater part of the copper came from Minong. Says the Father:

"Hitherto it had been thought that these mines were found in only one or two islands; but, since we have made more exacting inquiries on the subject, we have learned from the savages some of the secrets which they did not wish to reveal. It has been necessary to use artifice to elicit this information, and to distinguish the true from the false.

"Still we do not vouch for the truth of all we are about to relate upon their simple disposition, until we are able to speak with more assurance after having gone in person to the places referred to; and this we hope to do this summer, at the same time when we go in search of lost and wandering sheep all through the region of that great Lake."

Dablon describes Michipicotan island and tells the Indian legend concerning its store of copper. Continuing, he narrates:

"Advancing as far as the part called 'the great inlet,' one comes to an island three leagues from land renowned for the metal that is found there and for the name (Thunder), which it bears because it is said to thunder all the time.

"But farther to the west on the north side, is found the Island which is most famous for copper, and is called Minong; this is the one in which, as the Savages have told many people, the metal exists in abundance, and in many places. It is large and is fully twenty-five leagues long; it is distant seven leagues from the mainland, and more than sixty from the end of the Lake. Pieces of Copper, mingled with the stones are found at the water's edge almost all around the island, especially on the south side; but principally in a certain inlet that is near the end facing the northeast, toward the offing, there are some very steep clay hills where are seen several strata or beds of red copper, one over another, separated by other strata of earth or of rocks. In the water is seen Copper sand as it were; and from it may be dipped up with ladles grains as large as a nut, and other smaller ones reduced to sand. This large island is almost all surrounded with islets that are said to be formed of copper; they are encountered in various places as far as the mainland on the north. One, among others, is only two gunshots distant from Minong; it is between the middle of the island and the end that faces northeast. Again, on this northeast side, far out in the lake, there is another island, which, because of the copper in which it abounds, is called Manitouminis (i.e., "Island of the Spirit"); of this it is related that those who came here formerly, upon throwing stones at the ground, made it ring, just as brass is wont to ring. . . . ."Last Spring, we bought from the savages a slab of Pure Copper, two feet square, and weighing more than a hundred livres. It is not thought, however, that the mines are found in the Islands, but that all these Copper pebbles probably come from Minong or from the other islands which are the sources of it, borne upon floating ice or rolled along in the depths of the water by the very impetuous winds - particularly by the northeast wind, which is extremely violent."

(Jesuit Relation of 1669-70 as given in Vol. SVI of the Wisconsin Historical Collections.)

From which it would seem that the French possessed definite knowledge of some of the sources from which copper was derived. Why the deposits were not worked is a problem difficult of solution, for Dablon, in his description, says that he intends to visit the island during the same summer. Apparently he did not, for there is no record of any such journey.

Yet his description of Isle Royale is so exact, that if he did not see it himself, he must have obtained his information from some one who had been there. He has its distance from the mainland nearly correct, his length given for the island is not far from right, and in telling of the points at which copper was found in the greatest quantities, he states what has since been discovered to be the truth. These locations will be considered later.

After the time of the Jesuits, nothing is said or done about the copper until about 1847, when the first discoveries of "ancient mining" were made; these were found on Keweenaw Point, and subsequently some other workings were found on Isle Royale, but on account of its isolation, little attention was paid to them.

Henry Gillman in his article "Mount-builders and Platycnemism in Michigan," published in the Smithsonian report for 1873, says:

"In the year 1872 some of the most remarkable of the ancient works yet encountered were brought to light by a party of mining explorers on Isle Royale. The amount and character of the work here revealed was something so extraordinary as to almost exceed belief. . . .

"The works are generally pits of from a few feet to thirty feet in diameter; some being quite shallow while many reach a depth of from twenty to sixty feet. They are scattered throughout the island wherever the amygdaloid copper bearing rock is found, and are invariably on the richest veins; great intelligence being displayed in locating and tracing the veins and in following them up without interruption. This has elicited the astonishment of all who have witnessed it - no mistakes apparently having been made in this respect. The excavations are connected underground, drains being cut in the rock to carry off the water. Stopes one hundred feet in length are found. A drain sixty feel long presented some interesting features; having been cut through the surface drift into the rock, it had evidently been covered for its entire length by timbers felled and laid across. When opened the timbers had mostly decayed, and the center portions had sunk into the cavity, filling it for nearly its entire length with rotted wood. The amount of mining on three sections of land, at a point on the north side of the island, is estimated to exceed that of one of our oldest mines on the south shore of Lake Superior, a mine that has been constantly worked with a large force for over twenty years. . . . .

"At another point the excavations extend, in nearly a continuous line, for more than two miles, the pits being often so close together as to barely permit their convenient working. Even the rocky islets off the coast have not escaped observation, and where bearing veins of copper are generally worked. But it is probable that, including all the discoveries not one tenth of the excavations have been disclosed."

These two periods, that during which the French searched for copper in the seventeenth century, and the operations of modern miners during the nineteenth century, for operations were being undertaken at the time of which Gillman writes and were continued for about ten years, are the only attempts to seize the vast treasure that is yet believed to be hid in the rocks of the island.

It is possible that attempts at mining, of which no record is now known, were made during the eighteenth and at the beginning of the nineteenth centuries, for the Northwest Trading and Trapping Company had a station on the eastern end of Isle Royale, on Fish Island, one of the northern chain. This station is supposed to have been established in the eighteenth century, and today the logs of the old pier are to be seen beneath the surface of the water. The modern dock, built and owned by Herman Johnson, is placed on these old timbers. (Plate I.) Back in the woods can be seen the remains of an old root cellar; near by is an enclosed rectangle with a heap of stones at one side, the mounds forming the sides supposed to be the remains of the logs of the walls of a cabin and the stones, the ruins of the fireplace and chimney.

East of this cabin site, within a few feet of the shore, is a deep, square pit, presumably the opening to workings of considerable extent, for the amount of soil and rock thrown out is great. The pit is now filled with water.

All about over the main island are found excavations and holes of various sizes and depths. These are the test pits made by prospectors. (Plate 2.) It was impossible to obtain even an estimate of their numbers, but there are many of them, for the island has been thoroughly examined.

While the mining operations carried on during the seventies and eighties of the last century were quite extensive, employing hundreds of men, for some reason all work has now ceased. Today there is to be found only one of the many buildings erected by these early miners, and that the ruins of an old blacksmith shop about a mile from the head of McCargoe Cove. The other buildings have burned or have rotted away, even the pier on McCargoe Cove having disappeared.

At the time the copper veins were being worked, a tramway extended from the end of the Cove to the mine buildings. Mr. Chris Anderson said that once on this old roadway there would be no trouble in reaching the mine, for the ties lay plain to view in the open roadway. Mr. Anderson said that he had not been there for several years, but on his last visit he had found the trail as easy to follow as an open thoroughfare.

Yet when this point was reached, an almost primitive wilderness was found, showing the rapidity with which nature resumes sway on the departure of man. There was hardly a tie left, and the few that were found were crumbling heaps of rotten wood. There were spaces of over a hundred feet in which existed not the vesige of a tie; even the earthen mound that might be supposed to mark the decayed wood was wanting.

The new growth had sprung up and choked the old roadway; trees twenty feet in height, grew between ties. In fact, so thick was the shrubbery and brush, that the trail was soon lost, and the journey was continued by plunging north through the woods to the main chain of hills.

In the dense, primeval forest which covers most of the island, it is almost impossible to move about. Logs and decayed vegetation make movement one long climb, and to this is added the difficulty of walking several feet above the

real surface of the ground, for there is a network of moss and twigs over which
progress must be made, though at every few steps one crashes through this
flimsy covering.

About McCargoe Cove only was the walking found in any manner easy. Here
a fire had swept away the timber and through the grass, shrubbery and brush it
was comparatively easy to make headway. On the summit of the ridge to the
north, aside from the constant climbing up and down and over cavities, the
going was as easy as walking on a cement walk.

<u>Extent of the Ancient Workings</u>

In Gillman's report, quoted before, he gives a fairly accurate estimate of the
extent of the ancient workings about McCargoe Cove, save possibly his estimate
that only one-tenth of the pits have been uncovered.

Secretary Brown writes in the Native Copper Implements of Wisconsin:

"The aboriginal workings on Isle Royal are said to extend over some fifteen
or twenty miles of country. There can be no doubt but that a very large amount
of metal was obtained and distributed from these sources." (Vol. 6, No. 2,
Wis. Archeologist, p. 54.)

In "The Indian Authorship of Wisconsin Antiquities, Geo. A. West states:

"On Isle Royale, is located a chain of abandoned workings, occupying a
region about thirty miles long and five wide. From these two locations (the
Northern Michigan Region and that of Isle Royale) came all the copper used in
the fabrication of thousands of the implements and ornaments found throughout
Wisconsin and adjoining states." (Vol. 6, No. 4, Wis. Archeologist, pp. 232-33)

From these, and kindred references, the writer gained the impression that
the pits were so thickly scattered over Isle Royale that one could not move without stepping into a pit, or on ground thrown from a working.

Inquiry at the island revealed the fact that no one knew of such a plethora of
ancient diggings save at one point, that about McCargoe Cove. While those who
had investigated the workings refused to say that there were not pits scattered
all over the island, they insisted that every nook and corner had not yet been
dug into, and so no one could possibly confirm or deny their existence.

They did say that so far as knows, there was no modern working opened on
the island, and one in which copper was found, where the traces of the workings
of the aboriginal miners were not clearly apparent.

Mr. Alfred Merritt, who at present spends his summers in his cottage on one
of the islands in Tobins Harbor, and who was located on the island during 1873
and 1874, says that he never knew a place where copper was found by whites,
but what the red man had been there before them.

"I call to mind one instance," he remarked, "in which we thought we had
stumbled on a copper deposit not found by the ancient workers. At a point on the
north shore, near Lake Desor, we discovered copper on the southern slope of
the range. Yet when we had followed the vein a short distance inward we came
upon the pit of the old workers. This can always be told by the dark color of the
soil which fills it. They had started from the north, or lake side, and pushed
their way inward.

"The copper veins in the western half on the island are transverse, crossing
the main chain of hills. At the northeast they run parallel with the range."

As ascertained from various sources, the list given below comprises the
localities at which it is known ancient works are found. This is by no means
complete and as mining is resumed in future years, many others will probably
be brought to light.

1. Triangle Island, a tiny rock about a mile west of Washington Island, on
the western end of the main island. This is mentioned by Gillman in the

Smithsonian report for 1873, and was visited by the writer.

2. At the head of Washington Harbor where the Windigo Mining Company conducted operations.

3. At the Island Mine, located near the Big Siskiwit River in the south-western part.

4. At the site of the Ohio and Isle Royale Mining Company near Chippewa Harbor.

5. At another locality near Chippewa Harbor, though the informant was unable to give definite locations.

6. At the abandoned Saginaw Mine on Rock Harbor.

7. On a tiny island in the chain that forms the southern side of Rock Harbor, pits were found. This islet is a short distance northwest of Mott Island and is known as Hill's Island.

8. On the north shore near Lake Desor, as mentioned by Mr. A. Merritt.

9. The most interesting region of all, that about McCargoe Cove, visited by the writer.

The general trend of the ranges on the island is northeast and southwest with the south slope long and gradual and to north slope sharp and abrupt. This is an ideal section of the island looking along its greater length.

It can thus be seen that it would be almost a physical impossibility to work the north slopes, excepting where the weather and kindred forces have bitten deep into the rock. It is possible that the detrius at the foot of the cliffs may have been mined, though, so far as known, it has not been reported.

The region about McCargoe Cove consists principally of two high ranges of hills, both of which have been mined by the ancients. Mr. Chris Anderson says that the greatest amount of digging had been done on the south, or east side of the Cove but the ground on the south side of the range to the north and west of the harbor had been thoroughly exploited, also. The first mentioned hills are the higher of the two, and their north shore is higher and sharper, but even on the other range, the ridge falls sheer for from fifty to one hundred feet.

The pits are scattered all about the summit, and just below the summit on the south side, where the slope is long and gradual.

It is possible that they extend from the top clear down to the harbor front, or to the small creek that runs into it, but there is so much grass and shrubbery and in places the forest is so dense, that it is impossible to tell. The white men worked at a point about half way up the hill, as their dumps prove, but it was above these that the pits were most noticeable, and that the old hammer heads were found in the greatest profusion. At one point, where a log crossed an ancient mine, a dozen hammers were picked up beneath it and ranged on the trunk.

At another point an ancient pit had been re-excavated by the white men, for among the rock thrown out were found several of the broken hammer heads .

Several trees in falling had torn up soil and rock and almost invariably amond their roots were found the old stone mauls, sometimes as many as four being discovered in the roots of a single tree.

The Hammers

These hammers seem of a wonderfully uniform size, and would average about ten pounds in weight. Mr. Hart, who mined here during the boom period of Isle Royale mining, says that those he has seen, or the greater part of them, have grooves about them. None found by the writer have that characteristic, nor does Mr. A. Merritt agree with Mr. Hart about this. Mr. Merritt believes that they were used without a handle, being simply held in the hand, a conclusion well borne out by their size and weight. One of a very odd shape picked up by the writer, is unbroken and clearly shows marks of use on its point. It weighs about four pounds and is triangular in outline, but flat, while its surface is highly polished, as though it had lain in water for a long time.

No such stones as those of the hammers are found anywhere on the island, and it is supposed that all were brought from the Canadian shore. Mr. Merritt said:

"The Indian hammers which the natives pounded the native copper from the workings undoubtedly came from a point between Pigeon River and Port Arthur. This is the only place to my knowledge where they are found, and the natives no doubt took them from there to Isle Royale, and brought their copper back."

A reference to the chart accompanying this paper shows the area from which the hammers were gathered as being in very close proximity to the island.

Nearly all the hammers seen were broken. All exhibit the same general form of fracture, something as given in the sketches.

The break is almost always a side split, not a slivering from the point upward as might be expected if a strong, hard blow was struck directly downward. No such indication of a splitting from the point upward was discovered in the many broken sledges examined about McCargoe Cove. None of those illustrated in Holmes' article in the American Anthropologist, N.S., III, 1901, show the slivering action. All bear the same clear cut break across the maul.

It would seem that the blow struck was a turning or glancing one, such as is given with an ax in splitting wood. The tip of the blade enters the wood, then the ax is flapped sideways. A blow given with a hammer in this manner, would account for the transverse cleavages found.

The Copper

Copper is found in two general conditions: in quartz veins, and in masses. The old workers had no use for any save that in the solid form, and absolutely disregarded the quartz, no matter how rich it might be.

Mass copper was divided by the modern miner into two classes. Mass copper, huge nuggets which the aborigines found it impossible to move or cut up, and "Barrel copper," which latter term signified such small pieces as could be gathered up, thrown into barrels and conveyed to the smelters.

The mass copper, proper, was almost as useless to the Indian as the quartz, for he had to work around it and could only obtain such pieces as projected from it and which could be knocked off with the rude tools at his command.

Captain Francis says that the largest mass taken from this region weighed about three tons and was of the size of an old-style iron cook-stove. These huge nuggets bothered the modern miners as well as the savage workers until a method of cutting them up was devised.

From an archeological standpoint, "barrel copper." because of the probable uses to which the ancients could put it, should be divided into two classes, as the two forms in which it is usually found are nuggets, proper, copper in round, solid form, and the filigree shape, or copper which is in flat sheets and resembles wires interlaced or intertwined. In making implements and ornaments, much labor would be saved by making a judicious selection from either variety. If a flat tool or a breastplate were needed, the sheet copper or filigree work would answer the purpose and save much labor in pounding, while if a spear point, a chisel or a hammer head was to be produced, the round compact nugget afforded the best material to work with.

The Amount of Copper Mined

There is no certain method of determining the amount of copper mined by the aborigines, but some inferences, which will aid in forming conclusions, may be drawn; what became of the huge quantities gathered by the savages is a matter of conjecture.

Not only on Isle Royale, but in Northern Michigan as well, are pits found in great numbers. But even on this island alone the amount of copper mined must have been tremendous. Gillman says, p. 385 of the Smithsonian report of 1873:

"The amount of mining on three sections of land at a point on the north shore of th e island (Isle Royale) is estimated to exceed that on one of our oldest mines on the south shore of Lake Superior, a mi ne which has been constantly worked with a large force for over twenty years."

This is only on three sections, and there are several sections near McCargoe Cove which were as thoroughly worked, to say nothing of the other pits in the various parts of the island. Then, too, it must be borne in mind that the aborigines were working virgin soil; what must have been their finds when it has paid modern mining companies, employing high-priced labor, to rework the same ground.

At one time there were three hundred miners employed about McCargoe's Cove, and only on the north side, at that; another three hundred worked at the Saginaw Mine on Rock Harbor.

According to the U. S. Statistical Report of Lake Commerce, the valuation of copper since 1887 has varied from $190 per ton to $340 per ton, with a mean of $230. The price from 1887 to 1897 was constant at $200 per ton or ten cents per pound, so it is fair to assume that for the period at which mining was being done on the island, the price was about ten cents per pound. So , in order to make expenses, to say nothing of a profit, an average of at least thirty pounds per man must have been found each day, or with a crew of three hundred, the production must have been fully four and a half tons per day.

This inference is necessary in the absence of the exact figures of the production of the mines on the island. The mine at McCargoe's Cove was worked for a number of years, so that to meet expenses and make a profit, several thousand tons must have been produced from this one stand alone.

A comparison of the working of the modern with the diggings of the ancient miners shows that the work of the white man is only a small percentage of that of the older worker. So from this one locality alone, (the region about McCargoe Cove) thousands of tons must have been extracted by the old workers; for they had the unworked soil, teeming with nuggets, through which to run their drifts; they worked this area thoroughly.

It is interesting to note that the amount of copper passing thru the locks at the Soo was 35,000 tons in 1887 and had increased to over 150,000 tons in 1910. From 1898 to the present date the amount shipped has been constant; before 1898 the growth was gradual. The total value of shipments from 1887 to date is more than $550,000,000 during which time more than 2,500,000 tons were produced.

It is difficult to make an estimate of the total amount mined by the old workers, but taking at a guess the least given, or 35,000 tons, as the total found by them, there is a tremendous amount of copper yet to be accounted for. From the extent of the workings on Isle Royale, this estimate is extremely conservative. An estimate of one million tons would appear more nearly correct.

Should anyone uphold the contention, and there are reasons why he would be justified in so doing, that the ancients produced as much as have the moderns, then indeed is there a vast amount yet to be discovered.

<u>Methods of Working</u>

Archeologists are well agreed that the old miners ran their drift up to the rock surface and there built a fire. When the rocks were heated thoroughly, water was dashed on, and by the sudden contraction, as well as the chemical disintegration, masses were split away from the surface and were afterward removed and broken up by the stone mauls. Marks of fire on the walls, as well as cinders and charred wood on the workings, bear this out.

Yet, standing on the summit of the range, with workings all about, one difficulty presented itself. The water must come from somewhere, and it was a mile to the nearest pool. A creek ran thru the woods to the south, a small lake lay to the north, and McCargoe Cove was more than a mile to the east.

It is possible that enough water could be collected in the pits after each rainstorm to supply the demand, but this is not probable. As the workings are all near the summit of the ridge, there would be almost no surface drainage. As far as known there are no springs in this vicinity.

The burden of bringing water must have been enormous. If procured from the lake to the north, which was the nearest water supply, it would have to be carried up a height of more than two hundred feet, part of the way over a perpendicular wall of rock.

If brought from the creek, it must still be carried up a steep hillside, through a heavy forest growth. If water was invariably used, then the ancients were indeed marvels of energy and perseverance.

An investigation of the rock and its checking, stratification and weathering led to the conclusion that it might be possible to work the stone easily with simple hammers, sledges, wedges and levers. Checked and broken, it would be possible to work the stone easily with sledges and afterward break them up. Several pieces of native rock were tested. They were lying on the surface and had been subject to the action of frost, moisture and the sun, and when struck with the stone hammers readily crumbled into small pieces. The mauls, however, showed no deterioration. Probably native rock from the depths would have presented greater difficulties.

Both **Mr.** Merritt and **Mr.** Hart have seen the cedar shovels or paddles found in the depths of some of the workings. These invariably shrivel and decay on being exposed to the air. They have seen the remains of wooden bowls, and **Mr.** Hart has in his possession a birch bark taken from a pit and supposedly part of a basket or bucket used in removing earth or in bringing water. He also had a piece of rawhide thong found in the old workings.

<u>Signs of Habitation, Etc.</u>

Only one cache was reported. Mr. Hart tells of the finding of several copper implements beneath a tree near the mines; the owner probably hid them there and forgot the place or was killed. It is probable that when the island is thoroughly cleared up, many more will be found, for, compared to the country in Wisconsin where such finds have been made, the whole of Isle Royale is a vast, howling wilderness.

<u>Canoe Routes</u>

At the southwest end of Isle Royale is Washington Harbor, and at the Northeastern end, McCargoe Cove. Both of these must have been the points of departure of the old miners for the mainland, as they are the nearest sheltered harbors to the Canadian shore. This leads to the conclusion that the region about McCargoe Cove was the last one worked, or was in the process of being worked at the time of the coming of the French. For the hidden treasures had by no means all been found by the savages; as there was still plenty of copper here, it is unreasonable to suppose that a human being would take a trip of from fifty to one hundred miles on a dangerous and stormy sea to procure an article which existed in abundance near at hand. Such a trip would have been necessary to reach the workings on the southern shore. It is true that ore might have been carried overland, but aside from the small burden possible to be borne, is the immense difficulty in traveling through the woods of the island.

As there are no streams on the island which will float a canoe for any distance, there could have been no routes by boat through the interior despite the great number of large lakes found there.

The Trails

There are today, on the island, the remains of several trails. Whether they are made on the old ways of the original miners, or were entirely new, cannot be said. But in as much as they follow the best routes, some at least must have been located on the original paths, if such existed.

At present there are the remains of a trail from the east end of Washington Harbor to Lake Desor, and from Lake Desor to the north shore; one from the South shore at the east end of Siskowit Bay passing the Island Mine location; a trail also leads up the small river that drains Siskowit Lake. One of the principal paths lead from Rock Harbor at a point opposite its western entrance north to Sargent's Lake, thence west along the south and west shores of this body of water, finally cutting across to McCargoe's Cove at its southern end. A very short trail leads along the long finger to the north of Tobin's Harbor. This crosses at Monument Rock and is of use only to sightseers, as it does not reach the shore of Duncan Bay but terminates at Lookout Louise, a summit of a cliff several hundred feet above the Lake.

It is almost impossible for any one save an expert woodsman to follow these modern trails so well, in the few short years since they were opened, has time obliterated them. This being the case with those of comparatively recent construction it is an almost hopeless task to try and find the ones made by the ancient comers; only by making their location the result of logical reasoning can their course be estimated. As to hoping to find any such as exist in Wisconsin or the neighboring states where the feet of untold generations of redmen have worn deep paths along the more traveled routes, this is out of the question for there does not appear to be enough soil covering the rocks of the island to admit of a trail wearing down to such a depth; and it is doubtful if enough of the old miners walked over a given path long enough to give it character.

Village Sites

At present no sites of former habitations are known on the island, yet deductively, the presence of summer homes at least, can be established. The island is a continent in miniature, with a great lake system of its own on the interior; the climate at and around the coast is cool and chilly, especially at night, yet on the interior it grows intensely warm during the day and the evenings are not as cold as those on the shore where the breeze from the lake strikes and cools the land.

Besides, the coast is unsuited, in most places, to village sites. It is high, with little beach and almost no sand. The residents of the eastern section of the island said that no sand was to be found anywhere on the island, but Mr. Norman who has taken up a homestead at Long Point, says that there is plenty of sand down in that region.

174

If villages existed they were probably located on the interior, and if much
work is done near Long Point, sites may subsequently come to light in this
part of Isle Royale. Should any graves be found, they will probably be uncovered in this sandy section as there is hardly enough soil elsewhere on the island
to cover a body. Near McCargoe Cove are the graves of two white miners who
died during the operation of the mines. One is marked by a heap of stones.

The aborigines could very easily make their homes here, for the island
affords every means of subsistence on which the Indians habitually relied. The
best fishing to be found on the great lakes is in this vicinity. Years ago it was
far better than at the present. One of the fishermen said that, at a period only
ten years back, fishing with a hand line in a space of two hours he took over
sixty large lake trout, fish weighing from four up to forty pounds.

Mr. Hart tells that some twenty years ago when he had trout and herring
nets set, pickerel were so plentiful that in going over a single net stretched in
Duncan's Bay, he loaded his skiff three times and took the fish to shore, throwing them away for at that time there was no market for this variety.

If, as these tales indicate, fish were as plentiful in comparatively recent
times, what must they have been when the French first came to these shores.

On the island the great northern hare abounds, and consequently, mink,
lynx and other predatory animals are numerous. One trapper, in a single
season, captured eighty lynx, in addition to other fur bearers.

Caribou and moose were once found in large numbers on Isle Royale, and
even today a few caribou and at least one moose roam the fastnesses of the
hills.

Some edible plants and fruit were seen. At one of the small lakes flag was
noticed growing, and another plant which appeared to be wild rice; but the
shores were too marshy to admit of a close examination.

About McCargoe Cove strawberries grow in such profusion that it is impossible to move about without treading them under foot. They are large for
wild berries, and have a most delicious, sweet flavor.

A few wild raspberry bushes were found; blueberries are said to grow at
certain places in the interior; blackberries are found and also wintergreen.

A plant whose name cannot be learned, but which somewhat resembles the
wild geranium of Wisconsin woods, is found everywhere on the island. It has
white flowers with huge petals, and the berries it bears are monsters, nearly
two inches across. They are said by one to be white, and by another, red;
they are edible.

While the eastern end of the island affords scant soil suitable to cultivation,
on the south and west ends the old miners might have found situations favorable
to the growing of maize, melons, and tobacco.

If the natives did not remain on the island over winter, they probably made
it their summer home, especially when the above list of food supplies is considered.

Should other farms be taken up, more will probably be known about camp
sites within the next few years, but in the present state of the tangled forest,
investigations looking to the location of camping places are of little value.

Dablon's Account

As has been said before, Father Dablon in his account mentions the places
at which copper abounds. He says copper is principally in a certain inlet
where there are some very steep beds of clay in the hills. This can refer only
to McCargoe Cove, for there, and there only, is found the noticeable feature of
clay hills. As one enters the cove from the Lake, they appear especially
visible; here are found the greatest numbers of workings, and here, according

to Captain Francis, will be found the greatest and richest copper veins ever discovered.

Then the island only two gunshots distant from Minong (Isle Royale) and between the middle of the island and the end that faces northeast, can only mean Hill Island. The island far out in the lake may mean Passage Island, though Mr. Merritt says, "I have never known of any copper being found on Passage Island, and do not know of any evidences of any having been discovered there."

Or it may mean Gull Rocks, or Batteau Rock, thirteen and eighteen miles distant from the main island. This is yet to be determined.

The Miners

Who were the ancient workers? In the light of Dablon's account there can be no doubt that they were the various tribes of Indians of whom Father Allouez speaks when he says "This lake is the resort of twelve or fifteen distinct nations." For if Dablon had not visited the island, and his statement that he hoped to pay it a visit the same summer shows he had not, then his information must have been obtained from Indians, and he so states in the opening paragraph, who were perfectly familiar with the island, for even in his rehearsing of the fact gleaned from them he is so exact in his statements as to put to shame some of the later commentators.

If the Indians did mine the copper, and if their forefathers were the discoverers of the wonderful storehouse, the great question is, What became of the vast amount of copper they must have extracted?

It is true that copper from Lake Superior regions has been found in many and distant spots. P. V. Lawson in The Story of the Rocks and Minerals of Wisconsin says:

"The native copper for hundreds of specimens discovered in the mounds as far south as Florida, was obtained at the Lake. By extensive analyses caused to be made by Mr. C. B. Moore of specimens of the copper art obtained from the aboriginal mounds of Florida; little Etowah mounds of Ohio; float copper of Illinois; and numerous specimens of mined copper from Lake Superior, it was well determined that the undoubted source of most of it, and the probably source of all of it, was the native copper deposit of Lake Superior."

In addition, the natives at the mouth of the Mississippi told the French and Spanish explorers that the copper they had came from far up the great river, from huge seas of fresh water.

The area over which it was scattered was vast, yet such a comparatively small amount has been recovered, that there must remain untold numbers of specimens yet to be recovered, or - there must have been other savage markets to which the copper was dispatched.

Triangle Island

Gillman, in his "Mound-builders and Platycnemisn in Michigan," devotes much space to an account of a visit he paid to Triangle Island, off the western coast of Isle Royale. On page 288 of the Smithsonian Report he says:

"Triangle Island (he named it) is a sandstone rock with very little soil on any part of it. The rock, which is full of inequalities, fissures and clefts, is exposed over the greater portion of the island, though the northwest end, the highest part (18 feet above lake-level) is partially covered with bushes of Cornus stolofifera and a few stunted trees of very small size (little better than bushes) of mountain ash and poplar. The sides of the island rise abruptly, and there is no landing place for even small boats except for a small space on the northeast side and also a cleft like indentation on the south side. The natural conditions of the last-mentioned landing appear to have been improved by artificial means. It is twenty feet wide by about sixty feet in length, and has a gradual slope to the lake, the rock being generally smooth throughout. On each side are perpendicular walls of rock. Small boats could easily be hauled out here, especially with the aid of timbers laid for the purpose. Near it, and all along it, wherever there are indications of copper veins, are the circular pits of the 'ancient miners.' Though of small size they are remarkably distinct. At this place the rock is mostly as level as the floor of a room, and the well-like pits are immediately perceived to be the work of human agency.

"At two places at each end of the circular pits, the copper-veins in the well-like cliff had been attacked and partly excavated. The rock was discolored as if from the action of fire, and at the base of the more central point the sandstone was considerably hollowed. All these works exhibit the same roughish surface, totally unlike the action of water.

"Immediately at the end of the southern landing already described, is a marked circular depression, occupying nearly the center of the island, and presenting some indications of artificial origin. But about thirty five feet northwestward of the head of the landing occurs a more remarkable excavation. This is of rectangular form, twenty five by twenty feet, and with an average depth of nearly four feet. It was filled with water as were the pits. "

On the day in 1911 when pictures were secured, there was an extremely strong wind blowing, and great difficulty was experienced in reaching the island. A landing was effected on the northeast side and the boat drawn from the water and with much effort, up the declivity, being left on the steep slope which has a pitch of nearly forty five degrees. The writer was alone, and as the wind continued to increase in velocity fear of being marooned shortened the stay and as thorough an examination of the different points as should have been, was not made.

Grass and shrubbery still cover the summit of the island, but the southern slope is bare, indications pointing to this section of the island being swept by the seas. An old life preserver was found at almost the center of the island, apparently tossed there by the seas sweeping up the supposedly artificial landing.

No indications of the use of fire were observed nor does it seem possible that the discolorations could still be seen or would remain under the constant stress of weather. The rock at all points appeared to be smoothed by the action of the water.

The large square excavation was particularly noted. There was only a trifling amount of water on the bottom, not over half an inch, and the floor could be observed plainly. It is perfectly level with no observable marks of tools or digging.

The southern boat landing does have the appearance of having been formed artificially, because of its regularity, yet it is possible that it is a natural formation. It does not seem logical that Indians would go to all the tremendous labor necessary to work such an opening when the island is so small as to be unsafe for a residence, and when the copper yield could not have been great.

Modern Indians on Isle Royale

As the Northwest Trading and Trapping Company maintained a post there during the latter part of the eighteenth century, it is probable that Indians frequented the island at that time.

Only one instance of a visit of Indians during recent years was reported. Mr. Norman said that about fifteen years ago an aged Indian, his squa and his grown son came to and camped on the Amygdaloid channel of Fish Island for several weeks. They said they came to search for greenstones (chlorastolites) but it is peculiar that they should have made their permanent camp so far from the greenstone beaches. These are at the lower end of Rock Harbor, fully 25 miles from the camp site of the Indians.

NOTE: George R. Fox was Archaeologist and Director of the Edward K. Warren Foundation of Three Oaks, Michigan.

The exact reference of this paper is not known to the publishers.

ONTONAGON COPPER BOULDER
(Courtesy Smithsonian Institution)

HISTORY OF FAMOUS ONTONAGON COPPER ROCK
RECALLED BY SOCIETY'S OUTING
Samuel Brady - August 22, 1916
Mining Gazette

Apropos of the annual outing, at Rockland, of the Keweenaw Historical Society, the following article on one of the most romantic phases of early Copper Country history, the finding and removal of the celebrated "Ontonagon River Copper Rock,"has been contributed.

The history of the discovery of copper by the red as well as the white man is clouded in the obscurity of the past. In 1535, just 43 years after the discovery of America by Columbus, Jacques Carter, a noted French explorer, returned to his native country from his second voyage in search of the northwest passage, during which he ascended the St. Lawrence river as far as the present site of the city of Montreal, and brought with him the first news, gleaned by communication with the Indians, of the existence of great hills of copper farther to the west. The ushering in of the year 1540 witnessed the sailing of another expedition under Cartier and of the issuing of Francois de la Roque, Sieur de Roberval, letters patent, giving him supreme command as viceroy and lieutenant governor of the newly discovered lands belonging to France in the western hemisphere.

Roberval did not sail with Cartier but followed him one year later, arriving in New France after Cartier had sailed from home. The records in regard to Roberval's explorations are very scanty and he does not appear to have accomplished much either in the field of exploration or in carrying the Cross to the savages. The year 1547 found him in France organizing another expedition, which seems to have ended in catastrophe and the death of the entire party.

Fifty-six years later (1603) another expedition under command of the great Henry Champlain and the patronage of King Henry IV, set sail and resulted in the founding of the present city of Quebec and the establishment of a more permanent occupation of the country. Heit was who first explored the valley of the Ottawa to its headwaters in beautiful Lake Nipising during the year 1615, passing to within 180 miles of Lake Huron, which it is doubtful if his eyes rested upon, and then returning southward to the shores of Lake Ontario, he found himself to be the first white man to gaze upon its crystal waters as they poured their way through the many gateways of the Thousand Isles, toward the Atlantic.

The First Missionaries

The first missionaries to the shores of the great lakes were not Jesuits, as is generally supposed, but Recollet friars from Paris, an order of Franciscan monks, who as early as 1618 were placed in charge of missions in Canada by Pope Paul IV. They visited, and established, missions upon the eastern shores of Lake Huron, among the Huron Indians, under the care and guidance of Champlain. These missions were known to extend to the islands guarding the entrance to Georgian Bay, and as they were the only missionaries residing in New France, as it was then called, until the advent of the Jesuits in 1624, it is not at all unlikely that they were the first white men to tread the shores of this beautiful state. Many of these religious men lived and died among the savages.

One year later, says Mr. Utley in Michigan as a Province, Henry de Levy, a religious enthusiast, who was then governor and who had joined a monkish order, brought out from France five Jesuits to labor in converting the Indians.

In 1641, Charles Reymbault and Isaac Jogues established a mission at the head of Pentanguishine bay, and the following year coasted the shores of Georgian bay and the St. Mary's river as far as the Sault Ste. Marie, where they were well received by the Chippewas and learned from them of the existence of the great Kitchigammi or Big Lake, which they later gazed upon. They did not extend their journey farther, but returned that fall to Pentanguishine to pass the winter. The following year Father Raymbault passed to his reward from the effects of the great exposure and hardship he had endured and Jogues who had been captured by a roving band of Iroquois, was tomahawked at Gandaguem now Auresville, New York.

First White Man on Superior

In all probability the first white man who navigated Lake Superior was Jean Nicollet, who was born in France in the city of Cherbourg in 1598. Though not a member of any monkish order, he was said to have been full of the spirit of the true explorer and at the same time of a very religious nature.

Nicollet arrived in Quebec as early as 1618 and was sent by Champlain among the Nippissing Indians, where he remained nine years to learn their language, so as to be able to perform the duties of an interpreter.

In 1634 Champlain sent him upon an expedition westward to find the waterway leading to the China Seas and to establish a trade in furs and other peltries among the various Indian tribes. During the summer of that year he ascended the St. Mary's river to Lake Superior and later explored the Straits of Mackinaw and the shores of Lake Michigan as far as Green Bay. He had been told by the Indians of the existence of a strange people in these regions, called by them the "Tribe of the Sea," whom he imagined might prove to be Chinese and he is said to have provided himself with garments of china damask, decorated with birds and flowers of many colors in order to properly impress them with his importance when he was first ushered into their presence. It is recorded that his Tribe of the Sea proved to be Winnebagoes, whom he found clothed in skins like other Indians and not in the silks and satins of Oriental magnificence. After completing a treaty of peace with these people, he continued his explorations to the south, into the Illinois country and then returned the same year to Quebec, where he is said to have married a goddaughter of Champlain. He was drowned in the year 1642 while upon a trip from Three Rivers to Quebec.

Father Menard's Arrival

In 1660 Father Rene Menard, who for 20 years previous had labored with great zeal among the Hurons, early French settlers, near Three Rivers and among the Iroquois in northern New York, amidst untold hardships, left Three Rivers with an Ottawa flotilla on the twenty-sixth day of August, bound for Pikwakwewaming, now called Pequaming, upon the shores of Keweenaw bay, Lake Superior, where he arrived October 15 of the same year, after enduring great suffering and privations. His mission to these Indians appears not to have been attended with material success for upon the following year we find him, according to Father Verwist, in his life of Bishop of Baraga, leaving that place upon the thirteenth day of July, 1661, for a Huron village upon the headwaters of Black River, Wisconsin, to find a people more responsive to his teachings. When within about two days of his objective point, and while his party were engaged in making a portage, he disappeared and was never heard from afterwards. The effort of Father Menard to establish a mission upon the shores of Keweenaw Bay appear to have been the first one made in that direction upon Lake Superior. According to Charles E. Lawton, the place of Father Menard's disappearance was at the old portage between the west end of Portage Lake and Lake Superior, though other writers have considered that it was somewhere near Lac Vieux Desert.

First Report of Copper

In 1666 Claude Allouez, S. J., succeeded in interesting the Indians in religious matters to such an extent as to justify his remaining among them for a period of two years at La Point, upon the shores of Chequemagon Bay.

History records that he was an indefatigable worker in the field of missions and his record shows that he established them among nearly all of the Indian tribes bordering on the Great Lakes. Through him it is claimed we received the first recorded evidence of the existence of copper upon the shores of Lake Superior, from actual observation by a white man, though Charles Whittelsy published in the Smithsonian Contributions to Knowledte, V. 13, that Bouche, in his Historic Veritable et Naturelle, Paris, 1864, says "That the Frenchmen who went with Father Menard told me that they had seen a nugget of copper at the end of a hill which they estimated to weight more than 800 pounds. " It is very possible that this might have been the mass of copper which the late James Paull of Ontonagon claimed to have bought of an Indian which he stated was found on the west side of Keweenaw Point near the Portage, which was said to weight 800 pounds. Paull stated that he took it to Copper Harbor and that it was his impression that it later found its way into the cabinet of Yale college. It would appear that it would be interesting to determine if such an object can be found in the cabinet of that institution.

It was Father Allouez who renamed the great lake, Lac Tracy or Superior to honor a Monsieur de Tracy for possible contributions to the cause of religion. He undoubtedly made many excursions into the interior in pursuit of his labors and makes note of the existence of copper in the following language, says Mr. Utley. After stating that it frequently happens that pieces of copper weighing from ten to twenty pounds are found he says: "I have seen several such pieces in the hands of the savages who regard the metal as very precious and guard it with jealous care. For some time there was seen near the shore a large rock of copper, with its top rising above the water, which gave opportunities for those passing by to cut pieces from it; but when I passed that vicinity it had disappeared. " Some specimens were gathered by him and sent to the provincial administrator at Quebec. In collaboration with Father Marquette, who succeeded him in charge of the mission on Chequamegon Bay, he later published the first map of Lake Superior and the northern portions of lakes Huron and Michigan.

Alexander Henry Comes

Though the occurrence of copper in these regions seems to have excited the curiosity and wonder of the early missionary fathers, their reports of its presence did not result in stimulating research upon the part of the French, who seem to have been more greatly interested in trading for pelteries with the Indians, than in attempting to establish and work copper mines, in this, at that time greatly isolated region. Subsequent to the year 1678, there appears to have been a great relaxation in the spirit which stimulated the field of missions of 1640 down to that date, due no doubt to the long and almost continuous wars, which disturbed religious and commercial relations for about 100 years, as well as internal dissensions, existing between the Franciscans and the Jesuits. This long period of inaction in interest taken in the Lake Superior region was finally broken by an English trader by the name of Alexander Henry who while visiting Mackinaw in 1760, in pursuit of his occupation, learned of the existence of copper in this section. He visited here and later published a description of his observations and experiences, mentioning for the first time the great mass of copper, which he found as reported to him, lying in the bed of the west branch of the Ontonagon river, some 20 miles above its mouth, which he stated weighed probably about five tons. Henry later returned to England and organized a company to conduct practical mining at this place, which is stated to have been just ten rods east of the N.W. quarter of Section 6, T, 50, R, 40, on the site of the present dam of the Victoria Mining Company.

The First Practical Mining

Operations were started in the fall of 1770, he having transported a small party of miners from the Sault to the mouth of the Ontonagon river by means of a small schooner he had built for that purpose. After establishing a camp and laying out the work, Henry returned to the Sault for the winter. Upon the return of spring his schooner was loaded with supplies and dispatched to the mouth of the Ontonagon where, much to the surprise of those in charge they found the entire party awaiting their arrival. The miners had penetrated the bluff for a distance of some 40 feet during the winter and as the ground had been unsecured as soon as the frost disappeared the tunnel had caved in. Thus ended the first attempt at mining made upon Lake Superior. From the time of the abandonment of this enterprise upon the part of Henry and his associates nothing was heard of this float mass of copper until after the publication of the report of the expedition of General Lewis Cass, the then governor of the territory of Michigan, who was proceeding upon a tour of inspection of St. Paul via the head of the lake. This report was written by Henry R. Schoolcraft, the geologist of the party, who accompanied it to determine the truth of the reports concerning the mineral value of this region. To a very large extent the result of its findings were reflected in the later investigations of Houghton, whose more extended examinations lead step by step to the investment of capital and the development of one of the most productive copper and iron sections upon the face of the earth.

Governor Cass' Visit

Governor Cass accompanied by Mr. Scoolcraft and his party arrived at the meeting place of this historic mass of copper June 28, 1819. Of it he says: "I do not think the weight of metallic copper in the rock exceeds 2,200 pounds. The quantity may, however, have been much diminished since its first discovery as marks of chisels and axes upon it, with the broken tools lying around, prove that portions have been cut off and carried away."

It is very evident that the worthy gentleman was very much exhausted, and possibly disappointed by the arduous task of reaching this point and the comparatively small size of the piece of copper, for in writing of its surroundings he says: "Mostly immersed in water reposes the copper rock; on the left the little island of cedars divides the river into channels, and the small depth and rapidity of the water is shown by the innumerable rocks which project above its surface from bank to bank. The masses of fallen earth - the blasted trees, which either lie prostrate at the foot of the bluffs or hang in a threatening posture above - the elevation of the banks - the rapidity and noise of the stream, present such a mixed character of wildness, ruin and sterility, as to render it one of the most rugged views in nature. One cannot help fancying that he has gone to the ends of the earth, and beyond the boundaries appointed for the residence of man. Every object tells us that it is a region alike unfavorable to the productions of the animal and vegetable kingdom, and we shudder in casting our eyes over the frightful wreck of trees, and the confused groups of falling-in banks and shattered stones. Yet we have only to ascend these bluffs to behold hills more rugged and elevated, and dark hemlock and more forbidding to the eye. Such is the frightful region through which for a distance of twenty miles we follow the Indian guides to reach this unfrequented spot, in which there is nothing to compensate the toil of the journey but its geological character and mineral productions."

In 1826 General Cass and Thomas L. McKenney were authorized by the United States to negotiate a treaty with the Chippewa Indians at Fond du Lac. Subsequent to the execution of the same they ordered George F. Porter to accompany a detachment sent to the Ontonagon river to remove this mass of copper. The following is an extract from his report:

George F. Porter's Report

"We left Fond du Lac on the first day of August 1826 with two boats, containing 20 men, including our Indian and French guides, and after a short passage of something less than four days arrived at the mouth of the river. We immediately proceeded up the river. About 28 miles from its mouth the river divided into two branches of equal magnitude. We continued up the right branch for about two miles further, where we found it necessary to leave our boat and proceed by land. After walking about five miles further over points of the mountains from 100 to 300 feet high, separated by deep ravines, the bottom of which were bogs, we at length with some difficulty discovered the object of our search, long known as the 'Copper Rock' of Lake Superior. This remarkable specimen of virgin copper lies a little above low water mark on the west bank of the river, and about 35 miles from its mouth.

"Its appearance is brilliant wherever the metal is visible. It consists of pure copper, ramified in every direction through a map of stone (mostly serpentine, intermixed with calcareous spar) in veins of from one to three inches in diameter, and in some parts exhibiting maps of pure metal of 100 pounds weight, but so intimately connected with the surrounding body that it was found impossible to detach them with any instruments we had provided.

"Having ascertained that, with our means and time it was impossible to remove by hand a body weighing more than a ton (two-thirds of which I should have observed is pure metal) we proceeded to examine the channel of the river, which we found intercepted by ridges of sandstone, forming three cataracts, with a descent in all of about 70 feet, over which it was impossible to pass; and the high and perpendicular banks of sandstone rendered a passage around them impracticable. Finding our plans frustrated by unforseen difficulties, we were obliged to abandon our attampt, and proceed to Sault Ste. Marie."

Douglass Houghton's First Visit

It was visited again in 1840 by Bela Hubbard in company with Dr. Douglass Houghton, and it is believed to have been at this shrine that he received that inspiration which later was so strongly reflected in his opinions regarding the great future awaiting the copper regions of Lake Superior.

It remained for the skill and determination of one James Paull, a former Wisconsin lead miner, to remove this mass to the mouth of the Ontonagon river. In the spring of 1842 he proceeded to its resting place and with the aid of a small truck prepared for the purpose by him and the use of a windlass he succeeded in removing it to a point below the rapids where he conveyed it to the mouth of the river by means of a flatboat. Some writers claim that it was through the financial aid of Julius Eldred of Detroit, who supplied not only the equipment but the money as well that this work was accomplished and that Paull's part in it consisted principally in his taking charge of and directing the work, the enterprise having been inspired by Eldred. It is a pretty well established fact that Paull really came from Wisconsin for the purpose of removing this mass; that he set up a pre-emption claim to the land upon which the mass was found. That Paull did transport the mass to Ontonagon at his own expense is largely substantiated by the fact that Mr. Eldred, who came there in company with a Major Cunningham of the U.S.A. with the intention of seizing the same for the United States government, compromised with Paull by paying him the sum of $1,800 cash, which was later supplemented by a further payment of the sum of $400 after the claim made by Eldred against the government for the sum of $5,654.00 had been allowed for his services in this matter. The weight of the mass when brought to Ontonagon is reported to have been 3,708 pounds, it having no doubt been considerably reduced in size by the axes and chisels of the early explorers.

184

The End of the Big Mass

An extract from the Buffalo Gazette for the year 1843 says: "The copper was shipped from Ontonagon on the schooner Algonquin to the head of the Falls of St. Mary, where it was transferred to a Mackinaw boat and after passing around the rapids was shipped on the schooner Brewster to Detroit, where it arrived on October 11 last."

In the book entitled "Early Days in Detroit," written by the late Friend Palmer he says: "The Ontonagon river copper rock arrived in Buffalo when I was residing there. I think it came in the fall of 1843. While in transit from the revenue cutter Erie to the railroad depot on Exchange street, it was under the immediate charge of Capt. S. P. Heintzelman, United States quartermaster (since major general in the United States army, in the civil war) who was stationed at Buffalo at that time. The captain to gratify the curiosity of the citizens, had it paraded up and down the principal part of Main street and down Exchange street on a four wheeled truck, behind two span of horses and a driver. The horses were gaily decorated.

"Many of our citizens, eager to possess a clipping from the rock, as a souvenir, provided themselves with hammers and chisels for that purpose, hoping to get a clip at it as it passed through the streets, but they were foiled in this, as Captain Heintzelman was close to the rock on foot and it kept him busy keeping the people back.

"I have seen this rock many times at the Smithsonian Institution, Washington, as I presume many thousands have done, but I do not remember if it bore on its surface anything to indicate its strange history, and the various vicissitudes it had passed through before reaching its final resting place. If it does not, it seems to me that it should, considering the vast wealth it has already heralded, and the prospect of millions yet to come, the contemplation of which almost makes the senses reel."

This silent rock, in its bed on the rugged shores of the Ontonagon, bore on its metallic face its story and its significance. The untutored savage read it partly, but it was left for the Fur Trader Henry and Cass and McKenney, Schoolcraft, Houghton, Hubbard and others before them, who visited it from time to time, to read aright the tale it had to tell and its great import. It seems that no mineral specimen in the world at this day possesses the interest and significance that this rock of copper does now, reposing so quietly in the halls of the Smithsonian Institution in Washington, and there should be some fitting recognition of the great part it played in making known to the nation the vast wealth that lay hidden in the copper region of Lake Superior, only waiting to be sought after."

This article, which has been prepared for this meeting in a great hurry and in the midst of other pressing duties, is written merely for the purpose of trying to show what a great influence the erratic mass of copper which lay for so many ages in the bed of the Ontonagon river really had in directing attention to mineral wealth of northern Michigan.

(This paper was delivered at Keweenaw Historical Society Meeting of August 22, 1916, and published in Mining Gazette, Houghton, Michigan.)

MICHIGAN'S MOST ANCIENT INDUSTRY:
THE PREHISTORIC MINES AND MINERS OF ISLE ROYALE
By William P. F. Ferguson

In September, 1922, pursuing a quest which I had followed for several years, I found on Isle Royale in Lake Superior the remains of a Stone Age town or "city," evidently built and inhabited by the prehistoric people who worked the ancient copper mines of that island.

Speaking of a people who mined copper as belonging to the Stone Age may seem an error, but to these miners, it seems certain, copper was not a metal but a specially valuable stone, workable as they worked other stones. They probably had no knowledge of the art of smelting or of any other application of fire to metal.

The matter is not fully ripe for publication, for it will require a considerable work of exploration and excavation to determine the meaning of the find, but, since it has been the subject of many widely published news dispatches and is being discussed by "feature" writers all over the United States, it seems to be desirable to make a brief but correct statement of what seem to be the facts.

We should begin by recalling to the reader's mind the comparatively well known fact that Isle Royale, a large wilderness island of some two hundred and thirty square miles, in northern Lake Superior, lying close to the Canadian shore but belonging to the United States and a part of the State of Michigan, was the scene of extensive copper-mining in a remote past by a not easily identified people. It is not my purpose to attempt to designate dates or to assume that I am able to fix the identity of these miners. The most important testimony regarding their period of operations is found in the forests which overgrow their abandoned workings and the strongest clue to their identity is the character of the work which they did.

The best known of these ancient mines are in a section along the northern shore of the island in the vicinity of what is known as McCargoe Cove, where they cover several square miles. The workings, however, are found in all parts of the main island and on the adjacent islets. Everywhere they are overgrown and, when the white men first became acquainted with them, were overgrown with ancient forests, six-foot pines and cedars twenty inches in diameter growing in the pits and on the dump heaps. The age of these trees is a matter of dispute, but their presence may be assumed to indicate that the period of mining must have been not much less than five hundred years ago, while it may have been much earlier.

The work is of colossal magnitude. The mining method was exceedingly crude and appears to have consisted in heating the surface of the rock with fire, fracturing the heated rock by the application of water and breaking up the fragments with stone hammers. These hammers are natural pebbles of hard rock, brought across an arm of the lake from the Canadian shore and probably rudely fitted with helves withed or thonged to them. By this crude method, these ancient people dug circular pits from five to thirty feet in depth in hard rock strata, the pits sometimes so close together that it amounted to the turning over of the whole formation to their depth and moving many cubic acres - it would not be seriously extravagant to say cubic miles - of rock.

The object of their search was the so-called "float" copper pieces of the pure metal, ranging in size from a few ounces to several tons, found imbedded in the rock. Only the small pieces were of use to them; the large masses, after vain attempts to break them up, they left where they found them.

The present day visitor, who sees the workings only as he penetrates the forest, hardly realizes their enormous extent. They were more clearly seen by the early white miners who operated in the same localities. Interesting testimony to the impression made upon them comes from an elderly gentleman

who informs me that he visited the McCargoe Cove district while white men
were mining there, in the seventies, and asked the engineer in charge what
estimate he placed upon the time necessary for the digging of the ancient mines
in that locality. The engineer replied that he would take the night to think it
over and the next day said that, taking into account the transportation of the
stone hammers, the cutting of the wood for heating the rock, the providing of
food for the workers and the actual work of mining with the crude implements
employed, he did not believe that a force of ten thousand men could accomplish
the results which he had seen in that district in less than a thousand years.
He was speaking of only a small part of the ancient mines which exist.

The stone hammers themselves present a big exhibit in the case. Prof.
William H. Holmes, who made some slight explorations around McCargoe Cove
in 1892, estimated that the weight of the broken hammers found in that locality
would reach a thousand tons. The movement of such a mass from the Canadian
shore, in craft not much more cargo-worthy than the Indian birch canoe, speaks
of a great organized industry; and Prof. Holmes was considering only a small
section of the ancient workings.

The earlier observers attributed the Isle Royale mines to the Mound Builders,
and these latterly have been identified with the Red Indians. The conclusion
thus arrived at the Isle Royale antiquities are "just Indian work" had tended to
their neglect by archaeologists. Not attempting to argue the case, I point out
that the time period may easily have been much more remote than the Indian
days and that the character of the work speaks of a national industrial organization, quite beyond anything "Indian" of which we know.

It has usually been supposed that these ancient miners came to Isle Royale
only in the summer season, the island being wholly inaccessible in winter and
no signs of habitation being found. But, fifty years ago, a Mr. Henry Gillman,
who was a somewhat well known contributor to the current literature of that
day, in brief and vague paragraphs in two or three articles, referred to the
remains of a "city" on the south side of the island. The location was fixed
only by reference, giving the impression that Mr. Gillman was reporting some
unverified rumor or was withholding particulars in the hope of being able to explore the find.

When I found these paragraphs in the old magazines, some years ago, I had
already spent several summers studying the ancient mines and was naturally
anxious to find the "city"; but careful search in the vicinity of the only waterfall which I knew, while it discovered a few old workings, found no signs of
human habitations.

My first search in that field was in 1920. I returned to the same field in
1921, without further results, save the discovery of another waterfall; but in
1922 I found still another fall upon a stream which had been known on the maps
as the Little Siskiwit and which I have taken the liberty of mentioning the
Sibley, and upon both sides of this stream, at this fall, I found the "city."

The remains are numerous square or rectangular pits, dug along a ridge,
in a compact boulder formation. These pits were walled with the boulders excavated, surrounded by embankments to exclude surface water and provided
with roofs of some sort, making dwelling-places not unlike those used by some
of the western tribes of Indians and perhaps more like the dwellings of some
of the ancient peoples of Northern Europe. One of the larger of these pits,
upon the northern side of the river, is surrounded by what seems to have been
an earthwork, probably for defensive purposes. There are numerous small
pits but a considerable number of pits ranging from twenty-five feet square to
thirty by sixty feet.

These pits are easily distinguished from the mining pits by several features:
They are dug, not in the rock, as are the mines, but, as I have said, in a
boulder formation lying along the ridge, near the crest; they are rectangular,

instead of circular like the mines. Further, their position is not parallel to the axis of the ridge, as might be expected, but uniformly oriented to the points of a compass.

I was impressed with this fact at first seeing them and, after determining at night the variation of my compass from the North Star, found that, so nearly as the ruined walls could be traced, the north and south sides of the pits are true meridian to that star.

I have been quoted as saying that these remains cover "square miles." This is an exaggeration, yet they do cover several acres and are comparatively easy of access, the heavy forest having been burned away and the territory covered with a second growth. As in the case of the mines, the forests, of which huge stumps and fallen trunks remain, testify to the antiquity of the remains, large pines and cedars having grown since the work was done.

The location of this "city" has been something of a surprise to people who are more or less familiar with the existence of the mines from the fact that it is several miles away from the mines, from the fact that it is several miles away from the best known workings. A little investigation in the locality, however, discovered a number of old mine fields, some of them perhaps the most extensive yet found. The city may have served as a winter home for mine workers from the whole island or such of them as remained during the winter. There may, too, be other "cities" buried in the deep forests, unexplored by anyone who would recognize their character.

The site was probably chosen for two reasons: the first, that Hay Bay, opening out of Siskiwit Bay, with the wide estuary of Sibley River, makes the safest landing for small boats upon the south side of the island. Since the ancient miners probably came to the island in craft very like the Indian canoes with which we are familiar, this was important, a safe harbor being necessary to landing and to the shipment of copper carried away. The second deciding factor was probably the existence of the falls. In winter, the streams of Isle Royale and the bays, as well as the great lakes, are heavily ice-bound; but this fall would assure a water supply wholly or comparatively free from ice.

Speaking of a landing place, it is interesting to note that the left bank of the Sibley, just below the fall, where the land is only slightly above the water, appears to have been protected by an embankment or levee, three or four feet in height and running for something more than a half-mile. I say "appears" since, while I am convinced of the artificial character of the embankment, there has been no opportunity yet for examination which would warrant a definite assertion.

I had hoped, in event of finding the ruins this last autumn, to be able to do some excavating and to that end had provided a stock of tools and arranged for a small force of workers. One little oversight prevented the carrying on of this work to any extent. I had anticipated in the ruins nothing more difficult to deal with than the soil accumulated through some centuries. I found that the ancient dwelling-pits are more or less filled with the fallen walls of boulders which the action of frost and water and the growth of tree roots have precipitated inward. These could not be removed with pick and shovel; only by wheelbarrows or hoisting machinery, and for that I had not provided. We were obliged to content ourselves with mere surface digging and this was not prolonged, since the main work will require a return.

We were, however, able to assure ourselves that the pits were walled, but the only relics which we found were the well known stone hammers, of which, around the larger pit, which I have mentioned as surrounded by an earthwork, there were great numbers. Since I left the island, the game warden, who accompanied me in this search and who, with his wife, are the only year-around inhabitants of the island, has written me that, in the same region, he later found a stone axe, the first, so far as I know, to be discovered on the

188

island.

It would seem that the discovery of this town-site presents an opportunity for pushing the study of America's ancient history into a comparatively new field. We have here, I think for the first time, the dwellings of this prehistoric people, untouched since they left them, save by the hand of nature. Careful excavation, we are warranted in believing, will enable us to determine with considerable accuracy how their dwellings were constructed and will uncover many objects of use, abandoned when they left or broken or lost while they lived there.

If they had pottery, almost certainly there will be broken pieces in the trodden earth floors of these dwellings. In the soil around them or under their fallen walls, we are almost sure to find broken or lost weapons of great interest.

Complete exploration seems to me to be a scientific duty and the more because the performance of the duty, while in some respects difficult, presents no insuperable obstacles. Good water transportation will bring the explorers and the necessary tools and supplies to within less than a mile of the ruins. The workers can live confortably, particularly if the work is done in the fall months after the insect pests which are always met in the northern summer have gone. True, a substantial sum of money will be necessary for the inevitable expenses of such exploration; but that ought not to be difficult to provide with such a prize in sight.

It seems of importance, too, that this exploration be undertaken as promptly as possible, lest unqualified persons should disturb the field and destroy the opportunity without ability to avail themselves of it. It may be remarked that the owners of the land are willing that the exploration be made.

*

Michigan History Magazine - The Pre-historic Mines and Miners of Isle Royale; Vol. 7, 1923 - pp. 155-162.

THE FRANKLIN ISLE ROYALE EXPEDITION
By William P. F. Ferguson
Franklin, Pa.
Michigan History Magazine - 8 - 1924

By coincidence, at the very time when the MICHIGAN HISTORY MAGAZINE was presenting to its readers my report of the discovery of a prehistoric town on Isle Royale and my suggestion for exploration there (see July-October number, 1923), I was upon Isle Royale, at the head of the Franklin Isle Royale expedition, prosecuting the work suggested.

I had hoped to be able to begin work in the late August of 1923, but a variety of obstacles delayed the project, and it was not until the latter part of September that it could be undertaken. The major part of the expedition, with equipment and materials, reached the rendezvous on Thursday, September 20, but, owing to the failure of steamers to connect at Port Arthur, I, with my adjutant, Mr. Peter M. Lowry of Franklin, Pennsylvania, after a stormy voyage of nearly fifty miles in a twenty-two-foot motor boat, arrived late at night on Saturday, September 22.

Our camp, - Camp Franklin - was on the shore of Hay Bay, an arm of Siskiwit Bay, at the home of Mr. William H. Lively, the game and fire warden of the Island. We were provided with comfortable tents and utilized the warden's ample log cabin as a kitchen and mess hall. The expedition mobilized a working force of six able-bodied sappers, most of them recruited from northern Michigan and the Minnesota shore, with a qualified geologist, an accomplished forester, a prime cook and, in the commander, a hard-driving "boss." Our equipment was such as experience had taught me would be needed in the enterprise, including a good camp outfit, wheelbarrows, mattocks and shovels and planking for runways and platforms.

It proved fortunate that delays had occurred, for, while during several weeks preceding our arrival the Island had been deluged with rain, which would have prevented work, during the seventeen days of our stay there was no rain and the most suitable working weather was enjoyed.

There were two points for exploration in contemplation. Chief of these, of course, was the prehistoric townsite; but I was anxious also to do some work at a prehistoric mine about two miles distant from the town, which seemed to me to offer some features not found in the comparatively well known mines of McCargoe Cove of which I have spoken in the former article.

Our road from the camp to both of these points lay up Hay Bay and the broad estuary of the Sibley River, by boat, the town being reached by an easy trail of a half-mile from the landing but the mine by a trail of nearly three miles, through swamps and over exceedingly rough ground. The difficulty of transporting working outfit over this trail was by no means inconsiderable.

I will speak first, briefly, of our work at the mine, although it was done after our excavations at the townsite.

This old mine, which lies in the southwestern corner of Section 22 of Township 64N, Range 37W, according to the Ives Survey, is located at a point where a knoll of amygdaloid rock juts out from the side of a ridge, covering a base of perhaps five acres and rising to a height a little in excess of one hundred and fifty feet above the swamp at its base. Into this knoll the ancient miners drove five trenches, penetrating the rock, at points, to a depth of more than fifteen feet. The longest of these trenches is nearly five hundred feet in length, running from the southwest corner to the top of the knoll; two others run diagonally up the south side, while two more, one of them very large and deep, are driven from a ravine on the northwest of the knoll.

The method of operation was apparently similar to that which I have described in speaking of the McCargoe mines, though the traces of fire were not as numerous, and the stone hammers, which were found in considerable numbers,

were in the majority of cases more local boulders utilized for the purpose.
The characteristic hammer of diabase stone, brought from the Canadian shore,
was encountered, but less frequently, probably owing to the remoter location
of the mine from the source of supply for such hammer-heads, nearly seventy-
five miles away.

The magnitude of the work at this old mine was even more impressive than
that found in the McCargoe Cove district. No accurate estimate of course could
be placed upon the period of time necessary to complete the work; but I do not
believe that a force of twenty-five men could merely remove the debris from
the old trenches in six months of steady work.

It was impossible, too, to form any estimate of the reward, in the way of
copper found, accruing to the old-time miners. The rock of the knoll is shot
through with little veins of copper, along the line of which trenches were
driven. The showing we found was so rich that any prospector, unacquainted
with the unfortunate history of mining effort on Isle Royale, would be likely to
think he had found a bonanza. We found many small pieces of pure copper,
both in the rock and in the piles of debris through which we drove trenches.

I frankly confess that, from the standpoint of discovery, the work at the old
mine was wholly disappointing. I had hoped to find artifacts; this hope was the
brighter because of the finding, in 1922, of a highly polished ax-head of diabase
stone upon a rock overhanging one of the trenches, but aside from the broken
stone hammers and an unidentified fragment of which I shall speak, we found
absolutely nothing. If there exist here any of the huge unmanageable copper
masses found in the old pits at McCargoe Cove, we did not encounter them.

I shall have occasion, however, to refer to some of my observations at the
mine.

The old townsite, as surveyed by Uren and Dunston of our party, lies in
Section 24 and Section 23 of the same township. It is located on both sides of
the Sibley River, which at that point comes down, almost upon the section line,
by a series of beautiful small falls over heavy trap rock.

The remains are in two general groups, respectively upon the northeast and
southwest sides of the river. The principal feature of the first group is a
large pit-dwelling surrounded by a clearly traceable earthwork, probably of
defensive character. To the north of this is a cluster of smaller pits. Across
the river there are a dozen pits of considerable size with scores of small pits,
apparently mere holes in the ground, scattered over the rocky surface and
among the trees, so numerous that we did not even try to count them.

As I have explained in my former article, the terrain is a deposit of glacial
boulders and gravel, driven into what may be roughly called a depression at
the northeast end of one of the Island's numerous rock ridges. From a geological standpoint the mass is highly interesting, containing specimens which must
have come from great distances and over a vast area.

Our first excavation on the townsite was made at what I will call Pit No. 1,
the pit surrounded by the earthwork.

This earthwork is rectangular in form, the south embankment approximately
fifty-five feet long, the east and west embankments, less clearly defined, one
hundred and ten feet in length, with an outcropping of the rock ridge serving in
place of an embankment on the north.

The north and south walls of the fort, as of all the larger pits, so far as
these latter could be determined, lie, by our compass reading, declined about
10 degrees west, from true north.

The pit itself is located in the southwest corner of the earthwork. Before
the beginning of our work, this pit, surrounded by a group of second growth of
birch, spruce and pine trees, presented the appearance of an irregular truncated pyramid inverted. The western side was practically perpendicular, being
cut down in rock. The southern side was nearly perpendicular, although the

stone wall by which it was originally faced had tumbled down piecemeal into the excavation. On the eastern side, the wall had apparently been pushed in by the pressure of the earth, falling to pieces, so that only in spots were enough stones left together to be recognizable as part of a wall. On the northern side, where, at some seasons of the year, considerable volumes of water must pour down as the natural drainage of the old fortress, there has been something like a mass movement of the original debris from the excavation, so that it was impossible to locate the original position of that side.

At no place during the work could we find in the material handled any apparent difference between the virgin glacial deposit, the ancient dump piles and the debris involved in the movement of the sides since the pit-dwelling was abandoned. Apparently the time elapsed since both the natural sliding back of material and the original excavation has been so great that in all cases the materials have settled down to comparatively exact conformity to the geological deposit.

The excavation, as it existed when we were ready to begin work, measured substantially thirty feet east and west, twenty-five feet north and south, with a depth of nine feet below the apparent natural surface of the earth or fifteen feet below the top of the south embankment.

The bottom of the excavation was filled with a mixture of forest debris, loose stones and gravel to an irregular depth of perhaps eighteen inches. Below this was a layer of stones and gravel without forest debris, excepting that it was penetrated by a network of tree roots. These roots, it may be remarked, we encountered wherever we dug, to the very bottom of all our excavations. Below this layer, we encountered a dense mat of roots and rotted leaves which was removed in sections, sometimes as large as a bed mattress, six or eight inches thick. Below this was another layer of gravel and stones and another mat.

After a penetration of about five feet, we encountered the fire platform. Of this feature of all our excavations I shall speak more in detail hereafter. In this case, we were unfortunate in not knowing what we had encountered, mistaking first the stones of the platform for more fallen-in boulders and then supposing that we had found a paved bottom of the pit. Many of the stones removed before we realized what they were and it was the discovery of stones which had been acted upon by the fire which created the first suspicion of the real character of what we had found. Underneath the top stones of the platform, we found traces of fire, with burned sticks, taking out one stick, rotted to a pulp, nearly six inches in diameter and burned off as squarely as it could be cut with an axe.

The rotten condition of this stick was evidently caused by the presence of water which was plentiful in the bottom of this pit. We were inclined to believe this was surfacw water, since, although we were below the level of the river, it did not run rapidly when bailed out.

We excavated to a depth of substantially sixteen feet below the ground surface or perhaps two feet below the top of the fire platform, laying bare the bottom to an area of about fifteen feet east and west and ten feet north and south. During the whole of this excavation we frequently encountered broken stone hammers, about equally divided between the diabase stone and the boulders found in situ. None of these were grooved for helves but several of them showed the stain of rotted withes or thongs by which helves presumably had been attached. The presence of these was accounted for by the necessity of cutting down the rock in the west side of the pit. There were, however, a considerable number of small stone hammers, some of them showing marks of much use, which could not have been of any service in breaking rock. It suggested itself that these were probably employed in beating copper into weapons and utensils. Aside from the stone hammers, no artifacts of any character were found.

Along the east side of this excavation lay a large pine tree trunk which had grown upon the dump pile which may be assumed to mark the probably position of the northeast corner of this pit. The rotts from the stump of this tree grew down over the side of the excavation, showing that it had grown since the pit was dug, as was also shown by the fact that stone hammers were found under the stump, entwined around by a huge root. Of the meaning of the tree as an evidence of the age of the work I will speak later.

After this work on Pit No. 1, we crossed the river and selected from the large pits on the western side of Pit No. 2, one of three large pits lying in a line, as our next field of work.

On the west side of the river there is no sign of fortification of any sort and none of the pits are as large as Pit No. 1. Pit No. 2 measured substantially 17 feet east and west by 24 feet north and south, the north and south sides diverging westward from true north, as determined by compass reading, about 10 degrees.

The old walls of this pit remained in sections upon all sides, most markedly on the north side, which, as in the case of all the other pits excavated, was lowest and in this case had no deposit of debris, indicating that this was the entrance side. Assuming that the walls were originally perpendicular, they have been heaved in more at the bottom than at the top. It was suggested that this must mean that they were not originally perpendicular but sloped inward. I have, however, seen the same movement of walls in the old fashioned cellars of early settlers in the Catskill Mountains and believe that we may assume that they originally occupied a perpendicular position. In no cases did the corners remain clearly defined. The walls were built of small boulders, placed with some reference to the "face" of each stone, and in this pit were apparently only one stone thick.

Pit No. 2 was only a little more than six feet deep before the beginning of our work and at the depth of about three feet below this we found the fire platform.

These platforms, which we found in all the pits excavated, were apparently built up between eighteen inches and two feet from what appeared to be the floor of the pit, although in the gravel formation the floor was not easily identified. They were built of small boulders, laid together loosely, substantially rectangular and about three and one-half feet by four and one-half feet in size. They seemed to be placed diagonally upon a line from the northeast to the southeast corner of the pit in each case. There was no mark of fire upon the top stones nor were there arches or fire-boxes of any kind in them. But, below the top, the stones showed clear marks of fire, some of them being so burned that they fell to pieces with the slightest handling, while charcoal and partly burned sticks were found among these stones. The unburned portions of these sticks, as of two sticks driven into the ground at each end of the platform in Pit No. 2, were as solid and undecayed as one would find a tree limb that had been lying on the ground for a few months. All the sticks found were spruce.

These fire platforms were an unsolvable puzzle. At the first discovery of them, we supposed that they were places for supporting fires, similar to the fire banks found in Indian wigwams and tepees, where the fire is slightly elevated above the floor to promote draft. The absence of any sign of fire upon the top stones, however, banished this idea. The fires were evidently built on the earth floor, against the sides of the platforms. There was no evidence of large fires and less appearance of fire than would be consistent with long continued use.

There were a few stone hammers in the debris about Pit No. 2, possibly a dozen.

Pit No. 3 lies a few yards west of Pit No. 2 and is similar in every way, save that it is slightly larger. We excavated half of this, carefully, uncovering a fire platform, the lower layers of which showed marked signs of fire, though the top stones betrayed no acquaintance with heat. This pit afforded nothing new.

Pit No. 4 lies about thirty yards to the south of Pit No. 2 and before the beginning of excavation was in every way similar to the former pits, excepting that when we had removed the forest accumulation of leaves and brush, the walls were traceable in larger sections than we encountered elsewhere. Excavation proved that these walls were more carefully and solidly built, particularly on the south side, where they were two stones thick and had originally been comparable in stability to the stone walls built for fences by New England and York State farmers, excepting that they were built of boulders, there being no flat stones of building size in this formation.

We entered this pit from the southwest corner, carefully digging down to assure coming at the fire platform from the side, hoping to discover some solution of the problem as to the use of these. We were doomed to disappointment for, just above where we expected to find the platform and apparently resting upon it, we found the largest boulder encountered, a stone that would probably weigh a ton and a half, which must have rolled down from the debris pile. There was no way of determining whether it had originally been removed from the excavation, but that seems probably. It was so large, however, that in the absence of hoisting machinery it was utterly impracticable to attempt to remove it, and work on this pit was accordingly abandoned.

Pit No. 5 was selected from the group of pits lying to the north of Pit No. 1. These pits are slightly smaller and shallower than the others I have spoken of and I am unable to say whether all of them are walled. Pit No. 5, however, presented remnants of walls and a fire platform similar to the other pits but showing less signs of fire than we found elsewhere.

In addition to these, we excavated several of the numerous small pits found on the west side of the river. These present merely small depressions or holes in the ground, usually not more than two or three feet deep, ranging from six to ten feet across. They have no walls, but at a depth of from eighteen inches to two feet below the surface of the accumulation they all have rude fire platforms, - little more, however, than piles of stones, exhibiting evidences of fire, with bits of charcoal scattered through them.

In addition to these excavations, we dug over the surface of the ground about these pits to the extent of many square rods, in the hope of discovering artifacts or other evidence of occupation.

The reader may keep in mind that all this excavating work, which involved the removal of hundreds of tons of material, was done by hard labor. Nearly three-fourths of the volume of the matter removed was boulder, ranging in size from a double-fist to big stones weighing two hundred or two hundred and fifty pounds. The whole was penetrated with roots, a dense network which had to be cut with a mattock. Hardly a stroke could be taken that did not encounter a root. I may say in addition that much of the material was handled with hands and every shovelful of gravel or earth was carefully spread to prevent overlooking anything of importance. The mattock men watched the material moved with every stroke; the shovel men also watched carefully, and the barrow men, standing beside their barrows, inspected each shovelful thrown into them. Working at depth, another handling was necessary, the material first being shoveled up to a plank platform and from there to the barrows, affording another opportunity for inspection.

In all the work, however, aside from the stone hammers, the finds were exceedingly disappointing. We found no other tools, utensils, or weapons, either of stone or copper. We found no bones, such as we confidently anticipated to encounter about the pit-dwellings or around their fire platforms.

The only artifacts found, aside from hammers, were small pieces of red material which we at first fancied might be broken fragments of crude pottery but which, on a little closer examination, were pronounced bits of iron oxide, the suggesting being that they had been brought here to be used for paint. I was enough in doubt about this to bring home several pieces which I have submitted to chemical analysis and the chemists pronounced them fragments of burned clay, probably small pieces of pottery. They were, however, very few and were found not directly in the pits but in the loose debris outside and one of them in the debris removed from the mine. In no case are they large enough to give any indication of form.

The absence of artifacts around this old town was the more disappointing because in the McCargoe Cove district the early white miners made some very interesting discoveries. Two or three people in various parts of the country, learning of my work in Isle Royale through press dispatches, have written me descriptions of copper tools and weapons found in the old workings in that section. Particularly Mr. Emmet H. Scott of LaPorte, Indiana, who was financially interested in the Minong mines at McCargoe Cove, writes me of excellently made copper spearheads picked up there and showed to him when he visited those workings in the seventies. There is a tradition, too, told by elderly men who visited or worked in those mines, of a large finely-wrought copper knife blade. Unfortunately, all these finds seem to have been scattered. I am not able to learn that any of them are identified in any of the museums as coming from Isle Royale.

The problem presented by the absence of artifacts calls out several suggestions. First of these is the probably fact that these people, who apparently belonged to a period of development very close to what we know as the Old Stone Age, had few personal possessions of any sort, so that the chances of finding articles or broken pieces of any such would be small in any event and the more so because everything that they possessed must have had a high value and would have been carefully guarded.

A second consideration is that this townsite, as indicated by the small showing of fire around the platforms, may not have been long occupied.

A third is that, after the departure of the original inhabitants, whether of their own accord or because they were driven out by some other people, the ground may have been carefully gone over by people who picked up and carried away everything that they found.

We found no trace that white men had ever visited or noticed these old excavations, excepting that a cedar tree, some twelve inches in diameter, growing in Pit No. 3, had been cut down with an axe, apparently many years ago. There was no trace of the tree, aside from the stump. This is probably to be accounted for by the fact that some decades ago large buildings and docks were built by the white miners on the shore of the bay, some three miles from this point, and timber was cut for this work all along the side of the ridge. These pits were unmentioned in the field notes of Ives and have never been reported by timber cruisers or copper prospectors. The only known mention of them is by Mr. Gilman, in the magazine article, published more than fifty years ago, which I mentioned in my former article. For those who did not read my former article, I may repeat here that Mr. Gilman's article made very indistinct and vague reference to this townsite and that I made the discovery of it only after three seasons of exploring work in the Siskiwit Bay region.

It now remains to determine whether anything which has been found identifies the ancient inhabitants of this town and the prehistoric copper miners.

The prevailing theory, so far as there can be said to have been a theory, is that these mines were worked by the Indians and that the operation of them continued down to the coming of the white men. In confirmation of this theory there has been published by several writers references to the works of early explorers, particularly of the Jesuit fathers who penetrated the Lake Superior region in the latter half of the seventeenth century. A recent writer in a popular publication has also quoted Raddison, with the assertion that he found here the source of the Lake Superior copper and that he heard from the Indians stories about an ancient people who mined it.

Raddison in his curious narration, indeed, tells us of a visit to the western end of Lake Superior where he was perhaps the first, if not certainly the first, white man to penetrate, in 1664. He mentions without naming it, a large island which must have been Isle Royale, but he makes no mention of any copper mine there and gives no intimation that he visited the island or heard anything about its inhabitants. He apparently spent considerably more than a year in the neighborhood, and it is wholly improbable that had mining been going on at that time he would have failed to hear something about it.

The Jesuit fathers seem to have been very carelessly read by those who have quoted them. Their most extensive mention of copper is in the NARRATIONS for 1670. In these, Isle Royale is mentioned by its Indian name, Minong, and is spoken of as the probable source of some of the copper found around the lake. The writer of these NARRATIONS does mention "mines," but the passage clearly indicates that he was not speaking of worked mines but of mere deposits of copper. There is no intimation of any knowledge of the presence in Minong or elsewhere of workings, whether then in operation or ancient. All the copper spoken of is merely fragments, large or small, picked up along the lake shore, as they are picked up along the shores of Isle Royale occasionally even today.

Marquette is often spoken of as an authority for the Indian theory. Marquette did, indeed, draw a map of Lake Superior, fairly accurate, in which he located a large island, substantially where Isle Royale is located, although the outline of the island and its inclination to the main shore are wholly wrong; but there is no record that Marquette, in his brief missionary years, ever visited Isle Royale or knew of copper there. His field of labor lay to the south.

Unless some further evidence can be produced, I am compelled to believe that the Jesuit fathers never heard of the copper mines of Isle Royale, as mines; that these mines were not in operation in the Jesuit period and their time of operation was so long before that the work was overgrown by the forests and entirely forgotten, so that the Indians of the region, who visited Isle Royale and picked up copper along its shores but probably never had permanent habitations there, knew nothing about the ancient mines.

The one piece of local evidence so far available is presented by the forests. In the McCargoe Cove district, the early white miners found a forest of enormous pine trees growing over the ancient mine pits. Comparatively few of these trees are now standing, many of them having been cut down by the miners and others destroyed by fire, but old pine trees three feet and more in diameter, blown up by the roots, are found around McCargoe Cove with the ancient stone hammers held in the entwined roots. At other points on the island similar pine trees are still growing, but I have never felt at liberty to cut down a growing pine, which belongs to somebody, for the sake of counting the rings, nor have I had a force sufficient to do so at any time, excepting the past year, and, in that case, there were no growing large pines in the section where we worked.

I have already mentioned the large pine at the side of Pit No. 1 and have showed proofs that it grew since that pit was excavated. It is one of many hundreds of similar large pines lying fallen in this region. Believable tradition attributes their fall to a fire which swept this region, something like seventy-five years ago, when the early copper prospectors were at work. This tree was considerably rotted, but we were able to saw from the trunk, at a point which must have been nearly fifty feet above the ground, a comparatively solid section. This section presents a nine-inch radius, it being impossible to tell how much of the tree had been worn away outside this, by the action of the elements during the many years since it fell. Owing to the condition of the wood, I would not be willing to assert that I can count the rings absolutely correctly, but there seem to be one hundred and eighty-nine rings from the center to the circumference of this section. Standing near this fallen tree is a young pine, substantially fifty feet high; and two of my men who had been familiar with this northern country all their lives, one of them for thirty years owning a farm on which many such trees grow, asserted that a pine of that size was from fifty to seventy-five years old.

If now we estimate the growing period of this old tree at two hundred and fifty years (allowing fifty years for its growth up to the point where the section was taken) and remember that it has been lying seventy-five years in its present fallen condition, we have a period of three hundred and twenty-five years since this tree began to grow on the brink of this pit, which may even then have been long abandoned. In other words, we are justified in assuming that about the year 1598, or more than sixty years before the first white man reached western Lake Superior, this ancient pit-dwelling had been dug and probably had been abandoned.

At the old mine there was another interesting old tree, of which there remained only a long line of rotted pulp, where the trunk had lain, and the larger roots, still fast in the soil. The decay which had taken place would indicate that this tree must have fallen far more than a century ago; but underneath the roots we found the mine debris and two broken hammers. The tree was evidently much larger than the one at the pit. I do not believe anyone acquainted with forest growth and decay would doubt that it must have been growing at least five hundred years ago. It certainly began to grow after the miners had finished their work at that point.

This is about as far as we can go in fixing age.

I would make the collateral observation that the character of this work seems to me to preclude the supposition that it was done by the Indians. Even if we suppose that the Mound Builders were identical with the Red Indians, nothing which they are known to have done is comparable with the rock work of these old mines, while I am unable to find any record or trace of habitation left by the Mound Builders bearing any resemblance to the pit-dwellings.

Right here, in these pit-dwellings, with their fire platforms, it seems to me that we have found the one distinctive thing by which there may be some possibility of identifying or associating these ancient miners. The question is, Where else in the world has there lived a people who dwelt in walled pits, roofed undoubtedly with some perishable material, perhaps skin, perhaps bark, and built their fires about rude platforms, as these people did?

I confess I have turned very many thousand pages in the big libraries without finding any answer to that question. Perhaps some one else may be ready to give it.

For a little time it seemed that a parallel might exist in Europe, where some writers speak of ancient pit-dwellings; but the more recent authorities dissipate this hope and tell us that what were taken for pit-dwellings are in fact only ancient mining pits.

It would be premature to express any theory as to the identity of these ancient people. Their period, I believe, once having eliminated the theory of comparatively recent Indian origins, may be almost indefinitely remote. There is nothing to preclude the possibility that these old mines were dug and this old town inhabited a thousand or two thousand years ago. It is not probable that the miners were permanent inhabitants, either of Isle Royale or that part of the country. They may have come from very far away. There may have been

annual or occasional pilgrimages or expeditions from some more or less remote country to get this copper. I think, however, the pit-dwellings warrant
us in believing that, at least once, the miners spent a winter on Isle Royale.
The pit-dwellings would never have been constructed for other than winter
occupation. It has occurred to me that this town, as I mentioned in my former
article, may have been a sort of holding garrison to protect the landing in Hay
Bay or the mouth of the Sibley, which, as I have pointed out, is the best and
almost the only safe landing for frail boats to be found in this part of the Island.
As I have noted, the remains here do not seem to indicate long occupation; but
I may read the signs incorrectly and the town may have been occupied for a
long time.

What remains to be done in Isle Royale?

While I believe that our work this year was careful and exhaustive, I would
like to see further excavations and particularly further surface work done upon
the old townsite. I believe, too, there should be more systematic excavation
upon the site of the old mines, particularly of the mine where we worked this
year. But my brightest hope is that someone may yet discover another townsite, where, perhaps, there will be better opportunity for study, possibly because no conquerors or others have swept over the ground and removed lost or
broken relics.

In any event, it would seem to me that the field is so alluring that, whether
I am able to follow up this work or must rest content with what I have accomplished, somebody should at least try to delve deeper into this dimly written
chapter of ancient history.

****

It remains for me to ask permission to say, by way of footnote, a word about
the organization and personnel of my expedition.

In all, I spent in the 1923 expedition nearly fifteen hundred dollars. Of that
sum about six hundred dollars was subscribed by friends in Franklin, Pennsylvania, who were interested in my work. At their request I refrain from re-
cording their names but they have my warm gratitude and deserve the thanks
of all who are interested in uncovering the ancient history of America.

My thanks, too, are due to the Northern Navigation Company, both for
courtesies and for transportation assistance, and to the United States and
Dominion Transportation Company, which afforded me great aid. Mr. Hogsted,
their Duluth representative, purchasing and forwarding much of my equipment
for me.

There is none of the members of the expedition to whom I do not feel personally indebted for his work and his interest in the work. I want to record
my appreciation here of Adjutant Lowry, who went with me from Franklin and
who almost hourly relieved me of physical and mental care; of William H.
Lively and Mrs. Lively, whose home in the wilderness was our headquarters;
of William H. Uren, Jr., and William Dunstone, of the Michigan College of
Mines at Houghton; of John Jacobson, strong son of Norway and for thirty years
a fisherman-farmer on the Minnesota coast, and of Fred Jackson, a Minnesota
boy giant whose strength was a perpetual surprise and wonder. Nor should I
refrain from thanking the neighboring fishermen whose boats helped in landing
our expedition. It would be injustice, too, to forget Mr. E. A. Tripp of Cloud
River Bay, on the Canadian shore, who, in his little motor boat, brought the
adjutant and myself well toward fifty miles through fog and storm.

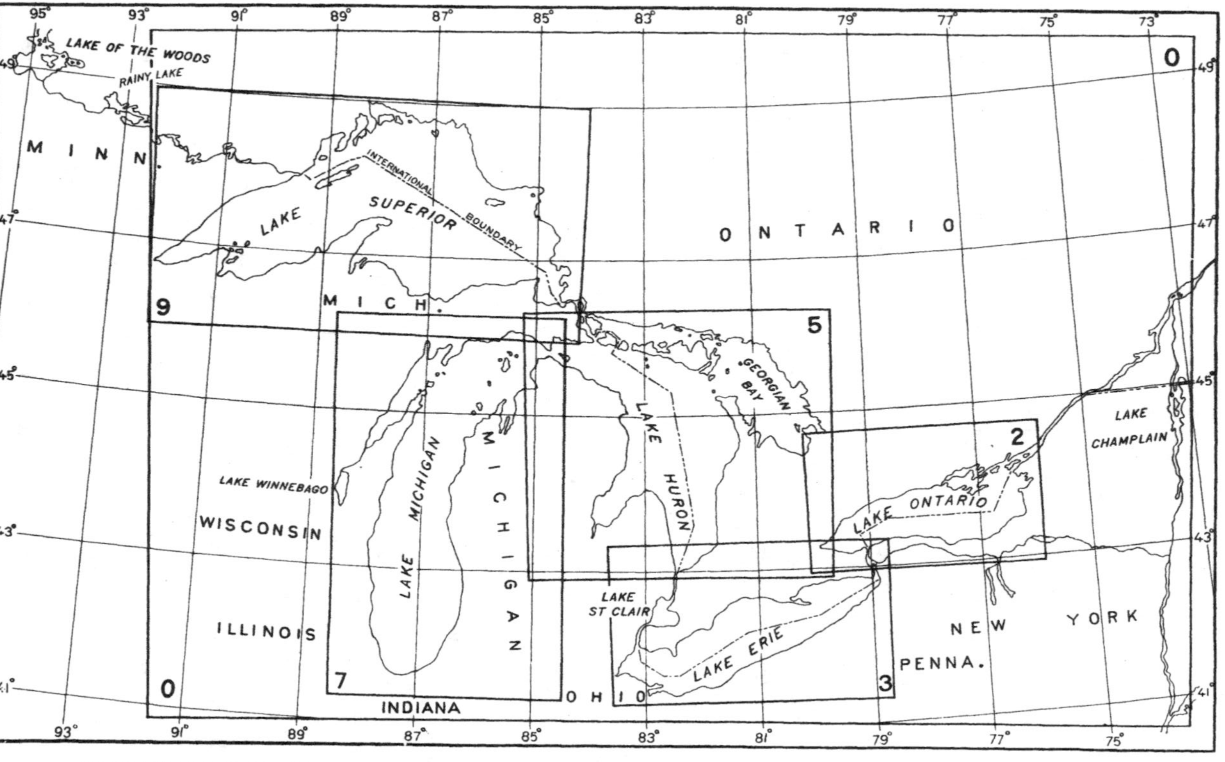

OUTLINE MAP OF GREAT LAKES. Numbers refer to general charts of the Great Lakes. The charts are available from U. S. Lake Survey, Corps of Engineers, 630 Federal Building, Detroit 26, Michigan.

HISTORICAL SKETCH OF LAKE SUPERIOR COPPER DISTRICT
Evidences of Mining Go Back Centuries; Long before Coming
of the North American Indians
By Professor James Fisher
Michigan College of Mining and Technology
Mining Gazette
September 7, 1929

Very few sections of the world's surface have given so much material to writers of picturesque romance, legend, adventure, successes and failures, as the Lake Superior Copper Country.

Copper, with its alloys, bronze and brass, was probably the first metal to be used for utilitarian purposes and it is possible that it even preceded gold for ornamental purposes. It is one of the six metals mentioned in the Old Testament, and the Bible names, "Tubal-cain, as instructor of every artificer in brass and iron." Copper was known to the Egyptians as early as 7000 B.C., and bronze relics have been discovered dating to the period of Menes, the founder of the First Dynasty, the first king of Upper and Lower Egypt, who reigned possibly as early as 5500 B.C.

Is there any more conjecture involved in assuming that the copper used by the ancient Egyptians came from the Lake Superior Region, the only place where native copper has ever been found in considerable quantity, than in assuming that these ancients were sufficiently advanced in the science of metallurgy to reduce the metal from its ores?

The evidences of the mining of copper in Michigan go back to the prehistoric times when a race of intelligent men of whom we have but little knowledge mined this metal with some system on Isle Royale on Keweenaw Point, especially in the neighborhood of Ontonagon. In the pits which they dug have been found masses of metal, some of enormous weight, accompanied by crude implements of stone and copper, and in some cases stone or timber platforms evidently used to assist in lifting the masses to the surface.

The civilization of this people was of a much higher order than that of the succeeding races generally referred to as the North American Indians. It may be possible that the extensive evidences of mining in the Lake Superior District are due to one of the Indian tribes, the Winnebagoes, who either inhabited or made frequent visits to this section before the advent of the Chippewas, also called the Ojibways, Iroquois, or Sioux. However that may be, there is so little of certainty known of them that we must be content to refer to them vaguely as the Mound Builders. That they lived many centuries ago is evident by the fact that the openings of their pits were found choked with debris and earth upon which grew the largest forest trees, requiring hundreds of years to mature.

Many of the Lake Superior beds were mined to a shallow depth for mass copper by this long-gone race. That they were good judges of mineral values has been proven by the making of good modern mines under many of these ancient pits.

Apparently the aboriginal inhabitants of what is now the United States were entirely unacquainted with bronze or brass and made but slight use of copper at the time of the discovery of the New World by Columbus. Both copper and bronze were used extensively at that time, in Mexico, however, where the superior Aztec civilization flourished.

The Ojibways, who were found in possession of the southern shore of Lake Superior by the first white men arriving at this inland sea, were but slightly acquainted with the practical use of copper and even had no legends regarding the mining done by their predecessors.

In 1536 Jacques Cartier explored the St. Lawrence River to the present site of the city of Montreal. He reported that the natives whom he met told him of vast seas of fresh water to the westward, and great hills of copper and precious metals, but he did not push forward to verify their stories. The first written account of the existence of native copper on the southern shore of Lake Superior is found in a book by Lagarde published in Paris in 1636. It is probable from this account that the existence of the metal was known only from the statements of the Indians made to the early French explorers, and that Lagarde had received the same information as Cartier. In the meantime the French fur traders, and the Jesuit missionaries had pushed westward and occasionally found it convenient to use the southern shore of Lake Superior as part of their route.

The next notation on Lake Superior copper deposits is found in the Jesuit Relacions for 1659 and 1660. At that time the Ojibways had a few crude utensils made from copper, but most of the metal in their possession was in the form of nuggets which the Jesuits said were worshipped and held in veneration as unusual works of the "Gitchie Manitou."

In the Jesuit Relacions for 1666-1667 is a portion giving the journal of the exploration of Lake Superior by Father Claude Allouiz, who seems to have been the first white man who, of a certainty, saw copper along the Southern shores of the Lake. In this relation of Father Allouez there is a chapter entitled, "Mines of Copper which are found on Lake Superior." He says "The first place where copper occurs in abundance after going above the Sault is on an island about forty or fifty leagues therefrom, near the North Shore, opposite a place called Missipicooatong (Michipicoten). Several other publications prior to 1750 speak of the masses of copper found in the region.

In 1763 and for several years following, Alexander Henry, an adventurous Englishman, who was in turn hunter, explorer, and miner, spent considerable time in this region, having come here soon after the conquest of Canada by the British. During the years 1765-1766 he was occupied in coasting along the shores of Lake Superior looking for mineral treasure and in the course of his voyage visited the mouth of the Ontonagon River. He writes, "I found this river chiefly remarkable for the abundance of virgin copper which is on its banks and in its neighborhood. The copper presented itself to the eye in masses of various weight. The Indians showed me some of twenty pounds. They were used to manufacture this metal into spoons and bracelets for themselves. In the perfect state in which they found it, it required nothing but to beat it into shape, --On my way back to Michilimackinac, I encamped a second time at the mouth of the Ontonagon River, and now took opportunity of going ten miles up the river with Indian guides. The object for which I more expressly went, and to which I had the satisfaction of being led, was a mass of copper, of a weight, according to my estimate, of no less than five tons. Such was its pure and malleable state that, with an axe, I was able to cut off a portion weighing a hundred pounds."

This mass of native copper is the historic "Ontonagon Boulder," derived from adjacent copper-bearing rocks and transported during the glacial period to the place where it was discovered. For ages it lay on the bank of the west branch of the Ontonagon river where it was known to, and worshipped by, the Indians. During the succeeding seventy-five years many explorers and scientists followed Henry's example, and the boulder became well known as a mineralological curiosity. It was transported in 1843 by James K. Paull, on a low truck with line and capstan, nearly three miles through a dense wood with numerous hills and valleys to the main Ontonagon River and floated on a batteau to the mouth. The Government, however, claimed ownership of the speciman and Lajoy Cunningham, officer in charge of Fort Wilkins at Copper Harbor, was instructed by the Secretary of War to secure the boulder and bring it to Washington. For a brief period it was placed on exhibition at

Detroit and toward the end of 1843 brought to Washington and deposited in the yard of the Quartermaster's Bureau of the War Department, where it remained until 1860, when it was transferred to the Smithsonian Institution where it now rests. This specimen represents the first considerable shipment of copper from the Lake Superior region, a district which afterwards became the most important copper center of the world.

Soon after disposing of the great mass Mr. Paull platted the present town of Ontonagon. He was a typical pioneer, devoid of fear, accustomed to hardship, a staunch friend but an uncomfortable enemy. He kept a hotel in Ontonagon until his death, May 1, 1881. He was the first white man to establish a permanent residence in the Copper Country.

In 1770 Captain John Carver published a book in London telling among other things of the native copper of Lake Superior, which, according to his account, could be had merely for the trouble of picking it up. This publication led to the formation of a mining company in London, the king of England being an official, and in 1771 there appeared at the Sault a party of "miners" sent over by the London Company. These men were provided with all the royal letters permitting them to mine for copper but they were inexperienced and had no notion that a knowledge of mining might be necessary. Alexander Henry, however, was acquainted with the region and versed in the Indian tongues, and had even brought some of the metal to the Sault with him, so he was engaged to assist in the enterprise.

During the winter of 1771-72 an edit was driven about forty feet into a clay bank on the Ontonagon, on the property of the present Victoria Mining Company. While they were working in winter no support was necessary for the frozen clay, but the spring thaw brought their operations to a stop. Thus ended the first "mining" operations by white men in the Lake Superior District, just as they had supposed, and hoped, that they were about to come upon a solid vein of copper, but in reality, just before they reached the red "Eastern" sanstone. No further attempts at copper mining were made in the Lake Superior Region for a period of about seventy years.

The Treaty of Paris in 1763 transferred the control of what is now the Upper Peninsula of Michigan from the French to the British. After the close of the Revolutionary War the treaty of peace of November 1782, made Michigan a part of the United States. The final treaty of September 1783 established the boundary line between the possessions of Great Britain and those of the United States. This line ran through the middle of Lakes Ontario, Erie and Huron, and their connecting waterways. Benjamin Franklin, a member of the boundary commission who had heard of the mineral wealth of Lake Superior, deflected his pencil to the north of the middle line passing through Lake Superior upon the crude map that was made the basis of delimitation, thereby including Isle Royale as a possession of the United States.

Because of long and vexatious delays in communication, and the reluctance of the military contingent to turn over their authority, the United States Sovereignty was not established over Michigan for a number of years. It was August, 1796, before the British flag gave place to that of the United States at Michilimackinac, the military headquarters for the Upper Peninsula.

In April, 1800, Congress passed a resolution for the appointment of an agent "who shall be instructed to collect all material information relative to the copper mines on the south side of Lake Superior." If such an agent was appointed he is not known to have reported the results of his investigation, but the action shows that even at that early date the attention of the government had been attracted to this region.

On the 24th of May, 1820, General Cass, who had been Governor of the Territory of Michigan since his appointment in 1813, set out with a well selected party on his important expedition of exploration, whose itinerary included the southern shore of Lake Superior. The objects of this journey were to examine the country so far as means would permit, and to select sites for one or more military posts among them. There was considerable conjecture regarding the existence of copper, and in a less degree, of other minerals; and it was among the chief objects of this expedition to make, as far as possible, geological and mineralogical investigations. Henry R. Schoolcraft, the topographer and mineralogist of the expedition, reports that in their journey along the south shore of Lake Superior they frequently found specimens of copper. The party passed through Portage Lake, thence up to the mouth of the Ontonagon River, which they ascended twenty miles in order to view the then celebrated "copper rock" that lay upon its banks.

In 1830 Schoolcraft organized an expedition for the discovery of the sources of the Mississippi River. This expedition, which included the south shore of Lake Superior as a part of their route, had as one of its members Dr. Douglass Houghton. Dr. Houghton was at the time of this appointment a physician in Detroit. He was a keen observer, much interested in science and a valuable member of the party as surgeon and botanist. Thus began the career of Douglass Houghton in this section where he was destined to render service of incalculable value. To him, more than to any other man must be given the credit for the early and rapid development of the copper industry.

On the admission of Michigan into the Union as a State in 1837, the first Governor, Steven T. Mason, recommended a geological survey of the State, and appointed Dr. Douglass Houghton as first State Geologist.

Although Dr. Houghton began his field work as State Geologist in 1838, it was 1840 before the exploration of the Lake Superior section was begun. The general results of this exploration were reported to the legislature in his fourth annual report as State Geologist, which bears the date of February 1, 1841. This report furnished the first definite information relative to the occurrence of native copper on Lake Superior. He saw very clearly the future importance of its mineral wealth, but was extremely cautious in his statements. He said,"The earliest, as well as all other travelers who have visited the district under consideration, have not failed to make frequent allusion to the loose masses of native copper that have been occasionally found scattered over it, nor has any one failed to allude to the large boulder or loose mass of that metal upon the Ontonagon River. Almost invariably the opinion has been expressed, from the frequent occurrence of these masses, that the metal must be abundant in the country. But after all, the true sources from which these masses had their origin, or the relation which they held to the rocks of the district, would appear never to have been understood, and all or nearly all that was known of their true relations was left to conjecture. The result of this has been that while some have excessively magnified everything connected with the subject of which, in truth, nothing was known, another class, equally far from what is really true, have regarded these masses of native copper as boulders transported from high northern latitudes."

In a letter dated December 26, 1840, Houghton wrote, "Ores of zinc, lead, iron, and manganese occur in the vicinity of the south shore of Lake Superior, but I doubt whether these, unless it be zinc and iron, are in sufficient abundance to prove of much importance. Ores of copper are much more abundant than either of these before mentioned, and a sufficient examination of them has been made to satisfy me that they may be made to yield an abundant supply of the metal. I do not mean by this that copper is to be found in that region, as is the popular opinion, pure and without labor but that capital may be safely invested in the raising and smelting of the ores, with profit to the capitalist.

"I brought from Lake Superior on my return to Detroit this fall, from four to five tons of copper ores, and am now busily engaged in making an analysis of them. Thus far they have proved equal in value to any ores I have ever seen, and their value for purposes of reduction cannot be doubted. The average of percentage of metal is considerably above that of the ores of Cornwall. While speaking of the ores I am reminded of the beautiful specimens of native copper which came out with the ores in opening some of these veins. They are not very abundant, but some of them are very fine. In opening a vein, with a single blast I threw out nearly two tons of ore, and with this were many masses of native copper, from the most minute specks to about forty pounds in weight, which was the largest mass I obtained from that vein. Ores of silver occasionally occur with the copper, and in opening one vein small specks of native silver were observed. There are as yet, however, no evidences of the existence of this metal in sufficient abundance to be of practical value.

"It has been my desire in all examinations connected with these important subjects to be sure and not deceive myself, and to draw no conclusions but such as are strictly based on observations."

The geological party that reached Lake Superior in 1840 consisted of Dr. Houghton, State Geologist; Bela Hubbard and Columbus C. Douglass as his assistants; Frederick Hubbard, in charge of instrumental observations; H. Thielson, civil engineer; Charles W. Penny, and six oarsmen.

The report of 1841 was the last one made by Dr. Houghton to the Legislature, the poverty of resources of the young State having compelled a suspension of the survey. Here again, Dr. Houghton showed his resourcefulness. The linear survey of the public domain was being made by the United States Government. These surveys had been in progress in the State of Michigan, as in other portions of the Nation's property not yet deeded to settlers. Dr. Houghton had found from time to time great advantage in his explorations by enlisting the intelligent minds of the public surveyors in the cause of geology and the related sciences. In fact, he saw in this union a rare chance to carry on his own scientific examinations on a large and permanent scale. His idea was to achieve a thorough geological, mineralogical, topographical, and magnetic survey of the new wild lands of the United States, contemporaneously and in connection with the government survey. In 1844, during the session of the forty-fifth Congress, the Doctor laid his scheme before the Secretary of the Interior. It was carefully considered, its objects approved, but its feasibility was questioned. Doubts were expressed whether deputy surveyors could be found sufficiently versed in the sciences to undertake such a work with any reliable prospect of success. In this dilemma, Dr. Houghton did not hesitate, but offered at once to take the contract himself, to complete the survey of the Upper Peninsula, comprising upwards of four thousand miles, at a price but one-half cent per acre in excess of the sum that would be paid for the linear survey. Dr. Houghton was assisted in formulating his plans and in carrying out the work by William Austin Burt. Mr. Burt came to Michigan as a young man in 1823. He had a strong constitution, a predisposition to work, six weeks of school education, and a capital yet to be acquired. He built mill buildings in many parts of the State, at the same time using his evenings and other leisure time studying mechanics, engineering and surveying. In 1835 he was appointed Deputy Surveyor, and entered upon a contract in the Upper Peninsula. Here he encountered the difficulties which led to the great work of his life, the invention of the Solar Compass.

Mr. Burt carried his surveys from the Lower into the Upper Peninsula in the year 1840, and had progressed to some extent up to the Spring of 1844, when Dr. Houghton's contract took effect. Mr. Burt entered heartily into the plans of Dr. Houghton and was equally enthusiastic in the prosecution of the work. He superintended the running of the township lines, while the running of the subdivision lines was allotted to deputies. Each surveyor noted in a book kept for that purpose all togography, including rock formations; he collected and carefully labeled specimens of minerals, veins, and all rock found in place, and recorded its dip and thickness, as well as its position on the surveyed lines. These men had to possess scientific knowledge of a high order, broad intelligence, and a degree of fortitude and perserverance which would command respect. Considering the slight supervision to which they were subjected, together with the inadequacy of their compensation, they may be regarded as among the most scrupulous and meritorious of public officials. They showed inflexible integrity in fulfilling their contracts in spite of many discouragements and temptations to slight their work; very few cases of fictitious field notes were ever reported. They would spend a whole season in the forest, far from human settlements, sometimes short of provisions and always without what we consider luxuries. Frequently they were obliged to carry their instruments, camp equipage, and provisions on their backs through places where neither horse nor canoe could penetrate. We cannot but admire them.

Excellent progress had been made in this work during 1844 and until the untimely death of Dr. Houghton, who was drowned near Eagle River, October 13, 1845.

The only vein whose location is definitely mentioned in the reports of Dr. Houghton is that of a green silicate of copper at Copper Harbor. It is reasonable to suppose that he knew the location of veins carrying native copper, but the survey had not been completed and the land had not been thrown open for settlement or even for exploration. The reports, however, called attention to the possibilities of the region, and numerous applications were made to the War Department, for permits to explore for minerals and to locate tracts of land in the district. By a succession of treaties with the United States the Indians relinquished their claims to the lands of the Upper Peninsula and Isle Royale, the final treaty being ratified March 12, 1843. This was the signal for the commencement of a wild rush to the district and a speculative craze that lasted for several years and which completely justified the anticipated fears expressed by Dr. Houghton.

The first permits to individuals to explore for minerals and locate tracts of land allowed the grantee to select a tract three miles square. About one thousand such permits were issued by the War Department and nine hundred and sixty selections were actually made. Sixty leases for tracts of one square mile were perfected and mining companies organized upon them. Many alleged copper deposits were "located" of which the succeeding generations of miners and geologists have been unable to discover the slightest trace. Copper was reported to have been found everywhere, from the beach along the lake shore back into the forest for as many miles as the prospectors had gone. Before the lands in this region were brought into market the permits issued by the War Department were the only titles which people could obtain to lands, and they were naturally not infrequently rated at a high value. The only people who really secured substantial profits from many of these mining concessions were those who sold them at fancy figures without development.

The system of permits adopted by the Government was not a success and after two years it was abandoned. In 1847 the Lake Superior Land District was established and the land sold, as surveyed, for five dollars an acre. Later this price was changed and a uniform price of one dollar and a quarter per acre was affixed to all government lands.

About twenty prospectors landed at Copper Harbor in 1843. From then on, for a period of about five years, explorers were abundant. The field was new, the uncertainties were great, and all were stimulated to a high degree with enthusiasm and eagerness to find wealth. Search for mineral wealth has in all ages impelled men to withstand privation and danger, and scarcely another motive can be found that has a corresponding influence. As is always the case in any pioneer district, so it was here, that men of enterprising minds, of unwearied zeal, of unflinching courage, were among the first to penetrate the wilderness.

Whether the pioneers arrived at Copper Harbor, Eagle Harbor, Eagle River, Ontonagon, or some other settlement, they were under the necessity of building their own houses. Fortunately, material was ready at hand and it required but strong and willing arms to speedily erect log cabins, rude in construction and design, but rich in their housings of brawn and brain and hope. The people were full of resource and under the circumstances accomplished great Hay Point, a copper-bearing vein was a conspicuous object known to the voyageurs as the "green rock," and had given a name to that beautiful harbor long before it became the center of the copper excitement. This point was included in the first lease issued to a Mr. Raymond. This lease, with two others, each of nine square miles, was disposed of by Mr. Raymond to some easterners who formed the Pittsburgh and Boston Company. Work was commenced by this company on Hays' Point in 1844 under the direction of Charles Avery, President of the Company, and John Hays, Agent. Theirs was the first mining shaft sunk in the District, and this company was therefore the pioneer in mining enterprise.

In preparing the ground where Fort Wilkins now stands, the soldiers had encountered numerous boulders of black oxide of copper, evidently belonging to a vein near at hand. A part of the mining force of the Pittsburgh and Boston Company was directed toward locating this vein, which they discovered December 5, 1844, and which proved to be a continuation of the one on Hays' Point. The vein was just a few rods east of the fort, and at the surface was from fifteen to twenty inches in width. The ore was mostly a black oxide of copper, with some silicates, red oxide, and native copper. It was of surpassing richness, yielding from sixty to seventy per cent copper. Mining was commenced here immediately; two shafts were sunk about one hundred feet apart, and the ore found in both. About thirty or forty tons of ore were obtained, but unfortunately it proved to be only a pocket which became exhausted at a depth of fifteen feet. The fissure and vein-stone continued, which induced the company to continue sinking in the hope that the mineral would reappear. The main shaft was sunk one hundred and twenty feet and levels driven each way, until it became manifest that it was unwise to proceed further. The company spent $25,000 at this place and on Hays' Point, while the net proceeds from the copper obtained were $2,968.70.

During the winter of 1843-44 the number of white men remaining in the Lake Superior District probably did not exceed twenty. A great deal of exploratory work had been done by individuals during the summer, some trying to locate ancient workings, and others actually trenching and sinking pits. The early explorations were mainly confined to the portions where the rocks were exposed, where bluffs, gorges, and river channels afforded the best opportunities for examination. Keweenaw Point, the Ontonagon district, and Isle Royale consequently received the most attention, and for several years prospecting was confined to these regions. Rumors of extraordinary finds were common, and eastern capitalists were attracted by the possibilities of the District. Associations of men were formed, leases were purchased, and experienced men were sent to look after further exploratory work.

The Lake Superior Copper Company was the first organized company in the District. As originally constituted on February 22, 1844, its possessions included seven of the three mile square leases, totalling, after deductions of overlapping claims, over forty square miles of territory, nearly all of which was situated in the richest portion of the then known mineral region. Several veins were located on the property but none proved successful and the property was sold to a new organization, The Phoenix Copper Company, which was granted a charter in March 1849. For a period of over forty years this company worked continuously. They were hospitable and the stranger was ever welcome if he was a manly man.

Lake Superior was the first of the great mining regions in the country to be exploited, the first in which was indicated the aptitude of the American for such preliminary work. The fever of exploration on permit culminated in 1848. The population had increased to a point where the true pioneer was beginning to feel that he was but one of a crowd. Rumors of the discovery of gold in California began to arrive and the Copper Country pioneers formed the nucleus of the California 'forty-niners."

The first locations made after the treaty with the Indians in 1843 were at Copper Harbor. This was natural because of the rock exposures in this neighborhood. On the point of land on which the lighthouse now stands, known as paying assessments of \$1,037,500 on the old Phoenix and \$1,350,000 on the new Phoenix Consolidated, hoping always for dividends, which, except for \$20,000 paid in 1877, never came. The company opened mines in the ashbed and in fissure veins and had some periods of prosperity when the product was comparatively large and profits correspondingly great, but the surplus was used in opening other and worthless veins, thus diverting the profits from the expectant stockholder. The "Phoenix" has recently been re-opened and at present is being explored by the Calumet and Hecla Consolidated Mining Company.

The Cliff mine was discovered in August, 1845, by a party of explorers working for the Pittsburgh and Boston Company. Following a narrow vein which outcropped on the summit and face of the greenstone bluff an adit driven seventy feet into the bluff encountered the first mass of copper ever found by systematic mining. This discovery was of the greatest interest and import- ance, not only to the company, but to the whole mining interest on Lake Superi- or. It gave encouragement to those engaged in prospecting and induced them to persevere. It also indicated the true source of the masses which had been found near the surface and in ancient pits. The \$60,000 paid in 1849 was the first dividend earned and paid by any mine in the District. During the period from 1845 to 1870, while the original company was working, over two and one-half millions of dollars was paid in dividends. This is over 2000% on the paid in capital and represents a dividend disbursement of 7.5 cents per pound of copper produced, the highest ratio for any mine in the district. This mine is also being re-opened by the Calumet and Hecla.

The wonderful occurrences of the great masses that were found in such quantity at the Cliff mine stimulated mining exploration and development in an extraordinary degree and the attention of explorers and investors was concen- trated on finding similar veins. Scores of test pits and trenches were made.

The Minnesota mine in Ontonagon County was opened on a strike fissure in 1849, and paid its first dividend in 1854. What is believed to be the largest complete mass of native copper ever found was discovered in this mine in 1856. This mass was forty-six feet long, its greatest thickness, eight and one-half feet. It weighed approximately five hundred tons. Twenty men labored fifteen months to work around and dislodge it from the rock. In doing this 2,750 pounds of powder were used. The mass was then cut into pieces small enough to be handled. Two men, expert with hammer and chisel, could cut about a square foot of groove a day. This mass cutting afforded a total of twenty-seven tons of chips. The cost of cutting the grooves through the mass averaged about twelve dollars per square foot and the statement is often heard that the mining of these large masses is unprofitable because of the enormous cost of cutting and handling. The truth is that the companies would prefer to find the same amount of copper in a form more convenient to handle, but it can be confidently asserted that no Lake Superior company dreads to find large masses for fear that they will be unprofitable; as a matter of fact, the value of the chips nearly equals the average cost of cutting. The large

Minnesota mass netted the company about $150,000.

The Central mine, operating on the Central fissure, seven miles east of the Cliff was discovered in 1854, made its first shipment of copper in 1856 and began paying dividends in 1864. It ceased operations in 1898, having produced copper and silver that marketed for nearly ten million dollars, $2,130,000 of which was paid up stock. No mining community in the District can boast of a more loyal group of employees than the Central. They were loyal to the company and the community, and though the location is now practically deserted the reunion is looked forward to and participated in by the old-time residents who are so situated that they can use this opportunity to revive acquaintance-ships and reminiscences.

Next to Copper Harbor and Ontonagon, the Portage Lake District was most accessible to the early explorer for copper, and during the summers of 1846, '47 and '48 this section was explored about as thoroughly as could be expected by individuals, unorganized and handicapped by limited capital. The explorers were looking for rich fissure veins and paying little attention to the amygaloid beds, even though these were known to contain some copper. The Quincy Mining Company was organized in 1848 and the Pewabic Mining Company in 1853. In 1856, after three years of exploration at the Pewabic location, and eight years at the Quincy, the great Pewabic amygadaloid lode was discovered by the Pewabic Company. The Quincy Company promptly followed the lead of the Pewabic, stopped work on the worthless cross veins, and concentrated their efforts on opening up the amygdaloid. These were the first successful mines on an amygdaloid lode, and served to divert some of the exploration activities from fissures to lodes. Both mines began paying dividends in 1862. The Quincy has operated continuously for over eighty years and has paid dividends, totalling $27,000,000 for a greater length of time than any other mine in the district.

A corporation known as the Ohio and Isle Royale began mining in 1845 on Isle Royale but transferred its base of operations to the south side of Portage Lake in 1852 and discovered the Isle Royale amygdaloid. Although worked intermittently by a number of companies no dividends were paid prior to 1913, although several tributers made profits during the times when the companies were inactive.

The Atlantic lode was discovered in 1864 and paid dividends of nearly one million dollars although the average copper content of the rock was less than fourteen pounds per ton.

The famous Calumet and Hecla conglomerate was discovered in 1864, and the Calumet and Hecla Mining Company formed by the consolidation of several companies in May 1871. Although this is the company most commonly referred to in conversation with visitors of inquirers, it must be recognized that it is not representative of the region as no other mine compares with it either in richness of rock, amount of production, or in profits. Dividends have been paid every year since 1870, a total of about $160,000,000.

Numerous other lodes have been discovered, the Kearsarge and Osceola in 1874, the Baltic in 1882, and so on; but in this brief sketch only incidents and properties have been selected that typify the district. Other properties could have been chosen and other incidents recited that might have been of greater interest to some. The Mass, Adventure, Ridge, White Pine, Nonesuch, and Victoria mines in Ontonagon County; the Allouez, Ahmeek, Mohawk, Seneca, and Copper Falls in Keweenaw County, the Winona, Mesnard, Arcadian, Old Colony, Centennial, and Wolverine in Houghton County, have received scant mention; the stories relating to the finding of masses of copper and pockets of native silver read like fairy tales; the biographies of the pioneers are full of romance; but the space allotted to this article is limited and many things must go unsaid.

More than one thousand permissions to explore for copper and develop the properties have been recorded in the district, and about two hundred companies have been incorporated to carry on this work. About eighty companies are listed as having produced copper in sufficient quantities to warrant stating the amount in the report to the stockholders. Thirteen of the eighty have returned to the stockholders more than the total amount of capital paid in. Approximately $80,000,000 in assessments have been coalled by all the companies and over three times as much has been returned in dividends. The Calumet and Hecla Company alone has paid in dividends double the amount paid in capital stock by all the copper companies in the Lake Superior District. It has been truly said, "It takes a gold mine to make a copper mine."

SELECTED BIBLIOGRAPHY
on
Prehistoric Copper in Keweenaw Peninsula and Isle Royale

Listed alphabetically by author
* Indicates paper is included in "Prehistoric Copper Mining in the Lake Superior
Region"

1. Adams, Charles C.
        An Ecological Survey of Isle Royale, Lake Superior.
        A report from the University of Michigan Museum, published by the
        State Biological Survey, as part of the Report of the Board of the
        Geological Survey for 1908. Lansing, 1909.

2. Barrett, S. A.
        Aboriginal Copper Mines at McCargo's Cove, Isle Royale.
        Yearbook of the Public Museum of the City of Milwaukee,
        vol. IV, 1924, pp. 20-36. Milwaukee, 1926.

3. Benedict, C. Harry
        Red Metal
        University of Michigan Press, Ann Arbor, 1958.

4. *Brady, Samuel
        History of Famous Ontonagon Copper Rock Recalled by Society's
        Outing
        1916, Mining Gazette

5. Brown, Charles E.
        The Native Copper Implements of Wisconsin
        The Wisconsin Archaeologist, vol. III, pp. 49-98, 1904.

        The Native Copper Ornaments of Wisconsin.
        The Wisconsin Archaeologist, vol. III, pp. 101-129, 1904.

6. Cooper, William S.
        The Climax Forest of Isle Royale, Lake Superior, and its
        Development.
        The Botanical Gazette, vol. LV, pp. 1-44, 1913.

7. Davies, A. C.
        *Antiquities of Isle Royale, Lake Superior.
        Annual Report of the Board of Regents of the Smithsonian
        Institution - for the year 1874, pp. 369-370. Washington, 1875.

8. Dee, James R. and Grover C. Dillman
        First Account of Copper Country Published in France in Year 1636.

9. Dillman, Grover C. - See James R. Dee

10. Drier, Roy Ward
        *Michigan's Most Ancient History is America's Prehistoric Copper
        Mines.
        Inside Michigan, July 1953, vol. 3, no. 7, p. 15.

210

Drier, Roy Ward (continued)
*Prehistoric Mining in the Copper Country

11. Draper, Lyman C.
Mode of Fabrication of Ancient Copper Implements.
From Report and Collections on the State Historical Society of
Wisconsin for the Years 1877, 1878, 1879. Vol. VIII,
Madison, Wisconsin: David Atwood, State Printer, 1879.

12. Ferguson, William P. F.
*Michigan's Most Ancient Industry: The Prehistoric Mines
and Miners of Isle Royale.
Michigan History Magazine, vol. 7, pp. 155-162, 1922.

13. Fisher, James
Historical Sketch of Lake Superior Copper District,
Evidences of Mining Go Back Centuries; Long Before
Coming of the North American Indians.
Mining Gazette, September 7, 1929.

14. Foster, J. W. and J. S. Whitney
Report on the Geology and Topography of a Portion of the
Lake Superior Land District in the State of Michigan.
In two parts, (Part I, Copper Lands, 230 pp. including
sketches). Executive document 69, House of Representatives,
1st Congress, 1st session, Washington, 1850.

15. Fox, George R.
*The Ancient Copper Workings on Isle Royale.
The Wisconsin Archaeologist, vol. 10, pp. 74-100, 1915.

16. Gannon, J. C.
*Prehistoric Copper Mines of the Lake Superior Region, 1953.

17. Gilman, Henry
Ancient Works at Isle Royale, Michigan.
Appelton's Journal, vol. X, pp. 173-175, 1873.

Ancient Men of the Great Lakes.
Proceedings, American Association for the Advancement
of Science, twenty-fourth meeting, held at Detroit, Michigan,
August 1875. pp. 316-331, Salem, 1876.

The Mound-Builders and Platycnemism in Michigan.
Annual Report of the Board of Regents of the Smithsonian
Institution - for the year 1873, pp. 364-390.
Washington 1874.

*The Mound-Builders in Michigan.
Michigan Pioneer Collections, vol. 3, pp. 202-213.
Lansing, Michigan, 1879-1880.

18. Holmes, W. H.
*Aboriginal Copper Mines of Isle Royale, Lake Superior.
American Anthropologist, n.s. vol. 3, pp. 684-696, 1901.

19. Jackson, Charles T.
    Report on the Geological and Mineralogical Survey of the
    Mineral Lands of the United States in the State of Michigan.
    Executive document 5, House of Representatives 31st
    Congress, 1st session, Part II, Washington, 1849.

20. Kenton, Edna
    The Indians of North America
    Selected and edited by Edna Kenton from "The Jesuit
    Relations and Allied Documents," etc., Harcourt, Brace,
    & Co., 1927.

21. Lane, Alfred C.
    Geological Report on Isle Royale, Michigan.
    Geological Surveh of Michigan, vol. VI, part I. Lansing
    1898. (Chapter 1, "Historical Introduction," pp. 1-26
    alone concerns the subject of this paper.)

22. Lathrop, J. H.
    *Prehistoric Mines of Lake Superior.
    The American Antiquarian and Oriental Journal, vol. 23,
    pp. 248-258, 1901. Reprinted from Northeast Magazine,
    February 1901.

23. Murdoch, Angus
    Boom Copper
    The Macmillan Company, New York, 1943.

24. Packard, R. L.
    Pre-Columbian Copper Mining in North America.
    Annual Report of the Board of Regents of the Smithsonian
    Institution - to July, 1892, pp. 175-198. Washington, 1893.
    Also in: American Antiquarian and Oriental Journal,
    vol. 15, pp. 67-79 and 152-164, 1893.

25. Pitezel
    Missionary Life, pp. 424-27, Chapter XXXI, Edited 1857,
    Published in 1857 by Walden & Stowe, Cincinnati, Ohio.

26. Reeder, John T.
    *Evidences of Prehistoric Man of Lake Superior.
    Michigan Historical Collections, vol. 30, pp. 110-118,
    Lansing, Michigan, 1903.

27. Savage, Dean James
    *Dug for Copper in Prehistoric Days.
    Sunday Mining Gazette, May 7, 1911.

28. Scherzer, Carl and Morits Wagner
    *Early Days in Ontonagon
    Translated by Samuel Brady from Chapter XX, Reisen in
    Nordamerika in den Jahren 1852 und 1853.
    Arnoldische Buchhandlung, Leipsig, 1857.

212

29. Scott, William P.
        Reminiscences of Isle Royale.
        Michigan History Magazine, vol. 9, pp. 398-412, 1925.

30. Smith, Samuel L.
        *Prehistoric and Modern Copper Mines of Lake Superior.
        Michigan Historical Collections, vol. 39, pp. 137-151,
        Lansing, Michigan, 1915.

31. Swineford, A. P.
        History and Review of the Mineral Resources of Lake
        Superior.
        The Mining Journal, Marquette, Michigan, 1876.

32. Thwaites, Reuben G.
        The Jesuit Relations and Allied Documents.
        72 volumes, Cleveland, 1896-1901.

33. Wagner, Morits
        See Carl Scherzer

34. West, George A.
        Copper: Its Mining and Use by the Aborigines of the
        Lake Superior Region: Report of the McDonald-Massee
        Isle Royale Expedition, 1928.
        Bulletin of the Public Museum of the City of Milwaukee,
        vol. X, No. 1, May 29, 1929.

35. Whitney, J. S.
        See J. S. Foster

36. Whittlesey, Charles
        *The Ancient Miners of Lake Superior.
        The Annals of Science (Cleveland Academy of Natural
        Sciences) vol. 1, pp. 15-18, and 27-30. Cleveland, 1852.

        Ancient Mining on the Shores of Lake Superior.
        Smithsonian Contributions to Knowledge, vol. 13, 29,
        Washington, 1863.

37. Winchell, N. H.
        The Geological and Natural History Survey of Minnesota.
        The ninth annual report, for the year 1880. St. Peter, 1881.
        The tenth annual report, for the year 1881. St. Peter, 1882.
        The fourteenth annual report, for the year 1885. St. Paul, 1886.

        *Ancient Copper Mines of Isle Royale.
        The Popular Science Monthly, vol. XIX, pp. 601-620, 1881.

        The Aborigines of Minnesota:
        A report based on the collections of Jacob V. Brower, and on
        the field surveys and notes of Alfred J. Hill and Theodore H.
        Lewis. Collated, augmented and described by N. H. Winchell,
        Minnesota Historical Society, St. Paul, 1911.

OTHER PAPERS - Authors unknown

> Ancient Mining on the Shores of Lake Superior
> From the Atlantic Monthly, 1865.
>
> Mineral Resources of Lake Superior
> A Geological Report Circa 1875
>
> Annual Report of the Commissioner of Mineral Statistics
> of the State of Michigan for 1880
> Lansing, Michigan, W. S. George & Co.

Addendum

38. Quimby, George Irving
    Indian Life in the Upper Great Lakes
    11, 000 B. C. to A. D. 1800.
    University of Chicago Press,
    Chicago 37, Illinois.
    182 pp (1960)

The following line drawings are taken
from plates published in "Report on the
Geology and Topography of a Portion of
the Lake Superior Land District, in the
State of Michigan" by J. W. Foster and
J. D. Whitney, United States Geologists
Printed for the House of Representatives
in 1850. In two parts. Part 1, Copper
Lands.

MONTREAL RIVER FALLS.

CARP LAKE, PORCUPINE M^{TS}

COLUMNAR TRAP, ISLE ROYALE

CONGLOMERATE HILLS, NEAR FT WILKINS.

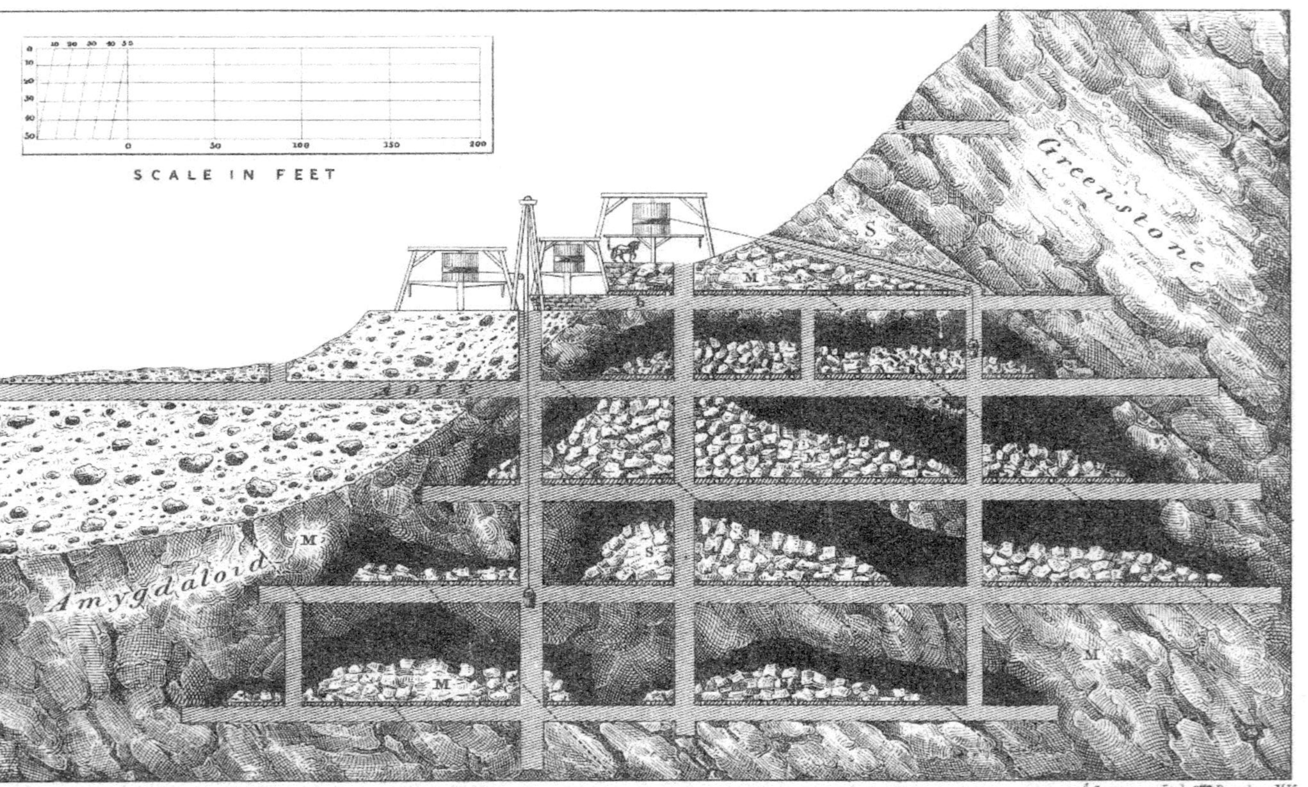

SCALE IN FEET
Greenstone
Amygdaloid
SECTION OF THE CLIFF MINE
Ackermann's Lith 379 Broadway N.Y.

CLIFF MINE, LAKE SUPERIOR.

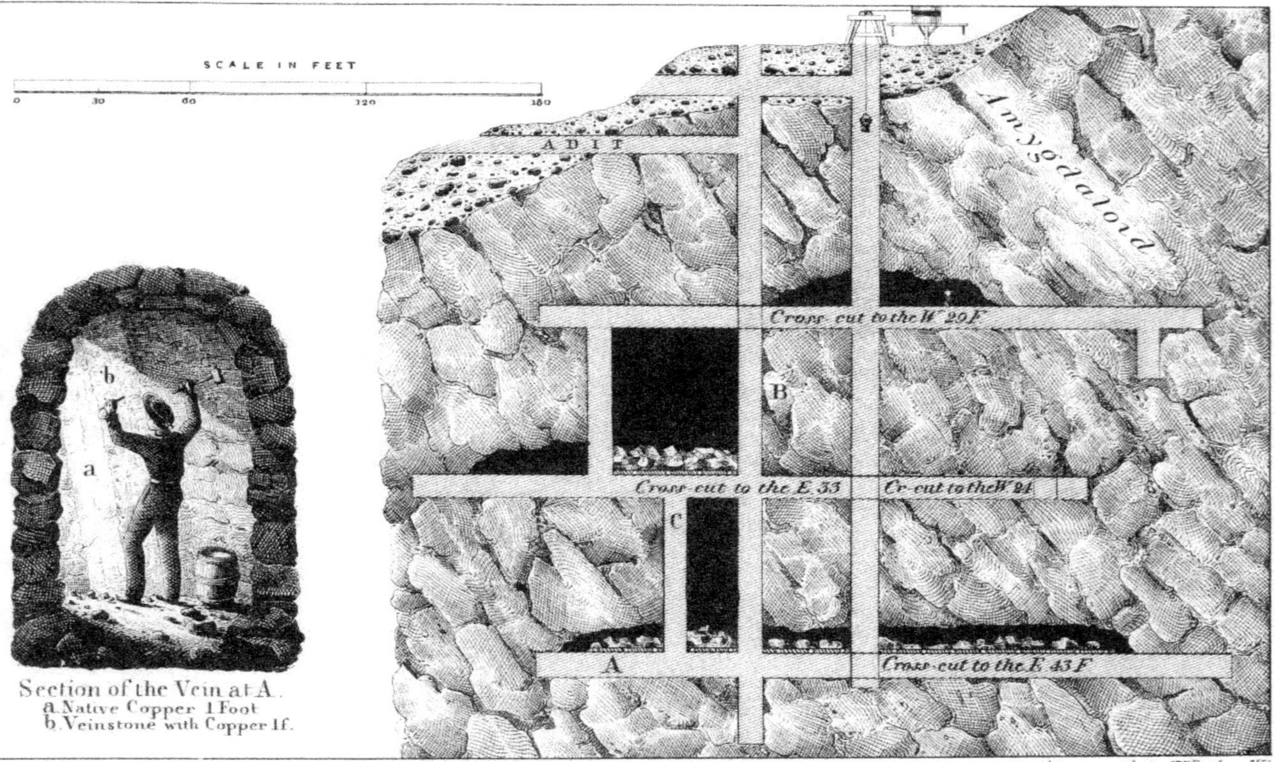

SECTION OF THE NORTH AMERICAN MINE

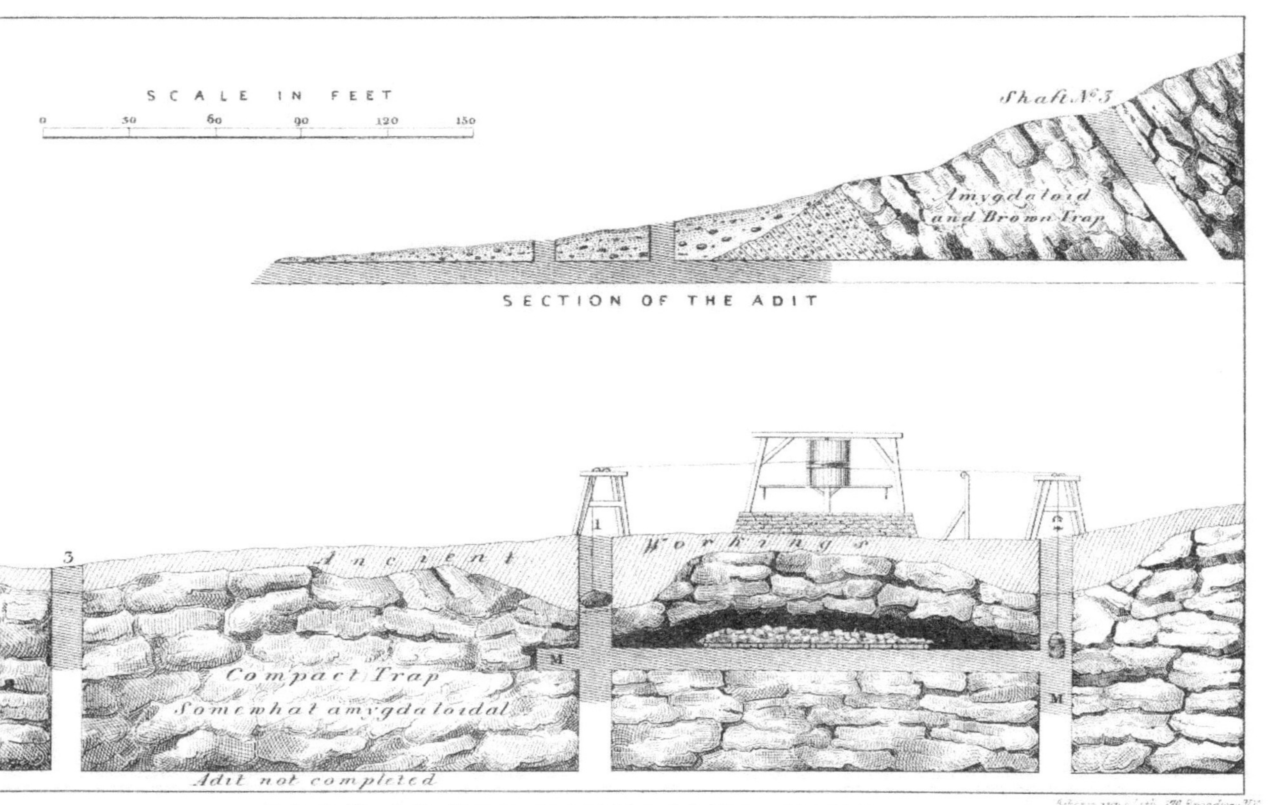

PLAN OF THE MINNESOTA MINE

www.ingramcontent.com/pod-product-compliance
Lightning Source LLC
Chambersburg PA
CBHW051511030726
47592CB00006B/2215